`Linux As No One Had Told You`

A text book for the Fundamental Linux course, intended for college students, who have little or no knowledge of Linux, and command line. With recognition of the rich and powerful Linux's GUI, this course is almost entirely focused on the command line and working with the shell.

San Diego, 2021.

Preface

This book is result of my experience teaching Linux fundamentals class in the local community college for quite some number of years. I did not plan writing this book. I designed this course to be very interactive and hands-on in class experience. But then the Covid pandemic struck and colleges switched to the distant online instructions. Thus, I had to convert my lectures to this new format. I designed this course to the people who have very little or not at all knowledge about Linux, or, even about computers (besides perhaps the cell phones; and yes, I had such students in my classes). We'll start with very simple things and will make our way to the level sufficient for a pretty comfortable navigation in this new world. This book is not a replacement for all those thick and heavy manuals and tutorials you will find elsewhere in abundant supply. But what it'll give you is a good place to start, and a good understanding of the Linux. So, welcome to the Linux world!

Lecture 1. Introduction to Linux OS.

First, let me introduce myself.

After more than 20+ years in the IT field, I retired from daily meetings and coding, and meetings, and another short meeting... and other routine. I've been a die hard Linux user for so long, so do not ask me to compare that with anything else... As a fair disclaimer, my answer would probably be biased.

My first home installation of Linux was one of the early version of Caldera (I do not even know if that company is still around) on a 60-dollars desktop from the second hand store. For years it was a trusted development machine for my moonlight projects. When after years of sitting in the corner, it was turned on for the last and final time to let me say farewell to all those lines of code I wrote back then... Well, enough to say it still worked perfectly.

I studied UNIX from people (both, my Professors and my mentors) whom I still admire for their immense knowledge and experience, even though I still occasionally wake up in the middle of the night in the fear that ***that*** test on the process scheduling algorithm in UNIX System V is to be due next morning... Yes, I know, I am probably done with my tests by now...

When I was going to build this course, I instantly knew, that none of those two-and-half-inches-thick books, describing the innermost details of how the OS works, or those, listing all the commands and options would be used in it.

The former did not belong to this fundamentals class. The later... they just were not suitable here.

This is a fundamental class. I wanted to build it to be suitable for the people who have very little (if any) experience not only with the Linux, but perhaps with the computers at all. I understand, that it may be a completely alien world for some of you, so I did not want to make it hostile. My goal was to show the beauty, the power and (contrary to the popular beliefs) the easiness of working with the Linux.

Because of that, I will go wide, not deep. I want you to have a general ideas of what the Linux is and what you can do with that (which is pretty much anything you want to). If at the end of the semester there will be one or two new converts to the Linux; people who would say: “That's it. Linux's forever”, that would be my accomplishment. If after the course ends, there will be one or two (or more than that) people who would say: “Done with that. Never again”, that would be... my accomplishment too. Because how can you know whether something is good for you or not good for you, whether it is suitable or not, before and unless you spent time trying that something yourself?

As for all those commands... There are hundreds of commands there. Each with dozens of different options. There is no way we can learn all of them. Nor that would be practical, because by the midterm you'd forget what we discussed during the first few weeks. But most importantly, that would be sooooo boring...

...And, honestly, not needed. We will cover some, which are, on my experience probably the most needed, and/or allow you to do most of your work on the system. So, again, the philosophy of this class is to go wide, not deep.

There probably are some people who think: 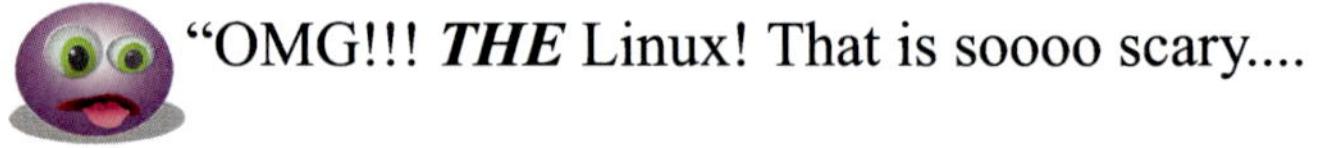 "OMG!!! ***THE*** Linux! That is soooo scary.... I never ….. " (fill in the blank).

I built that course to make it hard for you to fail. If you read the lectures, follow the examples, and generally pay attention to what I am saying, you should be reasonably good. People may ask: "What is the prerequisite for this course? There must be something. It cannot be otherwise.... for ***The*** Linux...."

Yes, there is.

You should be able to type on the keyboard. And probably be able to use web search.

That's it.

And since I am here, let me explain few things.

1. I built that course the way how I understand its logic, based on my experience, based on how my professors taught me.... So... if you don't like something here, do not blame me, blame my professors, because that's how I was trained. And, similarly, if you do like something, do not give credit to me. Give it to my teachers, because it is them, who made me what I am now.

2.  Contrary to the popular beliefs, Linux has very reach UI. Some of the most amazing contemporary features of the UI I saw on a Linux first, and only then on other systems. Yet, we will focus on the command line. Why? Because you cannot say you can work with Linux, if you cannot work with command line. Because on the interview you probably will not be asked what button to click; you probably be asked what command to type. Because you may not be able to use the UI at all. When you think "Linux", probably in 99% you think "server". And when you think "server", you probably think "remote server". Thus, no GUI may be available. All these would be good reasons. But I have another one still. I do not travel with the laptops anymore. They are big and heavy and bulky. I travel with tablets. Even they are big and heavy and bulky. I travel with the smart phone. And all the sudden I have the screen and terminal that resemble me those of the last century. Back to the ... past? Again? No, we will be focusing on the command line here.
3. ***Q***: What environment to use (what Linux distribution (AKA "Distro")) to use?
A: Any. You may have something already installed, or you may have a mac notebook.... or Raspberry Pi... anything you have, like, easier to you to install/configure.... Yes, there may be (or will be) differences in some tools or libraries, but those differences are not important. People who can work with one distro, can easily switch to another one. So... Anything you like.
4. Finally. I mentioned, that I am a hard Linux user, didn't I? Thus, it wouldn't probably be a surprise, if I say that I also have quite an experience with the Perl programming language. And I completely adopt the Perl's motto:

> There is more than one way of doing things.

That means, that if I do something in a particular way, that does not mean that you should do that something the same way. I encourage you to go and look and compare. You may find that some other way is better for you, or more easy, or more clear, or you just like it that way... all these are completely legitimate reasons in this class. As long, as you do it correctly.

Now, this class is not a hacking class. All the examples and explanations I give you here is for educational purposes only. The motto and condition for this course is:

> **Do no harm. Anything other than that does not belong to Linux or its community. In any case author is not liable for any your actions resulting out of reading of this book, separate chapter(s) or example(s).**

Welcome to the class and I look forward for the good semester.

1. Why Linux?

To answer that question, let's go back to the last millennium...

Actually, to the 70-80th of the last century, to be exact.

It was the time when people in Microsoft said that no personal computer would ever need more than 64 Kb of ram, and no browser or internet connection either. It was time when Apple was advertised as a kitchen devise to store recipes. It was time when 512 Kb of floppy disk was enough storage to keep all your data with some spare left.

It was on the PC side.

On the other side big businesses and universities were adopting a new OS, developed in cooperation/competition between Bells Lab and University of Berkeley. It was system made to live on the network, the system to manage many users at the same time, and manage many processes, running at the same time. It was safe, reliable, and very robust system. It was named UNIX.

Let's fast forward couple dozens of years. Anyone remembers or knows at all the Apple's OS 7 or 8? My personal experience was that it was a disaster. It froze, it crashed left and right. It was losing data. It was practically unusable – that's how unreliable it was.

At the same time Windows just came up with its most advanced OS they did at that time – Windows 2000. Finally it was a system, that could hold multitasking (khmmm... I recall an old joke... " – Is it true that this OS is truly multitasking?" " – Yes, it truly is" " – Can you show us?" " – Sure, let me just finish that task..."), that was reasonably integrated into the network, and that could handle more than one user in it. And let me pause here for a moment. Anyone experienced the situation when you were working (remotely) on a system (on a server) and all the sudden you got kicked off of it – because some one else just logged in? Think about it – you were in the middle of doing something and you are kicked off of the system... That was the windows' concept of multi user system.

So. Here we are in 2020. Let's old memories to gone. From the position and knowledge of today, let's try to enumerate, what would be your idea of a modern operating system? What would you put down as requirements if you were to design an modern operating system? From the position of today, what would you expect from the modern OS?

A complete list would probably fill the entire white board in the classroom, so let me just mention few items here.

So.

1. **Being safe**. What do we mean when saying be safe? No user exposure to the threats, nor user's **data** exposure to the threats. No viruses, no malware, no spying. No taking system's resources (the whole system, or its part) for doing something that you do not want to. Everything should be well protected. User does not need to be worried about all that...

– What? 

– Yes, I repeat. User does not need to be worried about all that.

What thing do you need to do first, when you start your computer for the very first time and before you make your way to the web? What they all tell you you have to do in the first place? Install and activate the antivirus. Configure a firewall. Right? That's what you've been told. That's what you've got used to. Right? You take it as reality. Yes, these days you cannot think of any computer that does not come with the antivirus or firewall. But that was not always the case. In fact, it took Government's regulations to push that through. These days we don't need to look for, install, and pay for the antivirus. But what is the cost of it? Even though, these days you'd get it for free? **What is the cost of the antivirus**? Forget about regular updates and running the scans. I repeat the question: What is the cost of the antivirus?

It takes computer's resources. You've got a powerful hardware and you need to slice off a part of it just because if you would not do that, there would be people around, who would share your computer with you and not always you might get the right share.

There was an old joke about one of the rather known antivirus – why does it protect your computer so well?.. When it runs, it takes the entire system's resources, and there is nothing left for the viruses. So there is a cost. It takes resources.

But what if you have a system, which is so hard to get it, that the cost of that far surpasses the potential benefits?

2. Let's continue with our list. **Being reliable**. What does it mean? After you configured it, it runs without interruption, with minimum interference and maintenance. In other words, the cost of maintenance is low. When you run server on a system, it needs to be reliable regardless whether you applied those patches and/or updates or don't. Because you may do that or may not. Because you may be able to do that or may not. Because you may want to do that or may not. Yet you want your services to be available still. Now, the services may become unavailable not because the system is down; the system may be up, but it runs very slow, making services not responsive, or response time that is not acceptable. In other words, if you have a fancy car, you want to drive it the moment you want to; not to see it spending time in the mechanic's shop.

3. That leads me to this. Your system should handle **multiple processes**, it should manage the memory, including the virtual memory, it should handle the other computers resources, so there is no resource leaks; it should be able to recover from the resource leaks without need to reboot the system. In general, you want the system to have minimum time between reboots and maximum uptime time.
4. And yes, You want to have ability to **support many users**. By that you mean not only having more than one user's account on the system. By that you mean that the system is capable of allowing more than one user to be logged on the system at the same time (which also includes ability to one user to log in from different location at the same time, however weird that may sound); not only logged in, but working on it. Including using the same software, programs, and tools. Can you start two office programs? Not two documents, but two instances of office? Many window's applications check for the running instances and exit if you try to launch second instance of the same application. But if you allow more than one user to be on the system, you should allow also more than one user to use the same program or application, right? Otherwise it makes little sense. And you see, how it circles back to the previous item – supporting multiple processes. The system should be able to do multi-tasking. You want to be able to write a report, chat with the friends, and listen to the music or watch the streaming movie at the same time, right?

And I want to elaborate a little more on couple of points above.

1. Being reliable and robust. That does not mean only ability to run without interruptions and degradation, as we just discussed above. It means ***ability to run***. Your hardware may be failing, your hard drive may be dying or already dead... it still runs off the memory. Interestingly, when in one of the classes I talked about that, one student shared exactly that experience they had in their organization with the mail server. So, to be reliable, it means: it ***runs***. In my years with Linux, I have not seen a performance degradation over the time or after the third party's software upgrades; I have not needed re-installing the system; I could install, upgrade, downgrade or remove the software without being worried about effect it'd take on the system.

It

just

runs.

You can leave system on for days, weeks, months, or years.

It
just
runs.

2. Talking about multi-user. How many users are many? I remember reading a topic on one board discussing how many are many. It went like that. Each user on a UNIX system has a unique user ***ID***. It used to be that UNIX reserved first 100 ***ID***s, including that one for the root, for the internal usage. It also released into the dynamic pool (for the processes) the ***ID***s beyond 500. That left numbers between 100 and 500 to be allocated for the users ***ID*** to be created on the system.

So, there could be potentially 400 users on the system, being able to login and to work on it simultaneously at the same time. Is it way too many? Too few? About right? The average classroom can accommodate probably 20-30 people. Therefore, 400 people would take about 20 average classrooms.

That would probably take 2 or 3 floors on the building. What about other buildings? Should there be one server for each building? With the maintenance cost, with the space, room, power cords, networking cables, separate IP addresses etc?

The discussion went – **it was way too low!** And because of that, the users' ***ID*** allocation was changed so that they are now allocated starting from 500, and apparently with no upper limit.

> When in Computer Science we say "no limit" or "unlimited", we understand, that there is still a limit. It is just that that limit is considered not to be reachable.

Now let's look at this from another angle. I mentioned that the average classroom or computer lab can accommodate 20-30 people. There is separate individual personal computer for each student in the classroom or computer's lab.

When I was a grad student, not **that** long ago, Computers' labs had terminals, connected remotely through the network to the server.

Each student in the lab was logged from that terminal to his/her account on the server.

All at the same time! All on the same server! Can you think – how robust the system has to be – managing processes, managing resources, network, memory, *CPU* etc – so that no one of those students ever could notice that there are other users on the same system; all working simultaneously without slowing it down. That's, Ladies and Gentlemen, how the multi-user and multi-tasking system should work.

Actually, think a moment about it. There is a powerful hardware, capable of a immense performance. If you confine it to a single user (what a waste of resources) in most of the time it would sit idle just because there is no enough work to do. You may be a very fast typist. But for your processor what you do

i s s o s l o w ! ! ! !

It makes a perfect sense to share the resources between multiple users. Have you heard about some projects that implemented the distributive computational power of peoples' PCs? For example there was a project to search for a near Earth potentially dangerous space objects. Any one can sign on and to allow his or her computer to be used as a computational power while sitting idle. That is the same idea of multi-user/multi-tasking – when you don't use the computer's resources, let it be used by some other tasks.

Alright. Let's return to our discussion of what features should the good OS have? Provide powerful shell interface, the collection of tools that allows user to do a large variety of work natively on a system. And while I am here, how about collection of packages; everything you possible need to, right out of the box:

1. How about mail server and mail clients? Not paying for each client's license, but shipped with the system?
2. How about services – web server, database server, file server, network server, network

file server etc? Not paid for, not needed to configure separately, but shipped with the system?

3. How about reliable storage? We'll talk about RAID later in the semester.
4. What else? Development environment. You have it. Complete with integrated dev environment, debugging, version control system for teams collaboration etc.
5. What else? Remote and safe access to the system. AND easy access to the system. Ability to integrate your system to the network, built-in firewall and networking tools etc, etc, etc... AND – remember – not to waste resources for the antivirus, because the OS is designed in such a way, with such security mechanisms, that you actually do not need the antivirus.

Good... That was a list of requirements and expectations what we would expect from our today's perspective and experience, listing the features a good OS should have. Now, can you imagine that all this was thought of and incorporated into the system designed and built... how many years? 50? 60? ago.

What the vision!

Now, you probably read or heard that Linux is very safe OS. Does that mean that Linux cannot be compromised? Of course not. There is no absolutely safe system. If you want an absolutely safe system, take the computer, turn it off, disconnect all the cords, and cables, and wires... And even that one would not be an absolutely safe system. Lock it in the enclosed cabinet, lock the door to that room... And...

> There is no absolutely safe system.

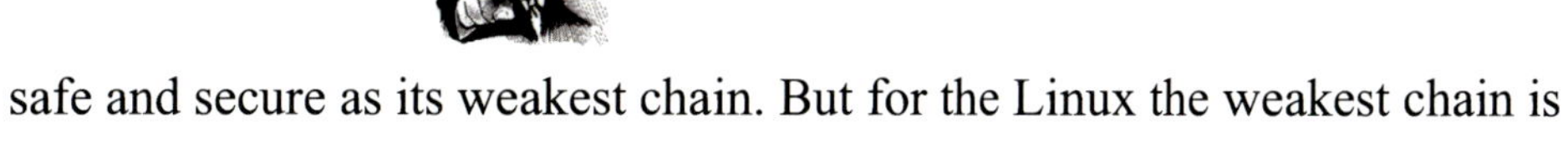

Every system is only as safe and secure as its weakest chain. But for the Linux the weakest chain is arguably the human.

If your password can be cracked by an 14-yeas old in 20 minutes, your password is not secure and your account is not secure. If you can call to the pretty powerful organization and convince them to reset the password for the pretty high ranking official, your system is not safe or secure.

As a user on a system, it is your responsibility to keep your account secure. It may be also your liability. Even if that is your home system.

The first day you get a job, you will be given a lot of forms to sign. Among those will be the forms from the IT. Make sure you read and understand those forms. Make sure you know, what they want, what their policies are, and what you can and cannot do with the computers. That may be your liability.

Couple of times I received a call from someone telling me he was from an IT and they needed to do a maintenance on my computer, so what was the password to my account? It was all wrapped into the very convincing form.

No.

There is no legitimate reason for anyone to ask for your password.

Besides... How would you prove, that you did not send ***that*** email coming out from your account, or did not visit ***that*** site?

Sometimes you need to make a decision.

In one organization I worked for, the management decided to conduct a sudden security audit of all the computers. They hired an outside company to do that.

Late in the evening our System Administrator received a phone call asking for the root's password.

No.

He was fired next day for the interference with the security audit. But, honestly, if he gave out the password, he should probably be fired on a spot for disclosing it over the phone.

Well, the last sentence I wrote was somewhat long. Let me correct it.

"... he should be fired for disclosing it."

Yes, sometimes you have a lose-lose situation.

Again, it is your responsibility to keep your account secure. Do not give your password to anyone. Do not leave your workstation unattended and unlocked, even if you just stepped out to the kitchen for the cup of tea... I may suffer from the professional deformation, but I lock my system whenever I am going to step aside, even though there is no one besides myself and my dog in my house...

... (continued) Do not login to your account if someone is watching over your shoulder. If you sit with someone and that person is about to login to his/her account, demonstratively and openly move aside and look other way – that is a general and common courtesy between people in the IT field.

So, can the user's account be compromised? Yes. But if it is compromised, only **that** account is compromised. Too bad for the user, but it does not mean that other users get compromised, it does not mean that the entire system gets compromised. To take control over the entire system – attacker needs to know or to guess the root's password. And ***this*** is what you particularly need to make sure it is a strong one, and ***this*** is what you need to make sure it is safe and secure.

Because... if the root's password is taken, the system is taken. That's it.

1.1. Why Linux (cont'd)?

Alright. We talked about many different things.

Let's backtrack and go to our main topic. Let me return to the landscape of the 1990-2000. Obviously, there were other Operating Systems, but let's limit our discussion by the three most known systems for the personal computers. We talked about Windows with W2K and XP and Mac with OS7 and 8. As I mentioned, the Apple OS was hopeless. And that what Steve Jobs realized, when he was brought back to the Apple – the very his company which he was expelled from. What he did, he scrapped completely the Apple OS and ported a Free BSD, which was a clone of UNIX on it. They put a nice graphical interface, which Apple is notorious for and that's how the contemporary MacOS X was introduced and new life of a Mac began.

At about that time, graduate student Linus Torvaldis was doing his research project – to port UNIX to the Personal Computers. Apparently, he was very successful in that his project. Because now we are here in this class discussing Linux OS.

What are the differences between UNIX and Linux?

1. UNIX is the system to run on the big and very powerful machines – You saw those pictures of a large rooms, people in white coats, huge metallic constructions, huge disks... I mean, physically huge...
2. Linux was made to run on the PC – lacking in power and specification – memory, hard drives, CPU.
3. UNIX was the system to control multiple processors. So when the more than one processor become available on the PC, Linux seamlessly integrated them.
4. UNIX is a proprietary system. Linux runs under the GPLs. Which means it is completely free. Which means, that you can get the OS for free, you can add some tweaks on it and you can even sell it or otherwise distribute it without paying royalties. This leads to another thing. There are many different discros of Linux, each tuned for some specific purposes. For example, RedHat, which positions itself as a server-grade disto. There are many other distros, nobody probably knows the exact number of those.

Let me circle back to the list of what are the features of the good Operating System.

There are couple more items, which I 'd like to mention.

1. Community support. Being under the GPL and being a community project from the very beginning, Linux has a great community support. These days you can find the online support for Windows and Macs as well, but Linux had this almost built-in from the very beginning of its existence. What it means for us – When you run into the problem, most likely someone else had that or similar problem, and it is very likely, that that problem was described and solution to it is put somewhere to the web. That means, that is you know the question, you can find the answer.
2. What other feature of good OS? Installation on a variety of hardware...

Suppose you have some really old computer, collecting dust somewhere in the basement. What shall you do with that? Install Linux on it. If not anything else, give it to your kids to learn how to program.

And we came to the topic that most of the books and tutorials start with:

2. Installation of Linux

Unlike those books and tutorials, I am not going to spend much time on it.

It used to be (despite the fact that Linux had always had a very good installation scripts) that installation of Linux was a fearful task.

If you wanted to really impress your friends, you would say:

– I spent this weekend installing Linux.

– Wow!!!

Not these days. These days that would be...

– So what... Boring.

I'll just mention couple of things (well, actually, three).

1. There are variety of options to install Linux. Network installation, installation on a USB flash drive, live system....
2. System will analyze your hard drive and suggest partitioning schema. You can accept that, but you also may want to create your own partitioning. If you do so, it would probably be a good idea to designate a separate partitions for the system, for the user space, for the data (if you will have a lot of data)... And don't forget the swap space (well, actually if you do, installation won't proceed). As general convention, the swap space should be the size of your physical memory.
3. It is very nice courtesy for the Linux users that distributors (be that OS or individual and separate packages) provide the checksum of the files to be downloaded. Do not proceed with the installation if the checksum does not match. **Just do not proceed.**

Next chapter following the Installation in all those books and tutorials is troubleshooting.

And here I am going to spend even less time on that.

Simply said, you will not.

I mean, how would that conversation with your friends ensue:

– So what... Boring.

– ...And it did not install!

– What??!!!

That will be all mine discussion about “what to do in case of troubles installing Linux”.

And that concludes today's lecture. Just to wrap it up, I'll say that I will be using my old trusted Raspberry Pi for all the future demonstrations.

Lecture 2. Navigating the directory tree, working with files and directories

1. Post-installation's first look at the system.

Alright. You have your new system. Let's take a first look at the file/directory tree that was created on a disk.

> In the Linux's world these things are called "directories", not "folders".

> We don't need to memorize the exact and entire structure below. For our discussions it would be sufficient to have a general picture of couple of things. That there is a ***root*** of the tree, and few (3 – 4) directories we will be visiting.

Since it is tree (not a graph), it has to be rooted, i.e. there is root on the tree ("A point of entry"). Here it is:

⟹ /

A single forward slash designates the root of the directory tree on a Linux. It is a top-level directory. Everything else is located below that (or under that if we have some regular files. But you probably never want to put a regular file directly under the root's directory).

Let's perhaps start looking at our tree with these things (since they maybe more confusing than other). Note, that it can be different and various combinations of the below, depending on the distro:

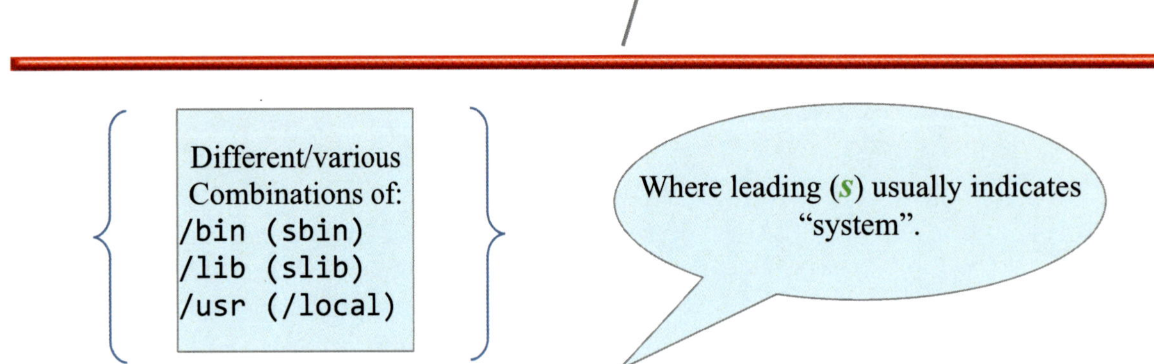

> The **(/s)bin** usually contains files, tools, and scripts, while **(/s)lib**, is a place for the libraries.

Those are place for the "system" files, and, separately, for everything else, including third party software. You probably do not want to install "everything else" into the "system" place. It probably would be better to install them into some other location, for example in here:

```
/usr/local/bin
```

(again, depending on system, the location may be different).

- Why don't place that into the system's directories (**/sbin** , **/slib**...)?
- We don't want to have any chance that during the installation, upgrade, downgrade, or removal of some tools or software, any of the systems' tools or libraries are affected... Or, any software for other users is affected.

For that reason, the above locations usually reserved for the system-wide installations, which is done by the ***root***. If you want to install something for yourself, it will go to your own place. That way you will know that you do not affect other peoples' settings and configurations, and likewise, other people will not affect your settings and configuration.

Continuing wandering around the directory tree.

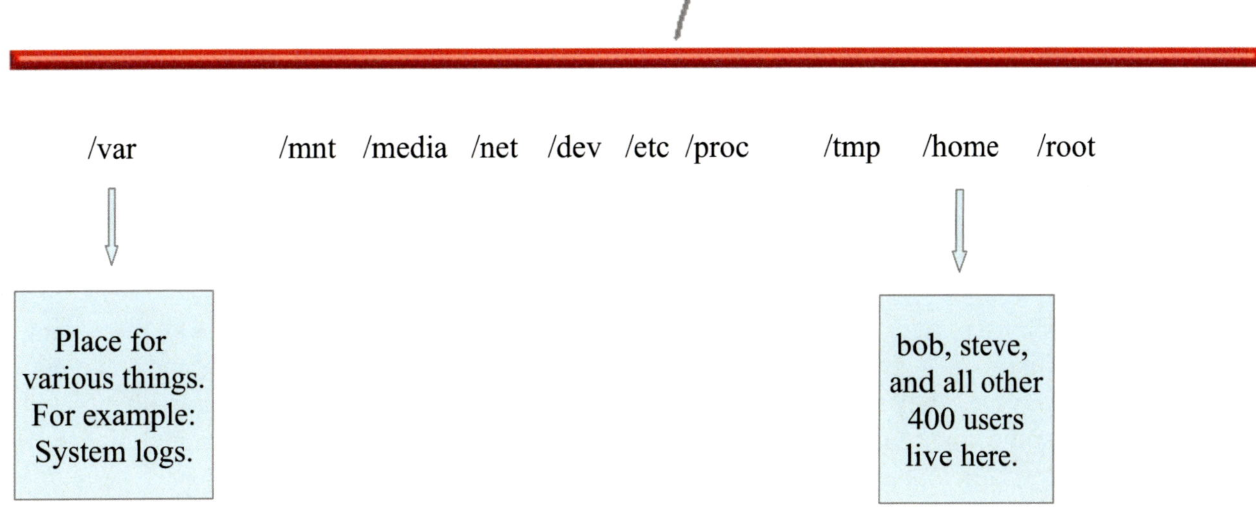

Let's formalize that a little:

/(s)bin – system files, scripts, and tools. ***/(s)lib*** – libraries (binary). You don't want to mess with them.

/usr (***/local***) – ***bin***, ***lib*** etc, is where you'd install third party software available for all users (system-wide).

/mnt – to mount devices, including USB, or to mount some other partitions, or parts of the directory tree (perhaps remote).

/media – where things like the optical drives are mounted, but distinction between ***/mnt*** and ***/media*** is not clear. Again, your system may have it differently. In any ways, this is generally just a guidance.

/net – where you mount network shares (and in that regard, the distinction between this, and the ***/mnt*** for mounting the remote file tree is not very clear either; you can have this or that, or both...)

/dev – all your devices, mostly harddrives. Note the difference with ***/mnt***. The later is the mount point of a “software” things we talked above. The former is what's you have on the system box (mostly hardware).

/etc – When UNIX was being developed, there were few files its creators did not know where a good place for them would be. So they made a special directory named ***et cetera*** and used it for those files. Over the time it became the place where important configuration files are located. It will be one of our favorite directory to visit in the second half of the semester.

/proc – another directory which we will visit in the second half of the semester. For now let me just say, that in Linux everything is a file. Let's just take a note of that.

/tmp – place to put all the temp files, or files which you want to share with someone else without opening your directory. It gives a full access to all users on a system, so if you want to share some file with someone, just drop it there and that other user will be able to get it from there....

But so the other users too!.

It is also a good place to put some of the logs and result of script execution – if you think those will be large files and you are concerned about your disk quota, the ***/tmp*** is probably the place. Just be aware, that it is probably the first place to get cleaned, so if you start the script overnight or over the weekend, and next day come to the office eager to see your noble prize results, you may be disappointed to see that it's all gone.

/home – where all the users live. Each has its own space, which they can configure the way they want to; they can install their own software, so for example Bob has Java 5, Steve has Java 6, and system-wide installation is Java 7. They all can run at the same time without interfering with each other. Moreover, Bob can run some tools using Java 5, and at the same time, from another terminal he can use system-wide Java 7, **but he cannot run** Steve's Java 6.

Again, each user has its own home on the system. It's located under the ***/home*** directory and usually goes by the user's name. Thus, if my user name is "***user***" or "***vladimir***", or "***bob***", my home directory would be:

```
/home/user
```

or

```
/home/vladimir
```

or

```
/home/bob
```

(**Not** the ***/home***).

- You mentioned, a user can install its own software. Where would it go?
- It would go under that user's home directory... For example:

```
/home/bob/bin
```

and the libraries:

```
/home/bob/lib
```

And here we finally arrived to the rightmost directory on our nice tree diagram.

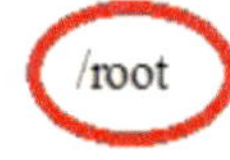

/root. It is the ***root's*** place. If Bob wants to see what ***root*** is up to, he can't. ***Root*** is a special user. ***Root's*** home directory is not under the ***/home*** as for the other mortals. There is special place. The ***/root***.

> So, we will use three meanings for the word "***root***":
> - Root as a ***root*** of the file and directory tree (A "point of entry" to the directory tree);
> - ***root*** as an owner of the system, and
> - ***root*** as a place where the ***root*** lives (home directory for the user ***root***).

Confusing? It is really not. From the context of discussion it should always be clear what meaning we use at every particular moment.

2. Navigating the directory tree.

To get from point A to point B you need to know couple of things.

1. Where the point A is, and
2. Where the point B is

Also, you need to have some navigational tools. It could be a sextant,

a map,

a GPS

or just description ("follow the yellow brick road").

And when we explain to someone how to get to that cinema theater or restaurant place, we could use two methods.

We can enumerate steps from that's person ***current*** location ("go down that street for couple of blocks, then turn right"), or we can tell to go to some "reference point" ("See that tall building?"), and then proceed from there.

In the first case we would give to the person the instructions that are ***relative*** to his/her current position (or to some known landmark).

In the second case we would give to that person the ***absolute*** direction. Which means, that next time that person is lost in other place, it is still possible to get to that tall building, and then repeat the previous navigation from there.

So, we have an absolute description (the ***path***), that starts from a certain point, and the relative description (the ***path***), that can start from anywhere. Interestingly, if you think for a moment, the absolute path is also relative to the certain point (to itself).

How does that apply to Linux?

In Linux the ***absolute path*** always starts from the ***root*** of the directory tree.

- And the relative one?
- The relative one starts from any place (including the root of the tree, however funny it is). You can build a path from your current location, or from any other arbitrary place.
- And how could I see if that is an absolute path or the relative one?
- That one is simple.

If your path starts with the forward slash : / that is an ***absolute path***. So, by just looking at the leftmost character in the path, you can always say which one it is.

Now, suppose user Bob wants to navigate from his home directory to the ***/tmp.*** If he asked for our help, what direction would we give to him?

Let's recall our drawing (we need only part of that):

First thing's first. Where is the point A?

It is here:

– And point B?

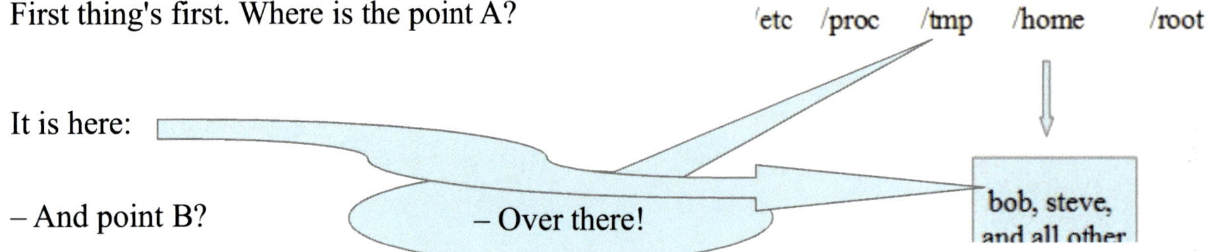

So, what would be our description, that we give to Bob?

Let's start with the ***absolute*** one:

```
/tmp
```

Note, that here we tell to go to the ***root*** of the directory tree (that tall building), and then make one step descending into the ***tmp*** underneath.

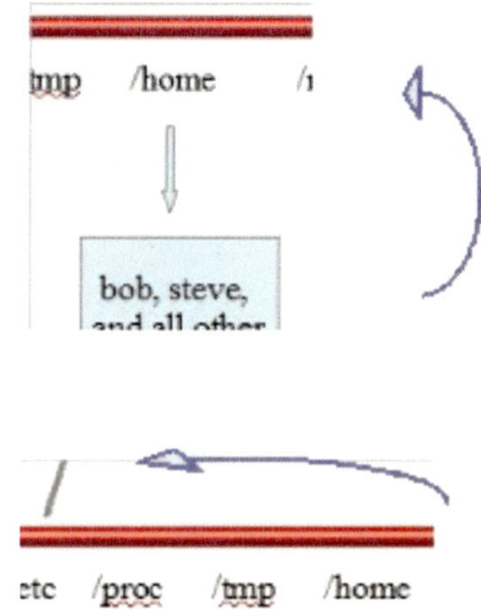

- And the one, relative to his home directory?
- That would be like this:

1. Go one step up from your home directory, which is

```
/home/bob
```

That would take you to the

```
/home
```

2. Then go one more step up to get to the ***root*** of the tree.
3. And then descend to the ***tmp*** (as we did first time).

- Hmmmm. Sort of confusing. How would poor Bob know all these locations?
- Linux wants to make things easy. Each directory, even the empty one has two special entries: The single dot (**.**) and the double dot (**..**). The single dot always refers to the "**this**" directory. Whenever you are on the system, it always refers to your current location. That is very useful, you don't have to remember that long path. Every time you want to refer to your location, you use a single dot (a "where am I" feature on the GPS).

The double dot always refers to the parent directory, or one level up from the current directory. It has meaning for all directories except the ***root*** of the directory tree. The ***root*** of the directory tree does not have anything above that, so there is no meaning for the double dot there.

Thus, our navigational guide (the ***path***) that we would give to Bob would be like that:

```
../../tmp
```

Where first double dot takes Bob to the **/home**, second double dot takes him to the ***root*** of the tree, and then descending one level down to the ***tmp***.

> Note, that the forward slash is also a path separator, i.e. it separates directories in the path.

> Note, that once I am at the ***root*** of the tree, to descend to the ***tmp***, I can use either : ***/tmp*** or ***tmp***. At that point it does not matter. It's like on the North Pole. All ways will lead to south.

And to conclude this section, I'll just mention, that when you log in to the system, you are taken to your home directory. So you start your new session in your home directory.

3. Finding your place and changing directories.

Alright, that was quite an introduction. Let's see some examples.

How to find out where on the directory tree you are located? There is a command ***pwd***: "path to the working directory", or "print working directory" – either one.

Let's see how it works (type a command on the shell prompt and hit <enter>)

```
cs130@raspberrypi ~ 2 pwd
/home/cs130
cs130@raspberrypi ~ 3
```

pwd with no arguments should give you **/home/<user>** (let's for now assume, that the users' home directories are under the /***home***, which is the default on probably most systems). Note, that the path printed out back to you is an ***absolute*** one (starts with the ***root*** of the tree).

Suppose I want to change to the ***/tmp***. There is a command **cd**, for "change directory". You need to provide path to the target directory as an argument of that command. Target directory has to exist.

> 1. In Linux almost all commands that take arguments (or parameters) use dash or minus sign followed by an argument. You can see both terms, I will almost exclusively use "minus" because I was taught that way.
> 2. Commands can accept an abbreviated parameters (a single character), or a verbose one (a word or more than one word). In the first case you would use them with the single minus, in the second case it would be double minus (--).
> 3. Please very carefully follow my syntax. To have that space or not to have that space may have a difference.

Let's use previous discussion and change to the ***/tmp*** few times.

Let's go from my home to the ***/tmp***. We can do it like that:

```
cd ../../tmp
```

```
cs130@raspberrypi ~ 6 cd ../../tmp
cs130@raspberrypi /tmp 7 pwd
/tmp
```

or like that:

```
cd /tmp
```

```
cs130@raspberrypi ~ 10 cd /tmp
cs130@raspberrypi /tmp 11 pwd
/tmp
```

> To execute a command on a Linux, type the complete command at the terminal prompt and hit <enter>

Note, that even though we are at the ***/tmp*** after the previous command, we still can run the second command, because of absolute path we use there. It will not change our place on the system, but it will be dutifully executed. But if we did these commands in reverse, depending on the location the first command would take us to, we could get an error on the second command. That is the difference between an absolute and relative paths. In the first case you can do it from whatever location. In the second case, you need to correctly provide it in reference to the starting point.

Let's see:

```
cs130@raspberrypi /tmp 12 pwd
/tmp
cs130@raspberrypi /tmp 13 cd ../../tmp
cs130@raspberrypi /tmp 14 pwd
/tmp
```

– Hmmmmm... I don't see any error as you promised. Do I miss anything?

– Actually, not. Can anyone tell me, why there is no error here?

– Maybe because at the top level the double dot has no meaning?

– Exactly. When we get to the top of the tree (or, to be exact, to the root of the tree), there is no more way up. But that does not mean, that for any other places it will work the same way.

When after we are done we want to return back to our home directory, we can again do it by several ways (type command and hit <enter>):

```
cd /home/<user>
```

- Hmmmm
- What?
- No, nothing.

Suppose, though, that your home directory is not ***/home/<user>***. Suppose, the system was configured differently. And.... you do not know what it is. Or... you do not want to type that entire path.

You can do:

```
cd $HOME
```

And let the system to resolve that.

```
cs130@raspberrypi /tmp 16 cd $HOME
cs130@raspberrypi ~ 17 pwd
/home/cs130
```

- Hmmmm
- What??!!
- Too much typing.
- Right. I see the Linux user.

> Linux users are lazy people. If they don't have to type even one extra character, they would do anything, but not type that one extra character.

> The more typing, the more chances for a typo. In the world that depends on correct paths, arguments, commands etc, that is important.

Alright. As you wish.

```
cd ~
```

```
cs130@raspberrypi ~ 18 cd ~
cs130@raspberrypi ~ 19 pwd
/home/cs130
```

Just as a single dot always refers to your current place, the tilde always refers to your home directory. Thus, if you are located somewhere on the system and want to copy something to home, or to place starting from home, or if you want to change to another directory, relative to the home, you don't need to type the entire path, you can use ~/

That is good, but not good enough. There are too many characters to type still. One too many to be exact. Let's do

```
cd
```

```
cs130@raspberrypi ~ 20 cd
cs130@raspberrypi ~ 21 pwd
/home/cs130
```

cd with no arguments will always take you to your home directory.

Alright. We finally managed to get back to our home directory without getting hopelessly lost, and after a while we want to change back to the one we were previously (in our case it would be ***/tmp***). You already may guess that there are few ways of doing that.

You can type

```
cd -
```

Note the minus sign at the end. That will tell ***cd*** to change to the previous directory, so you don't have to type that entire long path again.

- That's really cool! But what if I want to change to some other directory which I visited; and, since by this point I already feel myself as an accomplished Linux user in the sense that I don't want to type that many characters, I don't want to type all those?
- Sure. Let's do this.

```
history
```

3.1. History

As you can expect from its name, the ***history*** keeps history of the commands.

Here is how last few commands from my raspberry pi look like (note the last executed command is the ***history***). Note the commands are shown with full list of arguments and the commands' numbers, so that I can refer them by numbers too.

I believe the list in the history can hold as many as 1000 entries (by default), so you have quite some memory to keep history of what you've done few days back. That is convenient. Suppose, you ran some specific particular command with long list of arguments, typing a long line... By now you may not remember exactly what was all that. Having that entry in the history allows you to quickly re-run that command. Not only that. Having entry in the history allows you to run the command by its number, so you don't have to type everything back again. That is ***very*** convenient. Very!

How you do that? When in the history you see the command you want to execute (say, it would have number 123 in the history list), you type an exclamation mark followed by that command's number:

```
!123
```

And you actually don't have to type ***history*** to see the list. You can use up and down arrow keys to scroll through the history, and when you see the command you want to, just hit the <enter>.

It will not be practical to scroll through all 1000 entries,  but you definitely would do that for few most recent commands.

Again, that is ***very*** useful feature if you have a long command line with long list of arguments and you don't want to type them all (and to make typos).

> I will return to these words "***very*** useful" ***very*** often throughout the semester. It is only amazing, how creators of the Unix were thoughtful of human-computer interaction and system's usability. Well. They did the system for themselves to work on. That may explain few things.

Back to the ***history***. You can also do

```
!cd
```

That will execute the last command that starts from characters ***cd***.

You can also replace some string from the most recent command by something else:

^str1^str2^

Suppose you want to change directory to … say, ***/etc***. Your last command was

```
cd /tmp
```

so you would do:

```
^tmp^etc^
```

That one last example is rather silly, because it is easier to type just

```
cd /etc
```

But the intention here is to allow you to easily replace some part of the command – whether it be the typo you did, or change the argument, without necessity of retyping everything again from the start.

> More typing == more typos!

4. Autocompletion feature

> More typing == more typos!

So people tried to do everything they could thought of to reduce amount of typing. When you type the directory name or the file name, or (some) command, after just few characters you entered, shell may already recognize what you are typing. At that point, why bother typing all the rest of it?

Type few characters, and hit a <**tab**> key. If ***shell*** can uniquely recognize the word (the name), it will autocomplete the rest. If not, it will do nothing. But if you see nothing, don't stop there. Hit <**tab**> for the second time. If there are entries that begin with those characters, ***shell*** will show that list to you, so you can do intelligent checks. If after the second time ***shell*** shows nothing, there is no such things in the known inhabitable world and you may want to check your typing.

That is an immensely useful feature. It saves people from so many mistakes and problems!

When I am on a system, the <**tab**> key is almost my home key. I hit it at every occasion I can, and on those occasions I cannot, I still hit it, only harder. These days, other systems also adopted that feature, but it is amazing how people back .... in the dark ages could figure that one out.

5. Three things to always know while on the system.

Every time you work on a system, you need to know and remember three things:

- who you are,
- where you are, and
- what machine you are on.

– What? That is so silly! How can I not know, who am I?

Actually that's not that hard. And no, you don't need to go to another dimension. All you need to do is to work with several open terminals at the same time. Eventually switching directories, users, and machines. So, before you type the command and hit enter, you need to be very well aware: who you are, where you are, and what machine you are on.

There is no undo on Linux!

There is no undo on Linux. And the price of mistake can be... hefty. Here I will convey to you what my Professor told us:

You typed that command. Long line, lot of everything. Now. Take your hands off the keyboard, sit back and check it with your eyes. Everything is correct? All the paths, directories? Parameters, arguments? Files? Everything is correct? Sure?

Hit enter.

And there is no undo.

So, let's first find out who you are. Again, not because you forgot your name, but because you may get lost, under which login you are on that terminal.

As you can expect, there is a command for that:

whoami

```
cs130@raspberrypi ~ 22 whoami
cs130
cs130@raspberrypi ~ 23
```

(**cs130** is my user name on that Raspberry Pi, which I use for the demo).

Where you are:

```
pi@raspberrypi ~ $ whereami
bash: whereami: command not found
pi@raspberrypi ~ $
```

Ahh. That did not work......

Does that mean that we are limited in our creativity? Let's do something:

alias whereami='pwd'

```
cs130@raspberrypi ~ 23 alias whereami='pwd'
cs130@raspberrypi ~ 24 whereami
/home/cs130
```

And we should see the path to the working directory (again, given as an absolute path).

6. Aliases

Alias for the command is what it is. It allows you to make a new command, as we just did, or change the meaning of the existing command. For example, many people create aliases to include parameters they use most often, like that one below (we will talk about an ***ls*** command soon) :

alias ll='ls -l'

(Didn't I tell that the Linux people are lazy?)

I am not limited to just one command in the alias:

alias time='date;echo "time to go home"'

```
pi@raspberrypi ~ $ alias time='date;echo "time to go home"'
pi@raspberrypi ~ $ time
Tue Aug 18 05:48:37 UTC 2020
time to go home
pi@raspberrypi ~ $
```

Let's stop here for a moment and discuss what we see here.

First, I create an alias that executes a command ***date***. As you can figure out, that command sets/displays system's date and time. When run without arguments, as I just did, it runs in the display mode. Running it with arguments will set the time or date, and you need to be the ***root***. That command is terminated by the semicolon. People taking programming classes will recognize that syntax.

– But we did not use semicolon in the previous command!

- No, we did not. Nor we needed to because there was just one command there, and shell could figure that out by itself. But here we do need it. We need it for two purposes.
    1. To separate the commands and
    2. To run second command immediately after (**and no sooner**) when the first command completes. That is an immense feature. We will talk about that more than one time. Now proceeding with the rest of our alias.

After the ***date*** commands completes, the message is printed out on the screen by using an ***echo*** command. Again, as you could guess, the ***echo*** repeats on the terminal screen whatever argument I give to it. In our case it is a message telling me that it is time to go home. Note the placement of the single quotes and double quotes. I could just use all single quotes, but that would unnecessary complicate my syntax.

Here is the rule number one:

> **The simpler == the better.**

– What if I wanted to have some special characters there?

– Let's try. How about this:

alias whatamiinto="echo don\'t panic"

```
pi@raspberrypi ~ $ alias whatamiinto="echo don\'t panic"
pi@raspberrypi ~ $ whatamiinto
don't panic
pi@raspberrypi ~ $
```

Note the backslash to escape the meaning of the single quote, which has a special meaning in the shell. Again, people taking the programming classes would recognize the escape syntax. We will use that in our class too, although probably not that extensively.

How to see all the aliases you have? Just run the command without arguments:

```
pi@raspberrypi ~ $ alias
alias egrep='egrep --color=auto'
alias fgrep='fgrep --color=auto'
alias grep='grep --color=auto'
alias ls='ls --color=auto'
alias time='date;echo "time to go home"'
alias whatamiinto='echo don\'\''t panic'
alias whereami='pwd'
```

These are my aliases I created

As as side note, do you see all those escapes I would need to have typed myself if I went with all the single quotes in the previous example? But since I am.... oh, yes, so.... I did not want to get lost with all those, and simply used combination of single and double quotes, politely letting the ***shell*** to do the work for me.

Alright. The last three are mine. What about others? Those are set and configured during the installation (or later by the root) and are inherited by all users on a system.

I could also see if there is an alias already existed for the command I want to check. For example to see if there is (and what it is) the alias for the ***whatamiinto***, I would run this:

```
alias whatamiinto
```

And it should show me that (if that alias exists).

What if I don't want to have that silly alias? Who in the right mind would create one like that?

First, if I just made it, I can simply wait until the session terminates. All those settings are for the lifetime of the session only. When session ends, they are gone (we will talk how to make them persistent later). But if you need to remove it now, you'd do:

```
pi@raspberrypi ~ $ unalias whatamiinto
pi@raspberrypi ~ $ whatamiinto
bash: whatamiinto: command not found
pi@raspberrypi ~ $
```

7. What is the shell?

We already mentioned that word few times today. I guess we need to talk a little about what it is.

So we have the hardware. User does not interact with the hardware. When I type, I don't go inside to pull and push those dusty switches there; and when I read from the screen, I do not peek into the monitor to catch all those traces of light.

It is the OS that interacts with the hardware for me.

But user does not interact directly with the OS either. There is an additional layer there. When I interact with the computer, I interact with the OS through the ***shell***. Thus, the ***shell*** serves as my interface to the OS. Now let's look at the last picture again. :

Specifically, to here:

```
pi@raspberrypi ~ $ unalias whatamiinto
pi@raspberrypi ~ $ whatamiinto
bash: whatamiinto: command not found
pi@raspberrypi ~ $
```

What is that ***bash*** thing?

It is just the name of the ***shell***. There are at least few ***shells*** available. There used to be heated and involved debates:

– This shell is better, because....
– No, ***that*** shell is better, because....

Systems could ship with more than one ***shell*** installed, allowing you an option, as to which one to use, sometimes switching them during the same session...

These days, it seems that (one of) the most ubiquitous ***shell*** is the ***bash***. So, that line tells me that ***bash*** could not find the command that I tried to execute.

7.1. Subshell

If I had more than one shell installed I could switch to different one by simply typing its name and hitting the <**enter**>

What if I type the name of the ***bash*** and hit <**enter**> while I am already on the ***bash*** session?

bash <enter>

```
cs130@raspberrypi ~ $ bash
cs130@raspberrypi ~ $
```

Nothing visible happens, but silently, I am taken into new subshell session.

How do I know?

pstree <enter>

and find the branch with the ***shell***. Like that:

```
 ├─sshd───sshd─┬─bash───bash───pstree
```

You see, that I am on the second ***bash*** session.

Now let's run some commands under that subshell:

```
pi@raspberrypi ~ $ cd /tmp; cd / ; pwd;
/
pi@raspberrypi / $
```

Note, how I use the semicolon to run more than one command at the same command line. These commands run in the sequence, one after another. So what we see, is that I changed directory and printed the current path, which is ***root*** of the directory tree.

Now if I exit the subshell and print working directory from there, it will show me the place where I was before (let me skip the screenshot, you would take my word on it, right?). The command is: **`exit`**.

But that's not enough. Let's see the last entries of the history of the current shell session:

```
 645  bash
 646  pwd
 647  history
i@raspberrypi ~ $
```

There is no history of those commands that we did after opening a new bash session (#645). Remember, history keeps commands from the last session. Since we closed the subshell, but it was not the last session, its history is gone.

- Wait! Are you trying to hide something?
- No, no!
- What's the purpose of that then?
- If I am on a multi-terminal session, I can open a new terminal to run something with specific configuration, which I do not want to be for my main session. Or I may want to check some configuration before applying it to my profile. But I may not be on a multi-terminal session. I could be on a single-terminal session. I may also do some dull repeating task that I do not want to fill up the entire history (say, I compile code hundreds times per day while fixing bugs). In these cases, that option is quite useful.

And also, (and that is also very useful), I can do this as part of the script (or running a command), that opens a subshell, does some changes in configuration to run something else and then by exiting the subshell, everything is reverted back to normal by itself. Here is a very simple example, using what we already know:

Checking the existing aliases
Opening new session, creating alias, checking
Running command, exiting session
Checking aliases in the old session
Just to make sure: No, that session is gone.
cs130@raspberrypi ~ 17 alias
alias egrep='egrep --color=auto'
alias fgrep='fgrep --color=auto'
alias grep='grep --color=auto'
alias ls='ls --color=auto'
cs130@raspberrypi ~ 18 bash
cs130@raspberrypi ~ 1 alias mysillyalias='echo "never panic"'
cs130@raspberrypi ~ 2 alias
alias egrep='egrep --color=auto'
alias fgrep='fgrep --color=auto'
alias grep='grep --color=auto'
alias ls='ls --color=auto'
alias mysillyalias='echo "never panic"'
cs130@raspberrypi ~ 3 mysillyalias
never panic
cs130@raspberrypi ~ 4 exit
exit
cs130@raspberrypi ~ 19 alias
alias egrep='egrep --color=auto'
alias fgrep='fgrep --color=auto'
alias grep='grep --color=auto'
alias ls='ls --color=auto'
cs130@raspberrypi ~ 20
cs130@raspberrypi ~ 20
cs130@raspberrypi ~ 20 bash
cs130@raspberrypi ~ 1 alias
alias egrep='egrep --color=auto'
alias fgrep='fgrep --color=auto'
alias grep='grep --color=auto'
alias ls='ls --color=auto'
cs130@raspberrypi ~ 2

– Hmmmm. It's like a portal to other world to enter in and out....

Alright. Let's move on.

8. Listing the content of the directory

Now we can navigate our way through the space. But how to see what's around and near us?

The command to list the content of the directory is, as you may expect, is this:

ls

With no arguments it will print just the names of the files in the current directory.

```
cs130@raspberrypi ~ 8 touch myfiles{1..100}
cs130@raspberrypi ~ 9 ls
aliases     myfiles18  myfiles29  myfiles4   myfiles50  myfiles61  myfiles72  myfiles83  myfiles94
dir1        myfiles19  myfiles3   myfiles40  myfiles51  myfiles62  myfiles73  myfiles84  myfiles95
myfiles1    myfiles2   myfiles30  myfiles41  myfiles52  myfiles63  myfiles74  myfiles85  myfiles96
myfiles10   myfiles20  myfiles31  myfiles42  myfiles53  myfiles64  myfiles75  myfiles86  myfiles97
myfiles100  myfiles21  myfiles32  myfiles43  myfiles54  myfiles65  myfiles76  myfiles87  myfiles98
myfiles11   myfiles22  myfiles33  myfiles44  myfiles55  myfiles66  myfiles77  myfiles88  myfiles99
myfiles12   myfiles23  myfiles34  myfiles45  myfiles56  myfiles67  myfiles78  myfiles89
myfiles13   myfiles24  myfiles35  myfiles46  myfiles57  myfiles68  myfiles79  myfiles9
myfiles14   myfiles25  myfiles36  myfiles47  myfiles58  myfiles69  myfiles8   myfiles90
myfiles15   myfiles26  myfiles37  myfiles48  myfiles59  myfiles7   myfiles80  myfiles91
myfiles16   myfiles27  myfiles38  myfiles49  myfiles6   myfiles70  myfiles81  myfiles92
myfiles17   myfiles28  myfiles39  myfiles5   myfiles60  myfiles71  myfiles82  myfiles93
cs130@raspberrypi ~ 10
```

And we see another useful command. The ***touch*** "touches" the file(s) given to it as an argument to update the time stamp. If files not exist (and I don't know whether that was an intended feature, or not), the file is created (it is only logical), although it would be empty. Why this command needed is another story, just remember, that system was created by the programmers for the programmers. A lot of tools there are to work and to help working with the code. That particular command is very useful when you want to include some source files into the build but do not want to open and edit them just to change the time stamp. And also... there could be that I want to create a file, even a temporary one, and why would I have to fill it with something?

That was a side comment; But I used that command to populate empty directory with hundreds of files to see how the ***ls*** command works.

You see, that it lists the file names. By default it sort them alphabetically.

Let's see some of the flags for the ***ls***.

```
ls -l (a small el)
```

Generates a long listing (also sorted alphabetically):

```
cs130@raspberrypi ~/dir1 15 ls -l
total 0
-rw-r--r-- 1 cs130 cs130 0 Aug 19 03:36 myfiles1
-rw-r--r-- 1 cs130 cs130 0 Aug 19 03:36 myfiles10
-rw-r--r-- 1 cs130 cs130 0 Aug 19 03:36 myfiles100
-rw-r--r-- 1 cs130 cs130 0 Aug 19 03:36 myfiles11
-rw-r--r-- 1 cs130 cs130 0 Aug 19 03:36 myfiles12
-rw-r--r-- 1 cs130 cs130 0 Aug 19 03:36 myfiles13
-rw-r--r-- 1 cs130 cs130 0 Aug 19 03:36 myfiles14
```

… and you already see the problem: All these files do not fit into the screen. Let's list 10 files between 20-29:

```
cs130@raspberrypi ~/dir1 16
cs130@raspberrypi ~/dir1 16 ls -l myfiles2*
-rw-r--r-- 1 cs130 cs130 0 Aug 19 03:36 myfiles2
-rw-r--r-- 1 cs130 cs130 0 Aug 19 03:36 myfiles20
-rw-r--r-- 1 cs130 cs130 0 Aug 19 03:36 myfiles21
-rw-r--r-- 1 cs130 cs130 0 Aug 19 03:36 myfiles22
-rw-r--r-- 1 cs130 cs130 0 Aug 19 03:36 myfiles23
-rw-r--r-- 1 cs130 cs130 0 Aug 19 03:36 myfiles24
-rw-r--r-- 1 cs130 cs130 0 Aug 19 03:36 myfiles25
-rw-r--r-- 1 cs130 cs130 0 Aug 19 03:36 myfiles26
-rw-r--r-- 1 cs130 cs130 0 Aug 19 03:36 myfiles27
-rw-r--r-- 1 cs130 cs130 0 Aug 19 03:36 myfiles28
-rw-r--r-- 1 cs130 cs130 0 Aug 19 03:36 myfiles29
cs130@raspberrypi ~/dir1 17
```

What I actually typed was:

```
ls -l myf<tab>2*
```

Note the asterisk for the wild character.

Now let's look at that screen. Going from right to the left:

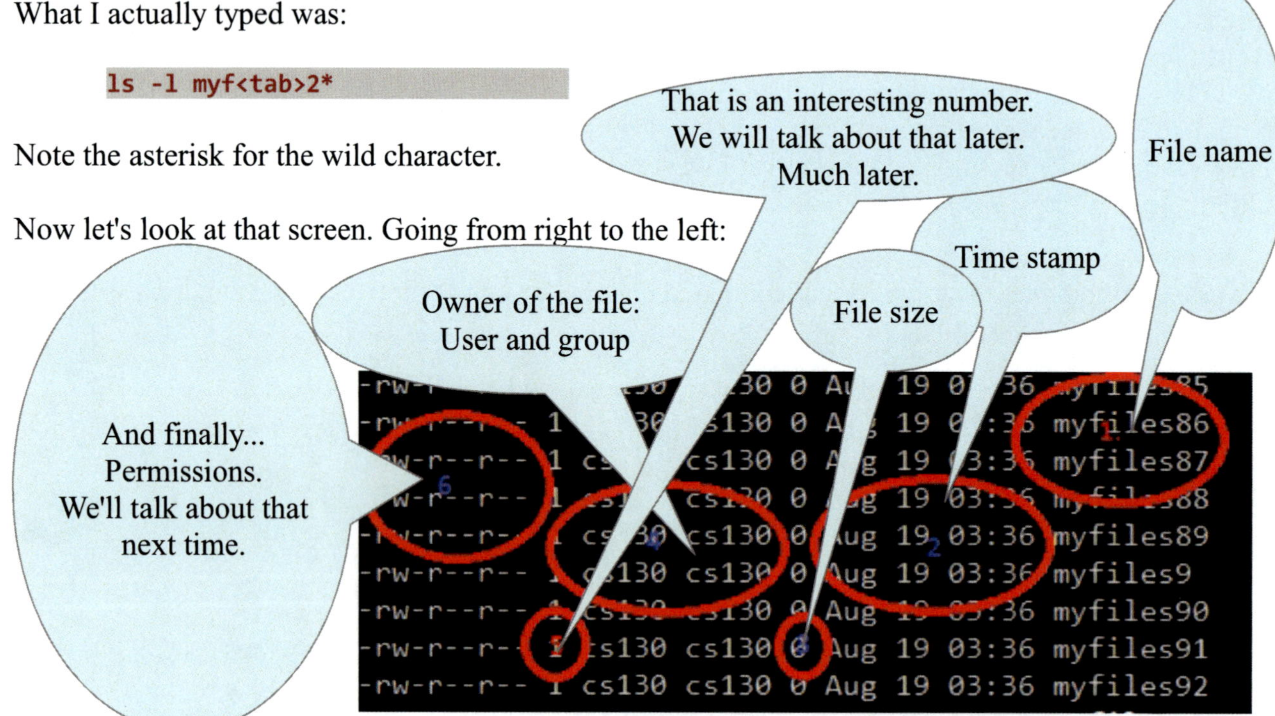

Let's return to the *ls* command. Since some time passed while I was making that great illustrations, I can now change the time stamp of a file for the next demo:

```
touch myfile29
```

and then do this:

```
ls -ltr
```

```
-rw-r--r-- 1 cs130 cs130 0 Aug 19 03:36 myfiles45
-rw-r--r-- 1 cs130 cs130 0 Aug 19 03:36 myfiles44
-rw-r--r-- 1 cs130 cs130 0 Aug 19 03:36 myfiles43
-rw-r--r-- 1 cs130 cs130 0 Aug 19 03:36 myfiles42
-rw-r--r-- 1 cs130 cs130 0 Aug 19 03:36 myfiles100
-rw-r--r-- 1 cs130 cs130 0 Aug 19 04:19 myfiles29
cs130@raspberrypi ~/dir1 19
```

I asked **ls** to give me a long listing (*-l*), sorted by time stamp (*t*), in the reverse order (*r*). And you can see the file that I accessed most recently is at the bottom of the screen.

I promised I would say words "that is very convenient" often. Here it is again.

One last thing here. People may recall me saying that every directory has two special entries: A single dot and a double dot. But we did a listing of this directory and did not see them. Where are they?

Let's add another flag to the **ls**:

```
cs130@raspberrypi ~/dir1 19 ls -a
.           myfiles18  myfiles29  myfiles4   myfiles50  myfiles61  myfiles72  myfiles83  myfiles94
..          myfiles19  myfiles3   myfiles40  myfiles51  myfiles62  myfiles73  myfiles84  myfiles95
myfiles1    myfiles2   myfiles30  myfiles41  myfiles52  myfiles63  myfiles74  myfiles85  myfiles96
myfiles10   myfiles20  myfiles31  myfiles42  myfiles53  myfiles64  myfiles75  myfiles86  myfiles97
myfiles100  myfiles21  myfiles32  myfiles43  myfiles54  myfiles65  myfiles76  myfiles87  myfiles98
myfiles11   myfiles22  myfiles33  myfiles44  myfiles55  myfiles66  myfiles77  myfiles88  myfiles99
```

(-**a**) flag tells **ls** to print all entries. In Linux, files starting with the dot are hidden files. They are not shown in the regular listing, but we can see them with the **(-a)** switch. Here you see the first two entries in the listing are our single dot and the double dot. So I did not lie.

Just to prove the point about hidden files:

```
cs130@raspberrypi ~/dir1 33 touch .another_file difffile
cs130@raspberrypi ~/dir1 34 ls --hide=myfil*
difffile
cs130@raspberrypi ~/dir1 35 ls -a
.              myfiles17  myfiles29  myfiles40  myfiles52  myfiles64  myfiles76  myfiles88
..             myfiles18  myfiles3   myfiles41  myfiles53  myfiles65  myfiles77  myfiles89
.another_file  myfiles19  myfiles30  myfiles42  myfiles54  myfiles66  myfiles78  myfiles9
difffile       myfiles2   myfiles31  myfiles43  myfiles55  myfiles67  myfiles79  myfiles90
myfiles1       myfiles20  myfiles32  myfiles44  myfiles56  myfiles68  myfiles8   myfiles91
myfiles10      myfiles21  myfiles33  myfiles45  myfiles57  myfiles69  myfiles80  myfiles92
```

look here

I leave it to you to figure out what I did with the commands ##33-35, and the output I got as result of that.

9. Working with files and directories

Now let's talk how to make directory, copy directory, remove it, and how to copy, delete, and rename files. Let's begin.

```
cs130@raspberrypi ~/dir1 40
cs130@raspberrypi ~/dir1 40 mkdir dir2
cs130@raspberrypi ~/dir1 41 ls
difffile     myfiles18  myfiles29  myfiles4   myfiles50
dir2         myfiles19  myfiles3   myfiles40  myfiles51
myfiles1     myfiles2   myfiles30  myfiles41  myfiles52
myfiles10    myfiles20  myfiles31  myfiles42  myfiles53
```

mkdir (no surprises here) makes a directory. Directory with such name should not exist in this location, or there will be an error:

```
cs130@raspberrypi ~/dir1 43
cs130@raspberrypi ~/dir1 43 mkdir dir2
mkdir: cannot create directory `dir2': File exists
cs130@raspberrypi ~/dir1 44
```

Did I mention that everything is a file in Linux? Here is one example of that.

Let's do the long listing on our current directory.

```
cs130@raspberrypi ~/dir1 45 ls -l
total 4
-rw-r--r-- 1 cs130 cs130    0 Aug 19 04:34 difffile
drwxr-xr-x 2 cs130 cs130 4096 Aug 19 05:18 dir2
-rw-r--r-- 1 cs130 cs130    0 Aug 19 03:36 myfiles1
```


Compare that with those for the regular files. See the difference? Here how we know which entry is a regular file (-) or the directory (d). Not by nice color. Your terminal may not support colors. But by the leftmost character in the long listing.

Actually... You know what? I don't like that name. Let's rename it.

```
cs130@raspberrypi ~/dir1 46 mv dir2 dir3
cs130@raspberrypi ~/dir1 47 ls
difffile     myfiles18  myfiles29  myfiles4   myfiles50
dir3         myfiles19  myfiles3   myfiles40  myfiles51
```

mv command moves file or directory from one location to another. It is also how you rename them. You do so by moving them from one name to another.

The order of the arguments for the commands involving source and destination is that: source → destination.

Now let me run these commands and then I'll explain what I did:

```
cs130@raspberrypi ~/dir1 48 pwd
/home/cs130/dir1
cs130@raspberrypi ~/dir1 49 mv dir3 ~/
cs130@raspberrypi ~/dir1 50 ls ~/
aliases  dir1  dir3
cs130@raspberrypi ~/dir1 51 ls
difffile    myfiles19  myfiles3   myfiles40  myfiles51
myfiles1    myfiles2   myfiles30  myfiles41  myfiles52
myfiles10   myfiles20  myfiles31  myfiles42  myfiles53
```

Let's follow that line by line.

#48: Check where I am (always know where you are on the system!)
#49: Moving the directory ***dir3*** to my home directory. Note how I refer the home directory! Again, no matter where I am on the directory tree, I can always refer to my home directory like that.
#50: Proving that home directory contains ***dir3*** here
#51: Proving that there is no ***dir3*** in my current location.

That's how I move directory from one place to another.

Actually, I changed my mind.

```
cs130@raspberrypi ~/dir1 52
cs130@raspberrypi ~/dir1 52 mv ~/dir3 ./dir5
cs130@raspberrypi ~/dir1 53 ls
difffile    myfiles18  myfiles29  myfiles4   myfiles50
dir5        myfiles19  myfiles3   myfiles40  myfiles51
myfiles1    myfiles2   myfiles30  myfiles41  myfiles52
```

#52: Moving directory ***dir3*** from home to the current directory and renaming it.
#53: Yes, it was moved to here and renamed to ***dir5***. Take my word that there is no ***dir3*** is in the home directory now.

Note the syntax! Note, how I use the single dot to refer to the current directory!

Ahhh. I am tired of that and don't want that directory anymore. At all!

```
cs130@raspberrypi ~/dir1 55 rmdir dir5
cs130@raspberrypi ~/dir1 56 ls
difffile    myfiles19  myfiles3   myfiles40
myfiles1    myfiles2   myfiles30  myfiles41
```

As you can guess, the **`rmdir`** command removes that annoying directory with no hope to resurrect it.

But actually I think I did it too soon. We need it for the following demonstration.

The history is our friend:

```
  540  ls -l
  541  mkdir dir2
  542
  543  ls -l
  544  mv dir2 dir3
  545  ls
  546  pwd
  547  mv dir3 ~/
  548  ls ~/
  549  ls
  550  mv ~/dir3 ./dir5
  551  ls
  552  ls ~/
  553  rmdir dir5
  554  ls
  555  history
cs130@raspberrypi ~/dir1 58 !541
mkdir dir2
cs130@raspberrypi ~/dir1 59
```

And now let's see how we can work with the files. Explanations below.

```
cs130@raspberrypi ~/dir1 59 cp myfiles1* dir2/
cs130@raspberrypi ~/dir1 60 ls dir2/
myfiles1   myfiles100  myfiles12  myfiles14  myfiles16  myfiles18
myfiles10  myfiles11   myfiles13  myfiles15  myfiles17  myfiles19
cs130@raspberrypi ~/dir1 61 ls myfiles1*
myfiles1   myfiles100  myfiles12  myfiles14  myfiles16  myfiles18
myfiles10  myfiles11   myfiles13  myfiles15  myfiles17  myfiles19
cs130@raspberrypi ~/dir1 62
cs130@raspberrypi ~/dir1 62
cs130@raspberrypi ~/dir1 62 mv myfiles2* dir2/
cs130@raspberrypi ~/dir1 63 ls dir2/
myfiles1    myfiles11  myfiles14  myfiles17  myfiles2   myfiles22  myfiles25  myfiles28
myfiles10   myfiles12  myfiles15  myfiles18  myfiles20  myfiles23  myfiles26  myfiles29
myfiles100  myfiles13  myfiles16  myfiles19  myfiles21  myfiles24  myfiles27
cs130@raspberrypi ~/dir1 64 ls myfiles2*
ls: cannot access myfiles2*: No such file or directory
cs130@raspberrypi ~/dir1 65 rm dir2/myfiles1*
cs130@raspberrypi ~/dir1 66 ls dir2/
myfiles2   myfiles21  myfiles23  myfiles25  myfiles27  myfiles29
myfiles20  myfiles22  myfiles24  myfiles26  myfiles28
cs130@raspberrypi ~/dir1 67
```

Let's follow that line by line.
#59: Copy files from current place to the directory ***dir2***.

##60,61: See that both, source and destination have these files.
##62-64: similarly, but instead of copying files, moving them.
#65: Removing files. Note the different command for files: **rm** , as opposed to **rmdir** for directories.

So you see, working with the files and directories are pretty similar. Alright. Now I am done and can remove that directory.

```
cs130@raspberrypi ~/dir1 67 rmdir dir2
rmdir: failed to remove `dir2': Directory not empty
cs130@raspberrypi ~/dir1 68
```

You cannot remove the non-empty directory. What to do? We can try to clean it first:

```
rm dir2/*
```

That should remove all files from that directory.... But what if there are other directories there, including hidden ones? It may be that manually removing all of directory' entries could be very tedious task.

There are couple of commands on the Linux that scary me to death every time I need to run them. One of them is that:

```
cs130@raspberrypi ~/dir1 68 rm -rf dir2/
cs130@raspberrypi ~/dir1 69
cs130@raspberrypi ~/dir1 69 ls
difffile    myfiles17  myfiles36  myfiles45  myfiles54  myfiles63
myfiles1    myfiles18  myfiles37  myfiles46  myfiles55  myfiles64
myfiles10   myfiles19  myfiles38  myfiles47  myfiles56  myfiles65
```

Here I recursively (-r) and forcefully (-f) remove all entries in the directory and the directory itself.

Why is that so scaring?

> Always know who you are and where you are on a system!

If, as a root I run a command, that resolves to this:

```
rm -rf /
```

.... After I hit <enter> , I would have enough time to prepare to the quickly approaching meeting with my manager, because this command will remove the entire directory tree.....

BTW, that is one of the attack on a Linux.

> Do no harm!!!

And finally, let me mention couple of useful flags for the copy command:

cp -p
keeps file attributes, including modification time etc.
cp -r
recursive copy (traverses all the directories beyond the current one)

For example, to create a backup copy of your directory branch, you would do:

cp -pr <your starting directory> <destination>

We will talk a little bit about copy and move commands next time, but for now that concludes today's lecture.

10. Summary and review

.	(single dot) current dir	**alias ls="ls -l"**; alias - shows all aliases.
..	(double dot) one level up.	
~/	Your home dir.	**history** – Keeps history from the last closed terminal, merging it with previous entries. Up/down arrows scrolls through the hist. !number, !string - repeat last cmd (number) or string ^str1^str2^ - substitute str1 for str2

Commands: ***cd, pwd, whoami, alias, ls, mkdir, rmdir, rm, mv, cp***

Lecture 3. Linux permissions, *PATH* variable.

Today we will discuss couple wonderful topics. But first, following the laws of drama, let's start with something ordinary. We will start with discussion on some features of copy and move commands that I purposefully left for this lecture.

1. Copy/move files (contd)

When last time we discussed how to copy/move files, we did not talk what would happen if the destination exists (in other words, when there is file or directory with the same name and in that same location).

Let me quickly run few commands one by one (you know that I use <*tabs*> key and scrolling through the history whenever I can, even if you cannot see that on the screen).

```
cs130@raspberrypi ~ 11
cs130@raspberrypi ~ 11 mkdir dir1
cs130@raspberrypi ~ 12 cd !$
cd dir1
cs130@raspberrypi ~/dir1 13 touch myfiles{1..5}
cs130@raspberrypi ~/dir1 14 cp myfiles1 ../
cs130@raspberrypi ~/dir1 15 cp myfiles1 ../
cp: overwrite '../myfiles1'?
```

You should understand everything did here with one exception at line #12. What is that funny looking weird thing there? there

What I asked ***bash*** for, was to repeat the last argument from the previous command. The last argument from the previous command was '***dir1***'. I did not want to type the ***dir1*** again because.... you know why, so I asked ***bash*** to do that work for me.

Back to the copying files. The last two commands on that screen copy the same file to the same destination. Thus, for the second time, that file should exist there. If your copy command is configured with default (-**i**) flag (for the information), or you made an alias like that:

```
alias cp='cp -i'
```

you will see the warning/request for confirmation like we see on that screen. Thus, you will not accidentally overwrite an existing file. Which is good. To continue you need to reply '***yes***' or '***no***'. That is nice. The only problem here, is that if these commands configured such and you need to copy hundreds of files over, you very quickly will give up hitting '***yes***' for every single one. You will probably interrupt the entire thing and overwrite the default option by running command with (**-f**) flag (to force). We saw that switch last time. Let's kill (interrupt) the command and do it with the **-f** flag, the only thing, I will use ***mv***, not a ***cp***. The flags are the same.

> To interrupt the active (a running) command, you send Ctrl-C keys combination, i.e. pressing the Control key followed by letter 'c'. That is also handy way if you have typed a long line and want to clear the prompt; you don't need to backspace all those characters; just send interrupt signal and it will clear the line.

```
cs130@raspberrypi ~/dir1 26
cs130@raspberrypi ~/dir1 26 cp myfiles1 ../
cp: overwrite '../myfiles1'? ^C
cs130@raspberrypi ~/dir1 27 mv myfiles1 ../
mv: overwrite '../myfiles1'? ^C
cs130@raspberrypi ~/dir1 28 mv -f myfiles1 ../
cs130@raspberrypi ~/dir1 29
```

Ctrl-C

You see, this time there is no complains/warnings, and file at the destination is silently overwritten.

Why did not I talk about that last time?

I wanted to have a reason to say this thing:

To be able to copy or to move file or directory to some other location, you need to have an appropriate permissions for that location (unless you are the ***root***). Let's see couple of examples:

```
cs130@raspberrypi ~/dir1 3 cp myfiles2 /tmp/
cs130@raspberrypi ~/dir1 4 cp myfiles2 /etc/
cp: cannot create regular file '/etc/myfiles2': Permission denied
```

We talked, that */tmp* is open for everyone. But that is not so for any other place. You generally have permissions for your place and for the places allowing your group(s). And that takes me nicely to the next topic.

2. Permissions

Linux's security is based on simple and clever design. Its efficiency proven by almost half of century history of Unix/Linux.

Instead of relying on user-level access schema, that necessitates having half-dozen of various users' roles, Linux deploys a file-level access. Every file on the system is set with just three grades of access:

- The user (owner) of the file;

- The group that user belongs to; and
- Everyone else (the “world”, i.e. everyone on the system).

Thus, each file is set with the certain permissions. The ***root*** has a full access to the entire system, but all other users are created equal.

> The simpler == the better!

How to set (and read) permissions in Linux?

As always, there is more than one way of doing things. Let me first show you the right way, and then we'll do the easy way.

2.1. Permissions Linux way

We need to recall how to count in binary. Let's draw some table. On the left column there will be the binary numbers, while on the right – the decimal ones. Let's go.

Binary	Decimal
000	00
001	01
010	02
011	03
100	04
101	05
110	06
111	07

We don't need many rows. We can stop here. And while we are looking at that table, I will mention one property of the numbers on the left:

Each combination of bits gives an unique number in decimal (on the right). Thus, there is one and only one combination of the bits at the left such that it corresponds to the number 7 on the right. And the opposite is true as well. If I select any number from the right column, it will map uniquely to a one and the only one row at the left. Again, that is an important property to remember.

The rest is simple. Let's re-draw that table with different header.

rwx	
000	00
001	01
010	02
011	03
100	04
101	05
110	06
111	07

...And I hope by now you already see where I am leading to. Each bit in the binary number sets or clears corresponding permission in the ***r***ead-***w***rite-e***x***ecute sequence of flags. Note, that read-write-execute are ordered from the left to the right, and bits counting goes from the right to the left.

Thus, if I want to set the executable permission, I need to set the rightmost bit in its binary representation. If I want to remove that, I will clear that bit (set it to zero). Let's see.

Suppose I want to give all the permissions: read, write, and execute. I need to set all three bits to do so. By looking at the table, the only decimal number that maps all three bits set is 7. Thus, I will use number 7.

Suppose I want to give read and write permissions, but not execute. That would be number 6. Correspondingly, if I want to give a read permission only, that would be number 4 in decimal.

And again, since we need to set permissions for ourselves (the user), for the members of our group, and for the world, we need to set three numbers. The command is ***chmod*** for change the mode. Let's do it. As always, explanation's below.

```
cs130@raspberrypi ~/dir1 3 ls -lrt
total 0
-rw-r--r-- 1 cs130 cs130 0 Aug 28 20:11 myfiles5
-rw-r--r-- 1 cs130 cs130 0 Aug 28 20:11 myfiles4
-rw-r--r-- 1 cs130 cs130 0 Aug 28 20:11 myfiles3
-rw-r--r-- 1 cs130 cs130 0 Aug 28 20:11 myfiles2
cs130@raspberrypi ~/dir1 4 chmod 777 myfiles2
cs130@raspberrypi ~/dir1 5 chmod 755 myfiles3
cs130@raspberrypi ~/dir1 6 chmod 644 myfiles4
cs130@raspberrypi ~/dir1 7 chmid 600 myfiles5
-bash: chmid: command not found
cs130@raspberrypi ~/dir1 8 chmod 600 myfiles5
cs130@raspberrypi ~/dir1 9 ls -lrt
total 0
-rw------- 1 cs130 cs130 0 Aug 28 20:11 myfiles5
-rw-r--r-- 1 cs130 cs130 0 Aug 28 20:11 myfiles4
-rwxr-xr-x 1 cs130 cs130 0 Aug 28 20:11 myfiles3
-rwxrwxrwx 1 cs130 cs130 0 Aug 28 20:11 myfiles2
```

#3. First thing's first. Let's see what we are going to work with.

#4. chmod 777 <filename> to give all permissions to everyone.

#5. chmod 755 <filename> to give all permissions to myself and read and execute, but not write to the group and to the world (everyone else).

> Write permission also allows to delete the file.

#6. chmod 644 <filename> to give read and write permissions to myself (owner, user), and read permissions to the group and to the world.

> "World" here means "everyone on the system".

#7. Finally you see why I want to do as little typing as possible. You will make typo. Some times it will be caught. Some other times....

Unfortunately, these "other times" will happen when you want them least.

Remember that famous Murphy's law:

> Whatever can go wrong, will go wrong.

And my extension to that:

> … and that will happen in the **least** appropriate moment.

#8. chmod 600 <filename> Same cookies for myself, nothing to the group and the world.

> Same things go to the directories, with the difference, that for the directories you can also apply changes recursively, and that the execute permission allows searching that directory.

That was the Linux's way. That's what you'll probably see in most tutorials and "How To..." guides.

One note before we proceed. You don't need to memorize that table. If it is easier for you, you can recall that when you move to the next bit in binary number, you do power of two. Thus, if you go from the right to the left, the first bit would be 1 (execute), the next bit would be 2 (write), and the third one would be 4 (read). Then you just need to calculate the sum of the combinations of bits.

Did I say that was easier?

Now let's see the easy way.

2.2. Permissions Easy way.

If you are not comfortable calculating bits, you can do it more verbose way. Let me run few examples, they are pretty straightforward and self-explanatory. Still, I'll explain few things:

```
cs130@raspberrypi ~/dir1 23 ls -l myfiles5
-rw------- 1 cs130 cs130 0 Aug 28 20:11 myfiles5
cs130@raspberrypi ~/dir1 24 chmod -v +x myfiles5
mode of 'myfiles5' changed from 0600 (rw-------) to 0711 (rwx--x--x)
cs130@raspberrypi ~/dir1 25 chmod -v go+rw myfiles5
mode of 'myfiles5' changed from 0711 (rwx--x--x) to 0777 (rwxrwxrwx)
cs130@raspberrypi ~/dir1 26 ^+^-^
chmod -v go-rw myfiles5
mode of 'myfiles5' changed from 0777 (rwxrwxrwx) to 0711 (rwx--x--x)
cs130@raspberrypi ~/dir1 27
```

#24. chmod +x <filename> to add executable permission to all. Also note me using the **-v** flag to ask for the verbose messages, so I would not need to do listing to see the changes.

#25. chmod go+rw <filename> giving read and write to the ***G***roup and ***O***ther

> In the verbose mode the terminology is changed. Since 'w' is used for the "write", we cannot use "world", thus we use "other" instead. But since we use "other", we cannot use "owner", so we use "user"..... Aghhrrr.

#26. No, I changed my mind. I don't want that. Note how I use string substitution for the most recent command so I don't have to type all that line.

OK, that was more verbose way. Just... You probably don't want to show that way on the interview. On the interview you probably want to show the first way.

2.3. Permissions for the Places from above

Now, when we understand the permissions, let's recall, that we left our discussion about permissions for various directories. Particularly, for the /***tmp***, /***etc***, and the /***root***. Let's look at them to understand why you can place something in some places but not in the other.

Since we know, that they all under the ***root*** of the directory tree, we need to look at that level. And while we are here, let's also check the permissions for the file we copied over into the /***tmp***. So:

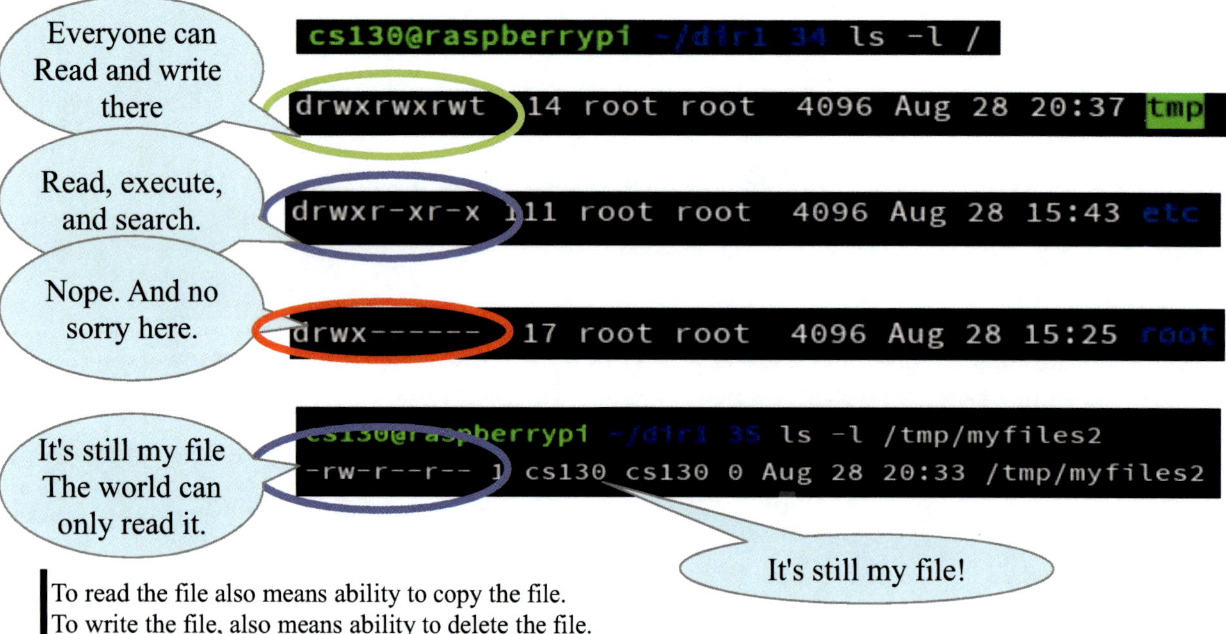

> To read the file also means ability to copy the file.
> To write the file, also means ability to delete the file.

As the owner of the file, I can set any permission for myself, even no permissions at all (0). I can always change them at any moment. Why I'd do that? Suppose I don't want to accidentally delete a file. I would remove the write permission. If later I need to edit/update it, I can add it with single command.

And since I expressed concern about accidental deleting something, I want to visit this picture again:

```
drwxrwxrwt  14 root root  4096 Aug 28 20:37 tmp
```

The last character (a "sticky flag") on the left column tells that the directory can not be deleted. That makes sense, because /***tmp*** gives a write permission to itself for everyone, and we already know, that that also means the permission to delete. By setting a "sticky flag" to the, the owner (the ***root***) made sure, that the important directory will not be deleted, even though it still gives ability to write to it.

3. How does the Bash (the shell) know what command to run?

– Hmmm. Indeed. How?

Actually, there is no magic involved. When the ***shell*** sees me typing some command, for example the **ls**, it starts thinking:

– Alright. The mortal wants me to run this. Where is that scratch of paper I scribbled down that list of locations on? Here. Let's see. Is that in the first location? Nope. Second? Nope. Third? Yes, it's there. Alright. I am done. I will run that command from that third location and will not bother checking the rest.

And if you want to know, which location the ***bash*** runs that command from (because there may be more than one locations with that command), you'd type:

```
cs130@raspberrypi ~/dir1 2 which ls
/bin/ls
cs130@raspberrypi ~/dir1 3
```

and now you know, that by default **ls** runs from the /***bin***.

What if you have your own version of **ls,** which you wrote yourself (or your friend gave to you), and which is much, much better than the one, shipped with the system?

You'd probably put it somewhere like **/home/<yourusername>/bin**. And to run it, you would need to tell ***bash*** that specific and exact place:

```
/home/bob/bin/ls
```

But if you do not provide the path, ***bash*** will look at those default places it keeps in its list.

4. PATH variable.

– So, if we have a list, that list should be stored somewhere.

– Yes.

That list is stored in the variable that keeps locations (***paths***), which ***bash*** will look at to find a command we want it to run. Because of that, that variable is called ***PATH*** (note all caps).

> Linux is case-sensitive. That is important fact to remember.

And because it is a variable, whenever we want to use it, we prep-end it with the dollar sign: ***$***. That is just syntax. Without that ***bash*** will not understand what we want it to do.

- If it is a variable, we should be able to look and see what's in there.
- Sure. Remember our friend?

echo $PATH

```
cs130@raspberrypi ~/dir1 $ echo $PATH
/usr/local/sbin:/usr/local/bin:/usr/sbin:/usr/bin:/sbin:/bin:/usr/local/games:/usr/games
```

Let's look at what's printed (your output ~~may be~~ will be different).

We know, that ***directories*** in the ***path*** are separated by the forward slashes. But there is more than one ***path*** in that list. We need to separate them. And we separate them by the colon (:). So here is the paths that ***bash*** will read from the ***PATH*** variable (going from left to the right):

1. /usr/local/sbin
2. /usr/local/bin
3. /usr/sbin
4. /usr/bin

Now the system files:

5. /sbin
6. /bin

And finally something not very important for some people, but extremely important for other:

7. /usr/local/games
8. /usr/games

So to locate the `ls` command from above example, ***bash*** had to check five locations before it found it in the /***bin***.

- That's interesting. But if the ***PATH*** is just a variable, can we perhaps modify it?
- *Yes, we can*.*

---

* Not a mine copyright.

And let me do it also to prove to you what I just said.

When you write a script to be executed in unattended mode, you want to minimize chances of it to be hijacked and exploited. Because of that, you want to minimize the possible access to the places that are not needed for the script to run (in other words, you leave only those, that needed by the script).

> Principle of a least privilege... That is a good principle to follow.

For now let me show to you how to completely reset the ***PATH***. We also do that because it is simple.

Like that:

export PATH=""

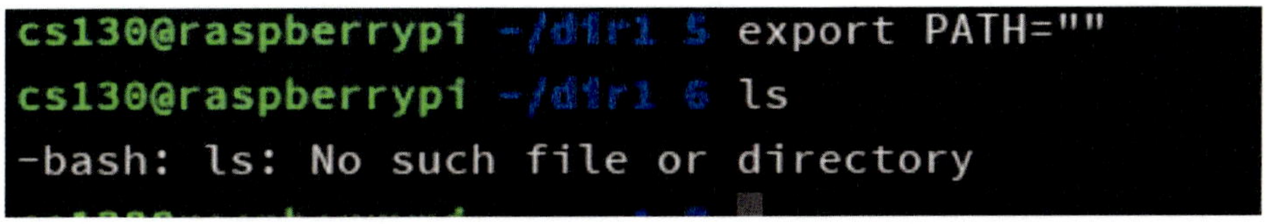

```
cs130@raspberrypi ~/dir1 $ export PATH=""
cs130@raspberrypi ~/dir1 $ ls
-bash: ls: No such file or directory
```

… And now when we try to run our `ls` command, the ***bash*** tells us that nope, sorry, cannot find it....

Let me return to the line #5 above.

```
export PATH=...
```

Probably in most (or at least in many) books and tutorials you will see different form of that command:

```
PATH=...<whatever>
export $PATH
```

But show me a Linux user who would run two commands when he (she) can do just one?

But I want to point out to something else. Let's look closely to the `export` command from my line and from the other. My line:

```
export PATH=...
```

The other line:

```
export $PATH
```

See the difference? Who is right, who is wrong?

The answer is: "Both are correct". To use the dollar sign or not to use the dollar sign depends on the context. In my command I create a variable (and immediately export that). When I create the variable, I do not use the dollar sign, because that variable does not exist yet. Whereas in the second version I do it in two steps:

1. Creating a variable (and no dollar sign is used there)
2. Exporting the (already ***existing***) variable. Because that variable already exists, I need to refer to that correctly by using a dollar sign.

That may be confusing, and people may need to get used to it, but … that's life. If we want the ***bash*** to understand us, we need to follow some syntax rules. People from programming classes should know the importance of syntax.

So. We reset the ***PATH***. And all the sudden we find ourselves not been able to run anything. Every time I want to run any command, I need to provide a resolving ***path*** to that location. To say that is inconvenient, it is... a little understatement.

– I want my ***PATH*** back! 

Well. First of all, do not panic. Just because you reset your ***PATH***, it does not mean it is lost... completely... yet.

Remember, all changes to the environment are for the duration of the session only (until you write them, which we did not... yet). So if you can allow that, you can just close the session and reopen it again; everything will be restored back magically.

If you work on a multi-terminal environment, you can open another terminal and copy the ***PATH*** from there.

> That is one of the several reason to always try to have more than one terminal open

Otherwise, let's try to restore that.

There should be no surprises, that environment settings should be stored in some files. The only problem, is that your environment is inherited from the skeleton's one of the system. Thus, we need to try to rebuild that skeleton environment first.

4.1. The *source* command

The ***source*** command reads the file given to it as an argument and tries to execute every line in it as if it was a ***shell's*** command. You can consider it as a "lite" version of running the script. We will use that to re-read and to re-build our profile.

Here are steps.
#1. I reset the ***PATH***
#2. Yes, it is empty.
#3. I read the skeleton's profile (on your system it ~~may be~~ will be different)

Yes, there are errors, but they are expected. Remember, we are re-building our profile.

After I re-read the skeleton profile, all my nice colors and command numbers at the prompt are gone. I am on a fresh basic profile. **But**! I was able to restore the skeleton's ***PATH***.

```
cs130@raspberrypi ~ 1 export PATH=""
cs130@raspberrypi ~ 2 echo $PATH

cs130@raspberrypi ~ 3 source /etc/profile
-bash: id: No such file or directory
-bash: [: : integer expression expected
cs130@raspberrypi:~$ echo $PATH
/usr/local/sbin:/usr/local/bin:/usr/sbin:/usr/bin:/sbin:/bin:/usr/local/games:/usr/games
cs130@raspberrypi:~$ ls
dir1  myfiles1
```

Next step, is to re-build my profile, which may also include some additions to the ***PATH***.

source ~/.profile (it could also be ***~/.bash_profile ;*** your file ***may be*** different, especially if you have different ***shell***)

```
cs130@raspberrypi:~$ source ~/.bashrc
cs130@raspberrypi ~ 7
```

And I am back to my profile (I did not need to ***re-source .bashrc***, because one file reads another, but... Oh well, I just did).
What are these ***.profile*** and ***.bashrc*** files that I ***sourced*** above? Those are files that store my ***bash*** profile. You can see that they are hidden. There are few files that keep your profile. On your system they may be different. If you want to see them, you can type (from your home directory):

```
ls .bash<tab><tab>
```

You need two tabs to see the list of suggestions. That list will consist of all files, starting with ***.bash***, and most of them deal with your profile one way or another.

But really... You see all the steps and troubles we had to take because we recklessly reset our ***PATH***?

```
Before you do changes to the system, make a backup copy!
```

- You did not tell us to!
- But I did:

```
cs130@raspberrypi ~/dir1 3 mypath=$PATH
cs130@raspberrypi ~/dir1 4
```

Just to verify:

```
cs130@raspberrypi ~/dir1 4 echo $mypath
/usr/local/sbin:/usr/local/bin:/usr/sbin:/usr/bin:/sbin:/bin:/usr/local/games:/usr/games
```

And after I am done with all those exercises, restoring the ***PATH*** back:

```
cs130@raspberrypi ~/dir1 7 export PATH=$mypath
cs130@raspberrypi ~/dir1 8 ls
myfiles2  myfiles3  myfiles4  myfiles5
```

And you can see, that it recognizes all the commands.

> Please again, carefully check out the placement and usage of the dollar sign for the variable name. Note, where I use it (if variable exists) and where there is no dollar sign (where the variable does not exist yet).

- OK, that example with resetting the ***PATH*** was kind of interesting, but not very useful. Can you give something that would be more practical?
- OK, as you wish.

4.2. Adding a reference to the current directory to the *PATH*

Suppose we have a script. A script is just the file with sequence of commands that ***shell*** can recognize and run. But that is not enough. To be able to run from the command line, the file has to be executable (has executable permission set).

Let's see some example:

```
cs130@raspberrypi ~/dir2 33 touch myfile
cs130@raspberrypi ~/dir2 34 chmod 755 myfile
cs130@raspberrypi ~/dir2 35 ls -l
total 0
-rwxr-xr-x 1 cs130 cs130 0 Aug 31 14:44 myfile
cs130@raspberrypi ~/dir2 36 my^C
```

Lines **##33-35**: Creating file, and adding executable permissions for everyone (all permissions to myself, and read and execute to the group and to the world). That makes this file executable (for everyone).

To run the executable file, you type its name, and hit <***enter***>, just as you do for any other commands.

#36. I started typing the name of the file and hit <***tab***> key... But... But ***bash*** does not recognize that as a command. Hmmmm.

Remember all our discussion how does ***bash*** know where to look at? Perhaps ***bash*** does not recognize my file as an executable because ***bash*** does not look at the correct place? Because in all those default places there surely no such tool. If so, we need to tell ***bash*** where to look at.

> I want to underscore this. If I used that file as an argument to any other command (for example, `ls`), ***bash*** would happily oblige. Because it knows that that is a regular file used as an argument to the command. But now we want to run it as an executable, and that imposes its own conditions.

Let's test it. Let me interrupt the current command (line) with the ***^C*** and try again, this time prep-ending the command with the single dot.

```
cs130@raspberrypi ~/dir2 36 my^C
cs130@raspberrypi ~/dir2 36 ./myfile ^C
cs130@raspberrypi ~/dir2 36
```

And when I hit <***tab***> key, ***bash*** was able to auto complete the command. So, my theory seems to be correct. With that, let's interrupt the command and modify the ***PATH***.

```
cs130@raspberrypi ~/dir2 36 export PATH=$PATH:.
cs130@raspberrypi ~/dir2 37 echo $PATH
/usr/local/sbin:/usr/local/bin:/usr/sbin:/usr/bin:/sbin:/bin:/usr/local/games:/usr/games:.
cs130@raspberrypi ~/dir2 38 myfile
```

Note the dot added to the ***PATH*** at the end (line **#37**).

And now, when I type the name of the file and hit the <***tab***> key, the ***bash*** successfully auto completes it. Note, that this time I do not need to prep-end the dot to the file name.
Let me explain, what I did on line **#36** above.

On the right-hand side of the assignment, I took the ***PATH*** variable. Since I used a dollar sign, to indicate that it is indeed a truly variable, ***bash*** will try to expand it. Thus, on the right-hand side the complete string containing all the ***paths*** will be used, even though ***we*** see it as a singular word "*PATH*". Next, I append that complete string with two characters: The colon (:), which is a path separator, and the single dot, which is reference to the current directory. I need to use a path separator, or I will corrupt the last ***path*** in the ***PATH***.

After that, I assign everything to the left-hand side of the assignment.

On the left-hand side of the assignment is a variable I am going to use to store that new value.

Incidentally, it's named... ***PATH***. That's fine. Nothing prevents me from using the same name.

People taking programming classes may recognize that it is very much similar to this statement:

```
a = a + 5;
```

So, nothing terribly awful here.

After that assignment my ***PATH*** has a dot at the end, which we see when we print it.

4.3. Adding an arbitrary path to the *PATH* variable.

Alright. That was good. And now we are ready for something else. Remember, you had your own version of the **ls** command, and every time you wanted to run it, you needed to provide a full ***path*** specifier, like that, or the ***bash*** would take it from the /***bin***:

```
/home/bob/bin/ls
```

Linux users are... yes, right. We need to do something about that. And that something is to modify the ***PATH*** variable by adding the above ***path*** to it. But... where to place it inside the ***PATH***? If we append it, like we did with the single dot, it will not help us, because when ***bash*** reads the list of ***path***s, it stops when the first match is found and that will happen before it reaches our custom location.

That means, we need to add our ***path*** at the beginning of that list. Let's do that.

```
export PATH=/home/bob/bin/:$PATH
```

We don't want to lose our original ***PATH*** value. We already saw what would happen if we did, and we don't want to repeat that experience again. That's why I included the $***PATH*** on the right-hand side of the assignment.

Here is what we have as result (I truncated the right edge of the picture, the one with the ***paths*** to the games... who needs them when we are talking serious things, right?)

```
cs130@raspberrypi ~ 1 export PATH=/home/cs130/bin:$PATH
cs130@raspberrypi ~ 2 echo $PATH
/home/cs130/bin:/usr/local/sbin:/usr/local/bin:/usr/sbin:/usr/bin:/sbin:/bin:
```

Note the first element in the list. It is our ***path*** to our local private ***bin***. Now we need to prove, that it works as we want to. How?

Since I don't have that cool version of the **ls**, as you do, let me, for the purpose of demonstration, copy a one from the /***bin*** and see which location will be used to run it.

I have a read permission for the /***bin;*** that means, I can copy files from there. Let's do that. But first thing's first. The destination has to exists:

```
cs130@raspberrypi ~ 3 mkdir ~/bin
cs130@raspberrypi ~ 4 cp /bin/ls !$
cp /bin/ls ~/bin
cs130@raspberrypi ~ 5 ls !$
ls ~/bin
ls
cs130@raspberrypi ~ 6 which ls
/home/cs130/bin/ls
```

#3. Making the private ***bin*** directory
#4. Copying **ls** from /***bin*** to mine's one.
#5. Verifying (always verify)

Yes, it's there

#6. Querying ***bash*** as to which **ls** it will use.

It is ours! We are good!

> 1. Depending on what you need to, you can modify ***PATH*** variable by different ways.
> 2. Always remember, that ***shell*** reads that list until the first match is found.

– And finally... Everything we did here was not really necessary. Well, sort of.

– What???!!! How do you....

– That was useful to demonstrate the concept, and also that's what you would do, if you just created your local private ***bin***. But if you already have that local private ***bin***, the ***path*** to it may likely be added to the ***PATH*** automatically when you start a new session.

– Is that another sort of magic?

– Not really. If you are interested how, look at your ***.bash_profile*** file.

5. Three types of quotes in Linux.

Wow! That was something. Now let me switch gears. And let me start this topic with examples.

```
cs130@raspberrypi ~ 7 echo $PATH
/usr/local/sbin:/usr/local/bin:/usr/sbin:/usr/bin:/sbin:/bin:/usr/local/games:/usr/games
cs130@raspberrypi ~ 8
cs130@raspberrypi ~ 8 echo "$PATH"
/usr/local/sbin:/usr/local/bin:/usr/sbin:/usr/bin:/sbin:/bin:/usr/local/games:/usr/games
cs130@raspberrypi ~ 9
cs130@raspberrypi ~ 9 echo '$PATH'
$PATH
cs130@raspberrypi ~ 10
```

What I do here, is I am printing the $***PATH*** as is, with double quotes, and with the single quotes.

As you can see, there is no difference in output of

echo "$PATH"
and
echo $PATH

But when I do

echo '$PATH'

I see a literal string “$PATH” printed out. Why?

When ***bash*** sees a dollar sign, it recognizes that following is a variable. Therefore, it takes that variable and substitutes it with the value that that variable stores in self.

> When ***bash*** sees a variable, it does a what's called “variable expansion”, i.e. it replaces the variable with its value.

That's why when we print the $***PATH***, we see the actual list of directories.

And the variable expansion takes place in our first two examples.

The single quotes, however, prevents variable expansion. Thus, you can print the literal string.

But what's the difference between

echo "$PATH"
and
echo $PATH

?

Why use double quotes if the result would be the same as without them?

Double quotes allow using a white space inside the variables. Linux does support white space in the file names or directory names. But.... since it may create complications writing the scripts, that is probably not a best choice. It'd probably be better to avoid white spaces. Still, Linux supports them. Let's see few examples:

```
cs130@raspberrypi ~/dir2 12 mypathwithspace="my path with space"
cs130@raspberrypi ~/dir2 13 echo $mypathwithspace
my path with space
cs130@raspberrypi ~/dir2 14 mkdir $mypathwithspace
cs130@raspberrypi ~/dir2 15 cd $mypathwithspace
cs130@raspberrypi ~/dir2/my 16 pwd
/home/cs130/dir2/my
cs130@raspberrypi ~/dir2/my 17 mkdir "$mypathwithspace"
cs130@raspberrypi ~/dir2/my 18 cd !$
cd "$mypathwithspace"
cs130@raspberrypi ~/dir2/my/my path with space 19 pwd
/home/cs130/dir2/my/my path with space
```

#12. Creating variable with spaces.

#13. Yes, it contains spaces.

#14. Let's create a directory with that name. Note there is no quotes there.

#15. Change to that directory.

#16. Printing path to that.
Oops.... There is only first word before space was used. Note, that for other commands we could easily generate errors here. Let's continue.

#17. Repeating the above, this time using the double quotes.

#18. You see why I prefer using that form, and not to type myself? The thing that I think it is and the real thing may not be the same.

#19. Printing path. This time it is what I wanted to.

That's the difference (and that's why you may want to avoid using the spaces in the names) between having the double quotes and not. What if we did not have the white space in the name, but still used the double quotes? Nothing special. No harm would be done, it'll just work as if there was none.

Other way of working with spaces in the names is to use a back slashes to escape the spaces (we talked about back slashes last time). But that would complicate your command unnecessary.

– And what about possible errors you mentioned in the comments to line #16?
– For example this:

```
cs130@raspberrypi ~/dir2/my/my path with space 20 ls ../../$mypathwithspace
ls: cannot access path: No such file or directory
ls: cannot access with: No such file or directory
ls: cannot access space: No such file or directory
../../my:
my path with space
```

– Why so?

When we run a command with the arguments, each individual argument in the array of those is separated by a white space. i.e. each word is taken as a separate parameter to the command. Without that ***bash*** would not know exactly, what we ask it to do. But if we use the space inside a single argument, that can confuse a poor ***bash***. It has a lot of work to do, let's be considerate to it....

Alright. That left me with the last type of quotes.

5.1. A back-quotes.

Back quotes run a command inside them, and return result of that command. It is sort of function in the programming. Note that on a (standard) keyboard back quote located on the same key as tilde.

Here is a very simple example:

```
cs130@raspberrypi ~/dir2 22 mydate=`date`
cs130@raspberrypi ~/dir2 23 echo $mydate
Mon Aug 31 14:26:18 PDT 2020
```

Here I run command ***date*** within the back quotes, save the result to the variable, and output its value.

Just to compare, here is what would be without back quotes:

```
cs130@raspberrypi ~/dir2 24 mydate=date
cs130@raspberrypi ~/dir2 25 echo $mydate
date
```

To say that back quotes are immensely useful in scripting and even in the command line, would still not be an accurate and complete description. That's how important they are and how they make a life easier for a command line and shell script user.

- Yes, it seems so indeed. Can you give us some more practical example?
- Sure. How about that one? Suppose I need to run a script that takes some time to execute. I launch it like that and leave for a lunch, hoping that when I am back at my desk, I can see when it started, and when it completed. Like that (with command ***sleep 20***, causing system to sleep for 20 seconds, to be used as a placeholder for an actual script):

```
cs130@raspberrypi ~/dir1 14 starttime=`date +"%H:%M:%S"`;sleep 20; endtime=`date +"%H:%M:%S"`; echo "start time $starttime"; echo "end time $endtime"
start time 16:35:51
end time 16:36:11
cs130@raspberrypi ~/dir1 15
```

Now, before we move to the next topic, let's do something simple

Alright, today it was an involved discussion. But still, I want to very briefly talk about the next topic in preparation to the next lecture.

6. How to read (or see the content of) the file?

6.1. cat

```
cat <filename>
```

You blinked, you missed it. Because ***cat*** dumps the content of the entire file to the screen. Be it ten lines or ten thousand lines, everything is dumped on the screen. Because of that it is not a suitable command to see the content of the large files. But if you know that your file is small, or you need just a small portion of your file to look at, that is a nice small utility. Its original purpose was to concatenate several files together, so you can give it more than one file name as an argument. They will be dropped on a screen one by one with no pause.

If you want an ability to look at the middle of the file, the one step away from very small and very simple utility is:

6.2. more.

Similarly, to the ***cat***, the ***more*** will display the content of the file (or files, since you also can give more than one file name to it) on the screen. But it stops after the screen is filled. To continue going screen by screen you hit the space bar.

If you want to have almost all functionality of a text editor, but without ability to edit the text (and often time you do want that, however strange that may sound: Sometimes you want to open the file and to be guaranteed, that you do not write to it, i.e. you want to open it strictly read-only), there is a tool for that:

6.3. less

Opposite to the ***more*** is ***less***.

Just few commands while in the ***less:***

Allows you to go back and forward (ctrl-u, ctrl-f or space), scroll up and down.
1g – jumps to the first line.
G – jumps to the end of the file
ctrl-g – displays file information (name, current position, what line you are in there)

You can search:

/ – forward
? – backward

n – repeats search.
N – repeats search backwards.
Search is case-sensitive, as everything in Linux.

One very useful feature – you can read and follow the file while it is being written!

G – jump to the end of file.
F – enters to the wait mode, waiting for the new data being written to the file, and displaying that data when it is written. This is very useful feature to monitor incoming data.

To interrupt: ctrl-c . To exit and close the file: 'q'

Finally, as with all that family, it allows you to open multiple files and switch between them.

And as an example for that section, here is the part of content of my ***.bashrc*** file dumped on the screen with the cat command where you can see the aliases setup:

```
# enable color support of ls and also add handy aliases
if [ -x /usr/bin/dircolors ]; then
    test -r ~/.dircolors && eval "$(dircolors -b ~/.dircolors)" || eval "$(dircolors -b)"
    alias ls='ls --color=auto'
    #alias dir='dir --color=auto'
    #alias vdir='vdir --color=auto'

    alias grep='grep --color=auto'
    alias fgrep='fgrep --color=auto'
    alias egrep='egrep --color=auto'
fi

# some more ls aliases
#alias ll='ls -l'
#alias la='ls -A'
#alias l='ls -CF'

# Alias definitions.
# You may want to put all your additions into a separate file like
# ~/.bash_aliases, instead of adding them here directly.
# See /usr/share/doc/bash-doc/examples in the bash-doc package.

if [ -f ~/.bash_aliases ]; then
    . ~/.bash_aliases
fi

# enable programmable completion features (you don't need to enable
# this, if it's already enabled in /etc/bash.bashrc and /etc/profile
# sources /etc/bash.bashrc).
if [ -f /etc/bash_completion ] && ! shopt -oq posix; then
    . /etc/bash_completion
fi
cs130@raspberrypi ~ $
```

7. Summary and review

Interrupt, Permissions, ***PATH***, types of quotes, reading files

Commands: ***export, source, chmod, cat, more, less.***

Lecture 4. Environmental variables. Find utility. Redirecting the file descriptors. Linux filtering, grep.

When people see or hear the words "Environmental variables" they become so scary, the next time I lose half of the class.

I don't want to lose half of the class.

Because of that, let me start with the far and slow introduction.

When we write computer programs, we use variables. We use variables to keep some values, to do calculations on those values, to print them out, to pass them to the procedures etc. If we did not use variables, we would not need computers. We could do most of the tasks with the calculators, because our programs would be just as simple. But with the variables we can write much more complex and useful programs than the calculator would allow us to, ***and***, we can exchange data with other programs to make it even more useful.

What kind of data can we store in the variables? If you write a program to compute the volume of the pool, you'd use some variables to store dimensions of that pool.

If you write program to keep and maintain the building, with the classrooms, you would probably need to have some variables to keep and store information about the state of that classroom. I.e, how many desks, the state of the white board, instructor's workstation, the state of the projector, its attributes – power consumption, lenses etc.

In short, all the information about the classroom's environment.

And because you use variables to store information about environment, those variables are called environmental variables.

Thus, environmental variables are the variables to store information about the environment.

So... Nothing scary so far.

How does it apply to us?

When you are on a system, the system needs to know quite some information about you and your profile: What is the session, what is your shell, your login, your paths... what is your display, your keyboard, your mouse..... A lot of things that you probably not even concerned about, but the system needs to know all that data to correctly run your session. To display right font, right size, right color on the screen. To write to the correct location on the disk... A lot of things. And not only for itself; it may share some of the information with other processes. And not only for the duration of your current session; Next time you open a new session, you want to have all your settings, all your fonts and colors and everything applied automatically. And because of that, all that information should be available, ready to use, and ready to share. And since these things are your session's environment, the system keeps all that information in the environmental variables.

Now I think we are ready to talk about

1. The Environmental Variables.

To see your Environmental Variables (***EV***), you'd run a command:

```
printenv
```

It prints all of them, which is a lot. Let me show you just few:

```
MAIL=/var/mail/cs130
PATH=/home/cs130/bin:/usr/local/sbin:/usr/local/bin:/usr/sbin:/
usr/games
PWD=/home/cs130
INFINALITY_FT_FILTER_PARAMS=11 22 38 22 11
LANG=en_US.UTF-8
```

And... Surprise! We see our friend ***PATH*** there! here

You can also see your current location, your language setup... All kept in the variables.

Let's print some:

```
cs130@raspberrypi ~ 9 printenv PATH
/home/cs130/bin:/usr/local/sbin:/usr/local/bin:/usr/sbin:/usr/bin:/sbin:/bin:/us
```

Note, that when I print *EV* with **printenv** command, I do not supply the dollar sign. When we did that with **echo**, we needed to tell bash that we wanted a variable expansion. But **printenv** knows, what we want to do, and thus, no special syntax is needed here.

It knows about me:

```
cs130@raspberrypi ~ 10 printenv USER
cs130
```

It knows about my ***shell***. (That's one of the way, how we can find out what is our ***shell***):

```
cs130@raspberrypi ~ 12 printenv SHELL
/bin/bash
```

… It does not know about my display:

```
cs130@raspberrypi ~ 11 printenv DISPLAY
cs130@raspberrypi ~ 12
```

It used to be that system needed information about your display. These days, apparently not any more. But there are still some tools that do need that information to correctly output to the screen, and in such cases you would need to set a display.

One other ***EV***, that we mentioned briefly in one of the past lectures:

```
cs130@raspberrypi ~ 1 printenv HOME
/home/cs130
```

The ***bash*** knows about your home. So, when last time we were adding the local private ***bin*** to the ***PATH***, what we could do instead was:

```
export PATH=$HOME/bin/:$PATH
```

Just... make sure that the $***HOME*** is not reset at the time when the $***PATH*** is under construction

Some ***EV*** may be set by some tools or processes to communicate to each other and are not intended to be read by the human. So there are a lot.

You are welcome to check and look at your system's ***EV*** just to see what it is.

One thing from our experience: You probably do not want to mess with the ***EV***.

One other thing, you may already noticed, that ***EV*** are all capitalized.

And now, when we officially introduced the ***EV***, let me return to the syntax from the last lecture:

1.1. Exporting to the Environment.

Let's recall couple of our previous examples:

```
(1): mypath=$PATH
```

```
(2): export PATH=/home/bob/bin/:$PATH
```

Q: Why in the (1) I do a simple assignment, while on (2) I use keyword ***export*** following the assignment?
A: In the (1) case, I just create a local variable for my own use. I am not going to share it with anything or anyone else. In the (2) case, after I created (updated) a variable by means of reassignment, I want to

export it to the environment, after which it will become a member of environment, i.e. an ***EV***. People, taking programming classes, may think about the ***EV*** as sort of global variables. And that would probably be a good analogy. Each your process, each your running tool will have access to your ***EV*** if needed (remember our brief discussion about limiting the access to the ***EV*** in the scripts and tools?)

Alright. That would be it for that. Let's move on.

2. A Find utility

Suppose, you do not know where the file is located, and you want to find that out.

There is a ***find*** command. That is powerful utility, with many options and much functionality. You can find files which modification time is before or after some certain time, which have certain size, or larger than certain size, etc. You can combine options, you can execute command on the search result. What it does, it recursively searches the entire directory tree (branch of the tree) beginning from the point you give to it, and applying the condition you supplied. In its simplest form it takes two arguments, the starting point, and the name of the file. Like that:

```
find <starting point> -name <file name>
```

If there is result matching your search criteria, ***find*** prints to you the ***path*** (or ***paths***) to the(those) file(s). A wildcard can be used in any part of the file name, in which case you need to include that into the quotes:

find . -name 'myfile*'

```
cs130@raspberrypi ~ 9 find . -name 'myfile*'
./dir1/myfiles4
./dir1/myfiles5
./dir1/myfiles3
./dir1/myfiles2
./dir2/myfile
./myfiles1
cs130@raspberrypi ~ 10
```

OK, that was a simple example. Let's do something more involved. Suppose you want to find all the xml files on the entire system. That means, you need to start searching with the ***root*** of the directory tree.

```
find / -name '*xml'
```

and hit <**enter**>.....

… And pretty soon you will discover couple of problem.

1. It keeps running, dumping a lot of output to the screen, and you have no ability to catch what's printed out.
2. You have a lot of errors like that:

```
find: `/var/lib/container': Permission denied
find: `/var/lib/polkit-1': Permission denied
find: `/var/lib/udisks2': Permission denied
find: `/var/log/lightdm': Permission denied
find: `/var/log/samba': Permission denied
```

... Permissions denied. We already know why is that. That means I don't have permissions to search those directories. One solution to avoid such errors could be to switch to the ***root***, but we work as regular user. And besides, we still need to do something about the first problem.

- Can we perhaps write the result to the file and then examine the file to solve the first problem.
- Every time on a Linux you ask "Can we...", the answer is most likely would be:

"Yes, we can"*.

---

* Not a mine copyright.

3. Redirecting output.

By default, the processes output messages to the ***standard output*** (***stdout***), which is our terminal screen. We can redirect that output to some other places, for example we can redirect it to the file.

Let's do that:

```
find / -name '*xml' > find_result
```

Here I repeat the previous command exactly (remember our friend – the up arrow key to scroll through the history), but I append it with the highlighted part. The Right Angle (or Greater-Than) button followed by a file name we want to redirect output to.

Couple of things:

1. If file does not exist, it will be created.
2. Otherwise it will be silently and without warning overwritten at the moment you hit the <***enter***> key.

Be aware of that. If you do not want that to happen, you need to be careful. One approach would be to hit <***tab***> key, while typing the file name. In that case, if the file exists, ***bash*** will auto-complete its name, and you will know that there is such file already. But, on the other hand you may want to overwrite it too.

There is other option. If you use double Right Angle, the file will be appended as opposed to overwritten. If it does not exist, it will still be created, as in the first case, so in that respect there is no difference between these two modes. Thus, to append to the file, you will do:

```
find / -name '*xml' >> find_result
```

Let's run it. Hit <***enter***>...

… and I still see those error messages:

```
find: `/var/cache/lightdm': Permission denied
find: `/var/lib/bluetooth': Permission denied
find: `/var/lib/lightdm': Permission denied
find: `/var/lib/container': Permission denied
find: `/var/lib/polkit-1': Permission denied
find: `/var/lib/udisks2': Permission denied
find: `/var/log/lightdm': Permission denied
```

What about my file?

It's there:

ls -lrt

```
-rw-r--r-- 1 cs130 cs130 80467 Sep  1 19:54 find_result
```

What's in there?

```
cat find_<tab><enter>
```

Yes, there are results of running of the ***find*** command:

```
/var/lib/gconf/defaults/%gconf-tree-ru.xml
/var/lib/gconf/defaults/%gconf-tree-it.xml
/var/lib/gconf/defaults/%gconf-tree-ko.xml
/var/lib/gconf/defaults/%gconf-tree-da.xml
/var/lib/gconf/defaults/%gconf-tree-ja.xml
/var/lib/gconf/defaults/%gconf-tree-th.xml
/var/lib/gconf/defaults/%gconf-tree-zh_CN.xml
/var/lib/gconf/defaults/%gconf-tree-eu.xml
/var/lib/gconf/defaults/%gconf-tree-cs.xml
```

So, what was on the screen then?

Every file (remember, everything in Linux is a file), has few file descriptors (***fd***). In our case we now are interested in two of them: ***standard out*** (we already talked about that) and ***standard error*** (***stderr***). We redirected the ***stdout***, but what's left on the screen was the error messages. And we did not do anything with them.

- We don't want those error messages on the screen. Can we get rid of them?
- Yes. Let's redirect them to the file also. To the errors file. Like that:

```
find / -name '*xml' > find_result 2> error_file
```

The ***stdout*** has a file descriptor 1 (***fd1***). But we usually don't specifically indicate that, because that is a default one. But for the ***stderr***, we need to indicate the file descriptor, which is 2 (***fd2***). Let's run it.

```
find / -name '*xml' > find_result 2> error_file
ls -lrt
```

And we see, that we cleared the screen from any messages, and there are two files created:

```
-rw-r--r-- 1 cs130 cs130 80467 Sep  1 20:07 find_result
-rw-r--r-- 1 cs130 cs130 59530 Sep  1 20:07 error_file
```

Again, to redirect the ***stdout*** you don't need to provide the file descriptor, while for the ***stderr*** you need to indicate it (number 2).

- Can we redirect everything into one file, so we could work with just one file later?
- Yes, we can*

---

* Not a mine copyright

We can do this like that:

```
find / -name '*xml' >> all_results 2>> all_results
```

Redirecting both file descriptors (***fd***) to the same file. Note, that I need to append that file for both file descriptors, because I do not know the order of the messages coming out of each descriptors.
So. We can use that command.

Nothing prevents us from doing that.

Except one thing.

If you show that command to someone, that someone would probably ask:

- Hmmm, errr, who, did you say, was your Linux instructor?

We are in the Linux class. We all saw those movies with guys in the hoods in the dark rooms typing on the screens something that no mere human can understand. We want to type something that no mere human can understand. That's why we are here, right?

Let me do something here and then I will explain what I did:

```
cs130@raspberrypi ~ 30 find / -name '*xml' > find_result 2>&1
cs130@raspberrypi ~ 31 ls -l
total 144
drwxr-xr-x 2 cs130 cs130   4096 Sep  1 20:20 bin
-rw-r--r-- 1 cs130 cs130 139655 Sep  1 20:20 find_result
```

Now, let me draw this picture

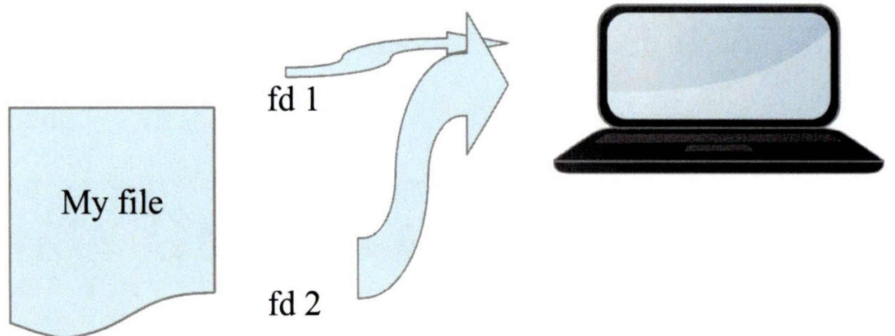

This is where both file descriptors (***fd***) point to by default (to the terminal screen).

Let's redirect ***fd1*** (first part of our command):

```
find / -name '*xml' > find_result
```

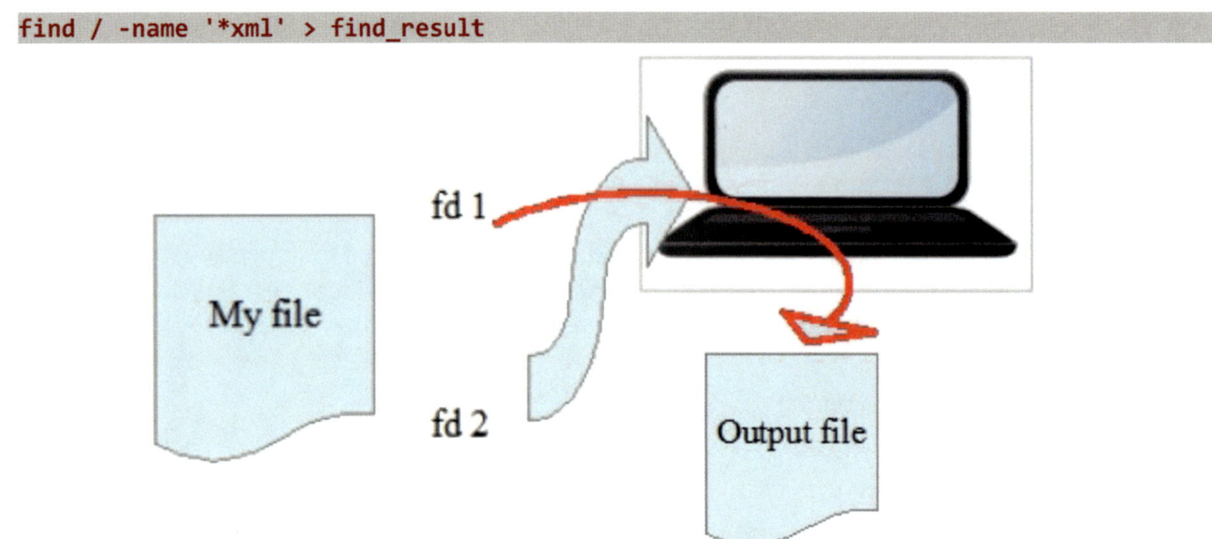

This is where the ***fd1*** points to after the first part of the redirection (to the output file):

Note, that the ***fd2*** (***stderr***) still points to the screen. That's what we saw when run the first example, with error messages on a screen, and result output to the file.

Now let's redirect the ***fd2***.

```
find / -name '*xml' > find_result 2>&1
```

We do it with the highlighted part of the command. Let's read it left to right. We take ***fd2*** and redirect it ***into...*** ***Into***(!) (see that ampersand?) … into ***fd1***.

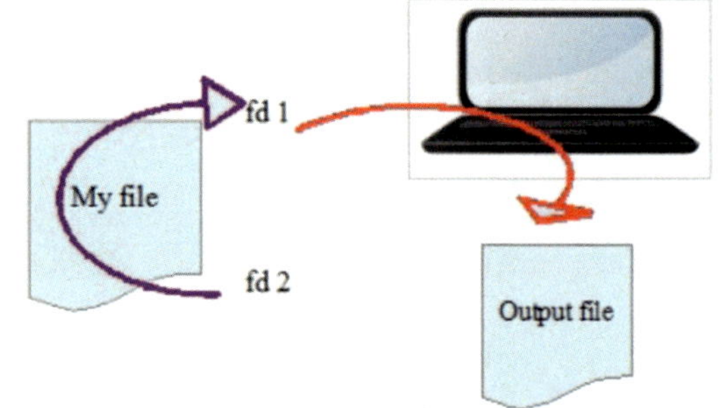

But... Where does the ***fd1*** point to now?
After our initial redirection it points to the output file.
Wow!!!

The order of opeations is important here. People, taking C or C++ may recall pointer reassignment. Your Professor probably drew something like that on a white board, while explaining these to you....

One thing to note is that such redirection lives only for the duration of the command. As soon as command terminates, all these clever redirection we did are gone with that command.

It is possible to make a persistent redirection, but that is well beyond our fundamental course. So I mention that just for your information.

- ... But... Actually. Why do you need to keep those error messages? They are from the locations, you have no access anyways; what's the point of that? Why keep all those files that are not needed?
- Do you mean we can...
- Yes. Let me do something.

3.1. Discarding (error) messages entirely (redirecting to the null device)

Let's run this command:

```
cs130@raspberrypi ~ 1 find / -name '*xml' > find_result 2> /dev/null
```

What I did, I redirected the ***stderr*** to the null device. The one of most usages of the null device is to serve as sort of a black hole. Everything, that got there is lost forever. I cannot prove it to you, because those error messages are gone. I cannot show it to you. Lack of the proof is my proof.

You will see that construct very often. Whenever you run a script in an unattended mode, or do command line, you will see that construct very often. In all the books and those tutorials. So. Here it is.

> Note, that I can redirect output not only to the file. Here I redirected output to the device.

And BTW, sometimes you want to keep the ***stderr***, and discard the ***stdout***. You still use the same construct.

Alright. That was something. I guess after such excitement, we need to talk about something dull, easy and boring. But first, one more thing about redirection – just for the completion.

4. Redirecting the standard input.

Cases when you (really) need to redirect the ***stdin*** are (very) rare. Examples of usage you'd see online could be (very) complicated. We will redirect ***stdin*** only once, at the end of this course. For completion reason and to demonstrate the concept, here is a very silly but simple example. Explanations below:

```
cs130@raspberrypi ~ 2 ls -ltr > myfile
cs130@raspberrypi ~ 3 cat < myfile
total 144
drwxr-xr-x 2 cs130 cs130  4096 Sep  1 20:20 bin
-rw-r--r-- 1 cs130 cs130 59530 Sep  1 23:10 error_file
-rw-r--r-- 1 cs130 cs130 80467 Sep  1 23:25 find_result
-rw-r--r-- 1 cs130 cs130     0 Sep  2 10:29 myfile
cs130@raspberrypi ~ 4
```

#2. listing the content of the directory and redirecting the output to the file (to get the file).

#3. running **cat** and redirecting content of the file from the previous step to the **cat**. By default, **cat** expects input from the ***stdin***, but here we redirected ***stdin*** from the file.

We see the content of the file dumped on the screen by the **cat**. Note, that I could just say:

```
cat myfile
```

But again, that was for the demonstration of ***stdin*** redirection.

5. (Some of the) Usages of the cat command

And since we used that command again, let's take a look at some usages of it.

5.1. Concatenating files together.

Last time when discussing the **cat** command, I mentioned, that it originally was intended to concatenate the files together. How?

That's actually simple. I also mentioned, that it can take more than one file as an argument, and that it dumps files on the terminal in the order of those arguments. Now the rest is simple. You would just run this command:

```
cat myfile1 myfile2 myfile3 > myfiles
```

And you don't need to open each of the file, copy it and paste it to another file. If you want to append something to something, here is the way.

– Nice!

5.2. Pasting content of the buffer to the file.

Suppose you copied something from the screen (web page, content of the screen), or from the file and you want to quickly paste that to another file. You do not need to open and then save and close that target file just because you want to put some text there... Why bother with so many unnecessary steps?

Here is what you'd do (supposing you already have the content to paste in the buffer):

```
cat > myfile
```

It opens the prompt and waits for your action.

You paste to that. You may need to interrupt (^C) or send end of the file (^D) to close the file. And here it is. You have that file. And(!) you preserved the **exact** formatting. That feature sometimes is more important than the entire ability to paste into the file.

– Very nice!

BTW, this is a good and quick method to create (or append) a file with some of your notes. You do

```
cat > myfile
```

And start typing. When you are done, you have that file. Some people even write simple programs or scripts like that! Just be aware that you can not go to the previous line.

– Very nice!

6. A Find utility (cont'd)

Let's rerun to the `find` utility. We were sidetracked by the involved discussion of the redirection, but here is one thing that we need to talk about.

Let's recall our example with the `find`. We wanted to find some files and here is the output we got:

```
cs130@raspberrypi ~ 9 find . -name 'myfile*'
./dir1/myfiles4
./dir1/myfiles5
./dir1/myfiles3
./dir1/myfiles2
./dir2/myfile
./myfiles1
cs130@raspberrypi ~ 10
```

As you see, it prints only the ***paths*** to the files found. That may not be sufficient for us. We may want to take the result of the `find` and do something with it. Just as a very simple example, we may want to see a long listing (for example to see the permissions, or time stamp, which may be important, as we may want to take the most recent file, etc).

Let's expand that command by adding few more instructions to it:

```
find . -name 'myfile*' -exec ls -l '{}' \;
```

```
cs130@raspberrypi ~ 3 find . -name 'myfile*' -exec ls -l '{}' \;
-rw-r--r-- 1 cs130 cs130 220 Sep  2 10:29 ./myfile
-rw-r--r-- 1 cs130 cs130 48 Sep  2 12:49 ./myfile1
cs130@raspberrypi ~ 4
```

The output is little different, because during that time I deleted these other directories.... Oh, well, that's not important.

What's important, is that we were able to apply another command at the result of the **find.**

Let's review what we did (starting from ***-exec*** option) step by step.

```
-exec
```

Tells to execute the following command. OK, that's easy, no big deal.

```
ls -l
```

Command to be executed by that ***-exec*** option. That's fine too. We saw that.

```
'{}'
```

That one is more tricky. What it does, it takes the result of the **find**, (which is list), and for each element of that list it applies the **ls -l** command. **ls -l** expects some argument. So, each element from the list returned by the **find** gets inserted (one by one) in the place of braces, and sent to the **ls -l** as its argument. The process stops when there is no more elements in the list. At that point we need to tell ***bash***, that we are done. We do so with that statement:

```
\;
```

We already saw the semicolon terminating the statements. People from programming classes do it all the time. Here we do it again. The only thing different is the backslash. Why do we need it? Because we ask ***bash*** to send the semicolon to terminate the processes flowing between **find** and **ls -l**. Thus, we need to tell, that it is not an instruction, intended to the ***bash***, but that we want it to be sent downstream the command flow. Thus, for the correct syntax we need to escape the original meaning of the semicolon.

And just for the completion reason... How do I know that **find** returns a list (besides of course the fact, that it prints the list of results on the screen)?

```
cs130@raspberrypi ~/dir1 3 ls
cs130@raspberrypi ~/dir1 4 touch myfiles{1..10}
cs130@raspberrypi ~/dir1 5 myfiles=`find . -name 'myfiles*'`
cs130@raspberrypi ~/dir1 6 echo $myfiles
./myfiles9 ./myfiles6 ./myfiles8 ./myfiles7 ./myfiles4 ./myfiles5 ./myfiles3 ./myfiles2 ./myfiles1 .
/myfiles10
cs130@raspberrypi ~/dir1 7
```

Here again we see usage of the back quotes. When we do **echo** for our variable, we see the list of file names, separated by a space. You see another reason why you may want to hold off of using the spaces in the file names?

OK, that was good.

Now let's see some of the real use of the ***find*** in combination with the **exec.**

It is not "***if***" it is "***when***"... At some point you do a listing on your directory and there you see some entry like that:

```
cs130@raspberrypi ~/dir1 17 ls -lrt
total 0
-rw-r--r-- 1 cs130 cs130 0 Sep  2 17:04 d
```

A file name containing (or consisting of) some of un-printed characters.

How can such file could be created? It could be errors in the command line: broken quotes, broken pipes, incorrect redirection... Anything.

(But don't ask how did ***I*** make it)

Now you look at that file and you realize that you cannot do anything about that. Because of un-printed character(s), no (usual) tool will take that as an argument. You cannot look what's inside that file, you cannot even delete it (with the regular tools). What to do? One option would be to leave it as is. But it really annoys you. There should be some way.

Actually, there is more than one way. But let me use that one for this discussion:

Each file has a special unique number associated with that. Actually, the human-readable file name is just for convenience of humans. Computers take it differently.

That number is called the "***inode*** number". To see it we need to add another flag to the **ls** command:

```
ls -i
```

```
cs130@raspberrypi ~/dir1 18 ls -i
43017 d
```

Here we see that number, which is 43017.

Good.

Now what we do:

```
find . -inum 43017 -exec ls -l '{}' \;
```

```
cs130@raspberrypi ~/dir1 19 find . -inum 43017 -exec ls -l '{}' \;
-rw-r--r-- 1 cs130 cs130 0 Sep  2 17:04 ./d
```

We ask ***find*** to do a search by the ***inode*** number, and to produce a long listing for that entry.

We want a long listing, to verify that we got what we wanted.

When we did our verification, what we do next is this:

```
find . -inum 43017 -exec rm '{}' \;
```

```
cs130@raspberrypi ~/dir1 20 find . -inum 43017 -exec rm '{}' \;
cs130@raspberrypi ~/dir1 21
```

And to verify that that annoying file is gone:

ls -l

```
cs130@raspberrypi ~/dir1 21 ls -l
total 0
```

We will return to the find utility again in a while, but for now, one note, is that the exact syntax of the last two parts may be picky for different systems. You may need to check your documentation for the exact implementation.

And that takes me to the next topic.

7. Online help and man pages

Every Linux's tool comes with the documentation. If you forget some command, or some options or flags, you can simply run this:

```
man find
```

to display documentation (manual) about the ***find*** command.

```
       This  manual page talks about `options' within the expression list.  These options control
       the behaviour of find but are specified immediately after the last path  name.   The  five
       `real' options -H, -L, -P, -D and -O must appear before the first path name, if at all.  A
       double dash -- can also be used to signal that any remaining  arguments  are  not  options
 Manual page find(1) line 1 (press h for help or q to quit)
```

And guess what? It opens in the ***less*** file reader, so that you can do full read, search, scrolling etc, everything you need while reading the file, but you cannot write to it. That is one example of usefulness of that tool (the ***less***).

Documentation can be very good and complete, or just a …. bare-bone skeleton, but. At least it exists.

And as always, there is a reach and a lot of various tutorials and helps available online. If you know the question, you can always find the answer.

8. Saving changes to your environment.

We talked about modifying the environment, like modifying the $***PATH***, or creating ***aliases***. At that time I said that the changes live only for the duration of the session. And I did not lie. Almost. Because there is obviously a way to make those changes persistent. All we need to do is to write them to our profile configuration file. We already know couple of such files. It would be ***.bashrc*** and ***.bash_profile*** (on your system it could be just a ***.profile***). Note that these files are hidden (the prep-ending dot in the file name). So. How to do that?

Now, when we know the redirection it should be simple.

> Note, that the way I will do it now, is for the illustration purposes, to show how to use **echo** to quickly append to the file without opening it. In many cases you will probably want to write to the profile files using the full text editor.

- But there are two files. Which one is which?
- It really does not matter. If you look at them carefully, one file reads another, so there is no difference where would you put it. But to be inline with the community, and other users' expectations, and to follow the yellow brick road, let's write ***aliases*** to the ***.bashrc***, and ***Environmental Variables*** to the ***.bash_profile*** (or ***.profile***).

> Before you do changes to the system, make a backup copy!

> You do not want to overwrite or otherwise mess with these files!!!

I repeat (with the <blink> tags):

> You do not want to overwrite or otherwise mess with these files!!!

> You do not want to make mistakes. But you will. And because you will, you should always do as much as work you can, as a regular user, switching to the ***root*** only when absolutely necessary. That should be your rule number one working on the system. Because cost of mistake of the regular user and the ***root*** is different.

Now let's write our ***alias***.

```
cs130@raspberrypi ~ 28 echo "alias mycoolalias='echo do not panic'" >> .bashrc
cs130@raspberrypi ~ 29
```

Let's check it:

```
cs130@raspberrypi ~ 29 alias
alias egrep='egrep --color=auto'
alias fgrep='fgrep --color=auto'
alias grep='grep --color=auto'
alias ls='ls --color=auto'
```

Let's ***re-source*** the ***.bashrc***

```
cs130@raspberrypi ~ 30 source .bashrc
cs130@raspberrypi ~ 31 alias
alias egrep='egrep --color=auto'
alias fgrep='fgrep --color=auto'
alias grep='grep --color=auto'
alias ls='ls --color=auto'
alias mycoolalias='echo do not panic'
cs130@raspberrypi ~ 32 mycoolalias
do not panic
cs130@raspberrypi ~ 33
```

Let's see if it persists in other session:

```
cs130@raspberrypi ~ 33 bash
cs130@raspberrypi ~ 1 alias
alias egrep='egrep --color=auto'
alias fgrep='fgrep --color=auto'
alias grep='grep --color=auto'
alias ls='ls --color=auto'
alias mycoolalias='echo do not panic'
```

- Cool! And the ***EV***?
- Same thing, it does not really matter where we put it, but to be consistent with other users and to follow the yellow brick road, let's put it into the ***profile*** file (in my case that would be a ***.profile***; your file may be different, for example ***.bash_profile***). Let me write a $***PATH*** with the single dot, added to the front of it:

```
cs130@raspberrypi ~ 3 echo 'export PATH=.:$PATH' >> .profile
cs130@raspberrypi ~ 4 source .profile
cs130@raspberrypi ~ 5 echo $PATH
.:/home/cs130/bin:/home/cs130/bin:/usr/local/sbin:/usr/local/bin:/usr/sbin:/usr/
local/games:/usr/games
cs130@raspberrypi ~ 6
```

here

And after I ***re-source*** the ***.profile***, I see my $***PATH*** containing the dot.

Again, that is for the demonstration of how you can quickly append to the file without opening it.

Alright. We had a little break; and now, re-energized perhaps are ready for the next topic.

The section we are approaching is one of the "***involved***" in this course (note me not saying "***difficult***"). People, who did not drop after hearing me saying word "***shell***", who did not drop after hearing me saying words "***Environmental Variable***", and who will still stay after the completion of this section have very good chances to successfully complete this course.

Let's start approaching that slowly.

9. Introduction to the Linux filtering. The grep utility

Suppose I want to find in the history lines with the command ***find***. Perhaps I want to re-run one of that command and do not want to type much myself, or maybe I want to refer to what exactly I did some while back. One method would be to dump the history, and to scroll through that history... All thousands of line of it.

That is not our method.

Instead, we would do this:

```
history > histfile; grep 'find' histfile
```

```
cs130@raspberrypi ~ 1 history > histfile; grep 'find' histfile
```

Well, actually we would ***not*** do this; we would do this differently, but give me some time, perhaps until next lecture. For now, we'd do this.

And we will have the list filtered out by the word "find".

```
345  find / -name '*xml' > find_result 2> error_file
346  find / -name '*xml' > find_result 2> /dev/null
357  cat < find_result
363  history > histfile; grep 'find' histfile
```

Now you can review the list (I displayed only the last part of that), and if you want to re-run some of the previous command, you'd simply do:

```
!346
```

This is an example or running ***grep***, the tool that does searching and filtering. The above was a demonstration of it running in the simplest form. We can use it to filter input from ***stdin***, or from the file. Let me run another example.

grep -i 'home' error_file

(Remember that file where we redirected our errors from the ***find*** exercises to? I kept it).

```
cs130@raspberrypi ~ 4 grep -i 'home' error_file
find: `/home/pi/.config': Permission denied
find: `/home/pi/.thumbnails': Permission denied
find: `/home/pi/.cache/menus': Permission denied
find: `/home/pi/.cache/chromium': Permission denied
find: `/home/pi/.cache/openbox/sessions': Permission denied
find: `/home/pi/.gconf': Permission denied
find: `/home/pi/.pki': Permission denied
find: `/home/pi/.gnome': Permission denied
find: `/home/pi/.local/share/icons': Permission denied
cs130@raspberrypi ~ 5
```

(-i) flag for the ***grep*** tells it to do a case-insensitive search.

Let's check couple other options

To display line numbers:

grep -n 'home' error_file

```
cs130@raspberrypi ~ 1 grep -n 'home' error_file
1207:find: `/home/pi/.config': Permission denied
1208:find: `/home/pi/.thumbnails': Permission denied
1209:find: `/home/pi/.cache/menus': Permission denied
1210:find: `/home/pi/.cache/chromium': Permission denied
1211:find: `/home/pi/.cache/openbox/sessions': Permission denied
1212:find: `/home/pi/.gconf': Permission denied
1213:find: `/home/pi/.pki': Permission denied
1214:find: `/home/pi/.gnome': Permission denied
1215:find: `/home/pi/.local/share/icons': Permission denied
```

Look at the line numbers on the left

To reverse (negate) the search. Here I will search for everything, that does not match word "find"

grep -v 'find' histfile

```
cs130@raspberrypi ~ 4 grep -v 'find' histfile
```

This results in a long list from the history entries that do not contain word "find". I'll show only small part of that.

```
358  logout
359  ls
360  ls -ltr > myfile
361  cat < myfile
362  logout
```

That option (-v) is very useful for a lot of applications. For example, I can easily remove the empty lines from the file:

Creating a file with some empty lines.

Using ***grep -v*** to remove them.

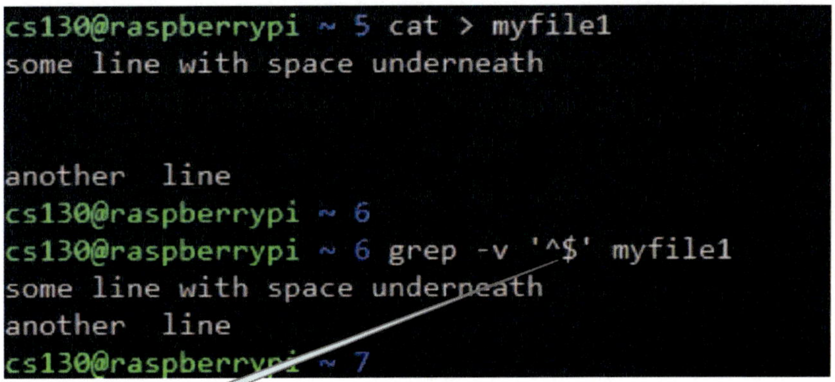

```
cs130@raspberrypi ~ 5 cat > myfile1
some line with space underneath


another  line
cs130@raspberrypi ~ 6
cs130@raspberrypi ~ 6 grep -v '^$' myfile1
some line with space underneath
another  line
cs130@raspberrypi ~ 7
```

Note the syntax here: here

The caret (^) anchors to the beginning of the line, the dollar sign ($) anchors to the end of the line (remember me saying that the dollar sign can be used to refer to the last argument? Let's remember, that the dollar sign can be used to refer to the last something).

When I ask to filter out (-v) line, that has nothing in between the beginning of the line, and the end of the line, I ask to remove the empty line.

With that let's pause until next time here. We have quite some information to read, understand, and memorize so let's pause and start big things next time

10. Summary

Writing environmental variables to the profile, redirecting the file descriptors, introduction to the Linux filtering, null device, inode, back quotes (again).

Commands:

find, grep, printenv

Lecture 5. Unnamed pipes

Without much ado and without special announcements we started a big part of our class.

The reason this is a big part, is this:

If you take the Linux exam, or you are going to the interview, you should very well expect ***at least*** some number of questions about that. (Did I say "at least?")

If you work with the Linux, depending on what you do, you may use those things occasionally, ***or*** on a daily and regular basis.

There is yet another reason for that.

It is in the syllabus.

Let's start (or shall I better say: "Let's continue").

1. Unnamed pipes

Last time we encountered a situation when we needed to run two processes in a sequence one after another. By itself it was not anything new, we did that many times already, and by now we know how to schedule two (or more) processes running in sequence.

But what was new last time, is that we needed to pass some information from the first process to the next one. Not only ***just*** some information, but information (the data) that the first process accumulated (produced), and that meant to be used (consumed) by the next process. That what was new for us. As you recall, we did it through the special file, that was created just for that purposes, i.e. to temporary store and pass the information down the chain of commands.

We did that with that construct:

```
history > histfile; grep 'find' histfile

130@raspberrypi ~ 1 history > histfile; grep 'find' histfile
```

And when I look at that line, I have three issues with that:

1. There is too much typing there.
2. We needed to create a temporary file just for the purposes of passing data from producer to a consumer. When we make a temporary file, we need to remember to clean up after the process finishes. And that's what we did. I mean, we forgot to do that.
3. And finally... It is just ugly.

- Can we...?
- Yes....

Let's re-write that command differently. Like that:

```
history | grep 'find'
```

```
s130@raspberrypi ~ 1 history | grep 'find'
```

Hey, I see that my command's here!

```
363  history > histfile; grep 'find' histfile
365  grep -i 'home' find_result
371  grep -v 'find' histfile
375  history | grep find
376  find . -name myfile*
377  find . -name 'myfile*' -exec ls -l '{}' \;
391  man find
392  find . -inum 43017 -exec mv '{}' dir1 \;
397  find . -inum 43017 -exec ls -l '{}' \;
398  find . -inum 43017 -exec rm '{}' \;
404  myfiles=`find . -name 'myfiles*'`
407  history | grep 'find'
s130@raspberrypi ~ 2
```

… And we see results from the ***history*** filtered by the word "***find***"

So. What we did here?

We used an ***unnamed pipe*** (that pipe character, which is on the same key with '\' above 'enter') to

1. Run commands in sequence (like the semicolon does)
2. Pass the data from the producer directly to the consumer without any intermediate steps of creating a file (that's what semicolon does not).
3. And we did (passing data) that without any programming, socket programming... by using just one key on the keyboard...

Just as with the semicolon we can bind together and assemble a pipe of arbitrary length (number of commands). Thus, we can create a pipeline of any complexity.

> When in CS we say "***any***", we mean "***any*** … reasonable"

As with other things, related to running commands, pipes in the pipeline exist for the duration of the command. As soon as commands completes, the unnamed pipe is gone.

Data flowing from the producer to the consumer supposedly should be in the format that consumer expects and can understand. But that is so for all other means of passing data, including the one we did with the file. Thus, it is your responsibility to build pipes with compatible "ends".

1.1. Some examples with unnamed pipes.

Let's do some examples.

Suppose, we want to find all the html files with word "***user***" either in the file name, or in the file path.

```
find / -name '*html' | grep user
```

```
cs130@raspberrypi ~ 5 find / -name '*html' 2>/dev/null | grep user
/usr/share/doc/adduser/examples/adduser.local.conf.examples/skel.other/index.html
/usr/share/doc/libfreetype6/reference/ft2-user_allocation.html
/usr/share/doc/fontconfig/fontconfig-user.html
/usr/share/doc/dillo/user_help.html
/usr/share/doc/base-passwd/users-and-groups.html
cs130@raspberrypi ~ 6
```

– That's cool! What if we wanted to find all files containing the word "user" ***inside***?

– Sure, no problem. We will need to modify the command a little.

We will need to build the list of the files, and then go inside each file and see if there is such word there. We could do that by something like that:

```
grep user `find / -name '*html' `
```

Note that I use a back quotes to get result from the **find**, and then use **grep** on that result. And again, the difference between these two commands, is that in the first case I filter for the ***file name*** (and path), while in the second case, I apply that filter to the content of the file, i.e. going ***inside*** of the files.

But actually, we don't want to run that command. Although you could. The reason I don't want to run that command, because of that same question:

– Hmmm, errr, who, did you say, was your Linux instructor ***again***?

No, I don't want to run it like that.

We will run it differently:

```
find / -name '*html' 2>/dev/null | xargs grep user | more
```

Let's see.

First, you'd see that I added part that discards the error messages for the **find**. You know, why. We are going to get a lot of files from all sorts of locations, so, expectingly, there will be error messages.

That was first part of our command before the pipe. Let's go to the middle part:

```
xargs grep user
```

The **xargs** command takes whatever input it receives, and tries to convert it to the argument to the command that follows self. i.e. to its own argument. Thus, it sort of transforms input to the arguments.

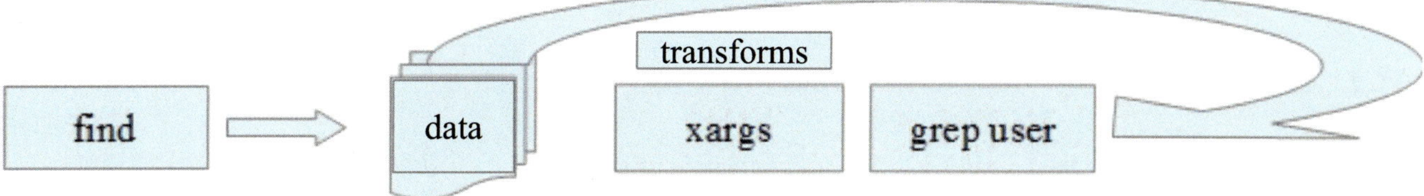

- So. What is the input does the ***xargs*** get?
- Whatever result the ***find*** returns and sends to the pipe.
- Good. And what is the argument to the ***xargs*** itself?
- The command to filter for the word "***user***": ***grep user***.
- Nice. So, we are mostly done with that part of the pipeline. What about the last part?

```
xargs grep user | more
```

I expect a ***lot*** of results. To be able to have at least some glance on it, such that it would make sense, I pipe the final result to the ***more***, and thus, am able to look at it screen full by screen full.

You will see the last (highlighted) part of that command (piping results through the ***more***) ***very*** often. Sometimes, though you may see that the ***less*** is used instead of ***more*** – just to add some more power to seeing and checking the results.

And here is the picture of a small part of my screen with the word "***user***" inside the files:

```
cs130@raspberrypi ~ 1 find / -name '*html' 2>/dev/null         grep user | more
grep: /opt/Wolfram/WolframEngine/11.0/SystemFiles/Inclu    s/XML/MathML2/html: Is a directo
/opt/Wolfram/WolframEngine/11.0/SystemFiles/Links/Datab seLink/ReleaseNotes.html:commands dire ly t
o Mathematica functions. Prepared statements allow users to easily integrate
/opt/Wolfram/WolframEngine/11.0/SystemFiles/Links/DatabaseLink/ReleaseNotes.html:Mathematica users w
ill find jumping into the database world quite easy with DatabaseLink. A
```

– Wait a minute! I just noticed … I think I saw an error message on the very first line. Here! How that could be? We discarded the errors to the null device haven't we?

```
cs130@raspberrypi ~ 1 find / -name '*html' 2>/dev/null | xargs grep user | more
grep: /opt/Wolfram/WolframEngine/11.0/SystemFiles/IncludeFiles/XML/MathML2/html: Is a directory
/opt/Wolfram/WolframEngine/11.0/SystemFiles/Links/DatabaseLink/ReleaseNotes.html:commands directly t
```

- We discarded errors from the ***find***. But that does not mean that the ***grep***, which follows that in the pipeline cannot produce its own errors. Remember, each redirection is for duration of the command only. If we want to get rid of the errors from the next command, we need to take care about that as well.

```
find / -name '*html' 2>/dev/null | xargs grep user 2>/dev/null | more
```

```
cs130@raspberrypi ~ 2 find / -name '*html' 2>/dev/null | xargs grep user 2>/dev/null | more
/opt/Wolfram/WolframEngine/11.0/SystemFiles/Links/DatabaseLink/ReleaseNotes.html:commands directly t
o Mathematica functions. Prepared statements allow users to easily integrate
/opt/Wolfram/WolframEngine/11.0/SystemFiles/Links/DatabaseLink/ReleaseNotes.html:Mathematica users w
ill find jumping into the database world quite easy with DatabaseLink. A
/opt/Wolfram/WolframEngine/11.0/SystemFiles/Links/DatabaseLink/ReleaseNotes.html:built-in database a
llows users to get acquainted with databases without needing to install a
```

- Wow! Wow! Nice!
- This is ***Linux***!

Alright. Let me do one other thing to finish this section.

Sometimes you are interested not in the actual files, or outputs, but in the ***number*** of those files or outputs. That is a very useful feature.

Is there such record or is there is no such record? How many users? How many active users? You don't want to do the manual counting. No, you do not want to. As you can imagine, there is a tool for that.

Let's re-run our last command and count how many times a word "***user***" is used in all those html files on the system, we have access to.

```
find / -name '*html' 2>/dev/null | xargs grep user 2>/dev/null | wc -l
```

The **wc** command (for "word count") used with the (-l) (a small *el*) argument counts number of lines in the input to self.

Thus, I just replaced the **more** command from the last run with the **wc -l**. And, as you may expect, I did not type that entire long line. What I actually typed was this:

```
^more^wc -l^
```

```
cs130@raspberrypi ~ 3 ^more^wc -l^
find / -name '*html' 2>/dev/null | xargs grep user 2>/dev/null | wc -l
1614
cs130@raspberrypi ~ 4
```

(in unison):

- This is ***Linux***!
- This is ***Linux***!

2. The head and tail tools

We saw how the **more** command works when we need to quickly examine output or file. But sometimes you do not need the full screen of the output. Sometimes it is enough to look at few lines, either from the beginning, or the end of the data. For example, if you want to quickly check the format of the file, you do not need to open it. Even such a simple tool as **more** would be too much for that.

Suppose, you want to quickly test, how your command works. Or, you are building a pipeline and want to test its parts, while gradually adding more and more chains to it. In all those cases a quick peek at the output data will be sufficient. And besides, you do not want your screen to be filled with something else that distracts you.

The ***head*** command displays first 10 lines (by default) taken from the argument to self. You can change that default by providing arguments. It is simple command, so let just see some examples, based on what we already did.

Instead of

```
find / -name '*html' 2>/dev/null | xargs grep user 2>/dev/null | more
```

Let's do:

```
find / -name '*html' 2>/dev/null | xargs grep user 2>/dev/null | head
```

```
cs130@raspberrypi ~/dir1 4 find / -name '*html' 2>/dev/null | xargs grep user 2>/dev/null | head
/home/pi/tiff-3.8.2/html/v3.7.0alpha.html:      supplied by user.
/home/pi/tiff-3.8.2/html/internals.html:available to a user and certain tag data may be maintained t
hat a user
```

(I displayed just few lines of the output here)

Let's change the number of lines in the output:

```
find / -name '*html' 2>/dev/null | xargs grep user 2>/dev/null | head -2
```

```
cs130@raspberrypi ~/dir1 5 find / -name '*html' 2>/dev/null | xargs grep user 2>/dev/null | head -2
/home/pi/tiff-3.8.2/html/v3.7.0alpha.html:      supplied by user.
/home/pi/tiff-3.8.2/html/internals.html:available to a user and certain tag data may be maintained t
hat a user
cs130@raspberrypi ~/dir1 6
```

Just a couple lines allow you to glance at the format of the file, or test your command.

Earlier, we saw example listing the directory with lot of files. Now we can do this:

```
ls -l | more
```

ls -l /bin | more

```
cs130@raspberrypi ~/dir1 8 ls -l /bin | more
total 5416
-rwxr-xr-x 1 root root 813992 Jan 11  2013 bash
-rwxr-xr-x 3 root root  30340 Aug 14  2012 bunzip2
-rwxr-xr-x 3 root root  30340 Aug 14  2012 bzcat
lrwxrwxrwx 1 root root      6 Aug 14  2012 bzcmp -> bzdiff
-rwxr-xr-x 1 root root   2140 Aug 14  2012 bzdiff
```

(Just few lines shown)
or this:

```
ls -l | head
```

ls -l /bin | head -5

```
cs130@raspberrypi ~/dir1 9 ls -l /bin | head -5
total 5416
-rwxr-xr-x 1 root root 813992 Jan 11  2013 bash
-rwxr-xr-x 3 root root  30340 Aug 14  2012 bunzip2
-rwxr-xr-x 3 root root  30340 Aug 14  2012 bzcat
lrwxrwxrwx 1 root root      6 Aug 14  2012 bzcmp -> bzdiff
cs130@raspberrypi ~/dir1 10
```

(Entire output shown)

And so on.

The ***tail*** is pretty much similar to the ***head***, with the difference, that, as the name suggests, it displays the last ten lines. As with the ***head***, that number can be changed with the argument to the command.

Just for fun, the interesting combination of head and tail can produce this:

ls -l /bin | head -5 | tail -1

```
cs130@raspberrypi ~/dir1 10 ls -l /bin | head -5 | tail -1
lrwxrwxrwx 1 root root      6 Aug 14  2012 bzcmp -> bzdiff
cs130@raspberrypi ~/dir1 11
```

Say, you want to display some lines in the middle of the output:

ls -l /bin | head -60 | tail -5

```
cs130@raspberrypi ~/dir1 14 ls -l /bin | wc -l
125
cs130@raspberrypi ~/dir1 15 ls -l /bin | head -60 | tail -5
-rwxr-xr-x 1 root root  42700 Jan 28  2013 ln
-rwxr-xr-x 1 root root  86672 May 19  2012 loadkeys
-rwxr-xr-x 1 root root  39232 Jun  5  2012 login
-rwxr-xr-x 1 root root  96340 Jan 28  2013 ls
-rwxr-xr-x 1 root root  39336 Dec 22  2012 lsblk
cs130@raspberrypi ~/dir1 16
```

Here is five files from within the middle of listing of ***/bin***.

Alright, that was a quick introduction to the couple of simple utilities.

3. The awk tool

Pretty much every (major) discussion in this course could be started with the words: "You cannot think working on a Linux without that...". The topic that follows in this section is one of the best proof of that statement.

The ***awk*** (named after the initials of its creators) is a full complete programming language. We will use only limited functionality of that to work on a command line. For us, probably the most useful feature, that ***awk*** provides, is the ability to work with columns (fields) in the file. We already saw ***grep*** to filter data. It is the great tool for that purpose. What it does, is searches the entire line to find a match. i.e. it works "horizontally". Sometimes we need more precision and more granularity, than matching the entire line. Sometimes we want the ability to look at and to work with separate fields and columns. When that is the case, we use the ***awk***.
General pattern how we write commands with the ***awk*** is a condition, followed by an action. The default action is print. So if we say

awk 'pattern',

it will print the lines that matches the pattern. Again, we don't need to say that we want to print it. It is built into the paradigm of the language.

When ***awk*** reads the input (file or input), it breaks it into the columns and assigns each column the indexes, starting from 1. Thus, to print first three columns from the file (suppose the file has more than three columns), we would say:

```
cat <myfile> | awk '{print $1 "," $2 "," $3}'
```

(We added comma to separate fields for readability of the output). Action in the ***awk***' statements should be surrounded by the braces, and single quotes ('{}'). Note the dollar sign. Remember... the variables!

Because ***awk*** works with fields (columns), and because it keeps track of each field (column) in the line, we can easily extract some columns, delete other, re-arrange their order, etc. We can match the entire line based on the fields and columns, and that provides a much better control.

Let's jump into the examples.

```
ls -l | awk '{print $3", "$9}' | head -5
```

```
cs130@raspberrypi ~/dir1 13 ls -l | awk '{print $3", "$9}' | head -5
,
cs130, difffile
cs130, filesls
cs130, myfiles1
cs130, myfiles10
```

This construct prints only third (user name) and the last (file name) fields from the output of ***ls -l*** command.

What we did here, we essentially deleted few columns from the output. And this is another usage of **awk:** to delete unneeded fields. We can also concatenate two columns together:

```
cat users_phone_numbers | awk '{print $3$4}'
```

and, generally re-format the fields:

```
cs130@raspberrypi ~ 9 echo -e "(760) 123 45 67\n(858) 432 44 55" | awk '{print $1" "$2"-"$3$4}'
(760) 123-4567
(858) 432-4455
```

(Note the **\n** to insert a new line).

So, next time when your Customer Service Department complains about difficulties working with non-uniformed and non-compatible phones records, you know how to fix that.

We can also change the field separator in the output:

```
cs130@raspberrypi ~/dir1 14 ls -l | awk '{print $3":"$9}' | head -5
:
cs130:difffile
cs130:filesls
cs130:myfiles1
cs130:myfiles10
```

Or re-arrange columns in the file:

```
cs130@raspberrypi ~/dir1 15 ls -l | awk '{print $9"->"$3}' | head -5
->
difffile->cs130
filesls->cs130
myfiles1->cs130
myfiles10->cs130
```

So, you already see that it is quite a useful tool. But that is not all. As I said, probably the most value for us is its ability to match input based by the fields.

Suppose, I have a files that have ownership by a mixture of groups: user (myself), sqluser (people from the sql database group), and webuser (people from the web development group).

```
-rw-r--r-- 1 user user 0 Aug 19 04:34 difffile
-rw-r--r-- 1 user sqluser 0 Sep  4 20:20 filesls
-rw-r--r-- 1 user user 0 Aug 19 03:36 myfiles1
-rw-r--r-- 1 user webuser 0 Aug 19 03:36 myfiles10
-rw-r--r-- 1 user user 0 Aug 19 03:36 myfiles100
-rw-r--r-- 1 user user 0 Aug 19 03:36 myfiles11
-rw-r--r-- 1 user user 0 Aug 19 03:36 myfiles12
-rw-r--r-- 1 user webuser 0 Aug 19 03:36 myfiles13
-rw-r--r-- 1 user user 0 Aug 19 03:36 myfiles14
```

Suppose, I want to filter these files to see only those, from my own group (user). What I would do is this:

```
ls -l | awk '$4 == "user"'
```

```
cs130@raspberrypi ~/dir1 8 cat filesls | awk '$4 == "user"' | head
-rw-r--r-- 1 user user 0 Aug 19 04:34 difffile
-rw-r--r-- 1 user user 0 Aug 19 03:36 myfiles1
-rw-r--r-- 1 user user 0 Aug 19 03:36 myfiles100
-rw-r--r-- 1 user user 0 Aug 19 03:36 myfiles11
-rw-r--r-- 1 user user 0 Aug 19 03:36 myfiles12
```

(Output truncated)
What the command after the pipe tells is to take each line in the input and match its 4th field to the word "***user***". If match is found, print that line.

Note, that I could achieve the same result with the ***grep***:

```
ls -l | grep -v 'webuser' | grep -v 'sqluser'
```

```
cs130@raspberrypi ~/dir1 9 cat filesls | grep -v 'webuser' | grep -v 'sqluser' | head
total 0
-rw-r--r-- 1 user user 0 Aug 19 04:34 difffile
-rw-r--r-- 1 user user 0 Aug 19 03:36 myfiles1
-rw-r--r-- 1 user user 0 Aug 19 03:36 myfiles100
```

But how much longer that command would be, and, most importantly, it is not practical. I can do this to filter out couple, maybe three different conditions, but what if I had dozens? But most importantly, what if I had an "sqluser" in some other field, not on the 4th one? It will be filtered out as well. No, that is not practical. Whereas with the ***awk*** I can achieve that precisely and with one simple command.

And to see my last point: What if in addition, to the different groups, I had different users like that?

```
-rw-r--r-- 1 webuser user 0 Aug 19 04:34 difffile
-rw-r--r-- 1 user sqluser 0 Sep  4 20:20 filesls
-rw-r--r-- 1 user user 0 Aug 19 03:36 myfiles1
-rw-r--r-- 1 user webuser 0 Aug 19 03:36 myfiles10
-rw-r--r-- 1 user user 0 Aug 19 03:36 myfiles100
```

A ***grep*** would not distinguish between these fields (unless you write a rather involved condition). Whereas, again, with the ***awk*** I can achieve that match with one simple command.

```
cs130@raspberrypi ~/dir1 11 cat filesls | awk '$4 == "user"' | head
-rw-r--r-- 1 webuser user 0 Aug 19 04:34 difffile
-rw-r--r-- 1 user user 0 Aug 19 03:36 myfiles1
-rw-r--r-- 1 user user 0 Aug 19 03:36 myfiles100
-rw-r--r-- 1 user user 0 Aug 19 03:36 myfiles11
-rw-r--r-- 1 user user 0 Aug 19 03:36 myfiles12
```

We did fields re-arrangement. Let's do this for our user group only:

```
ls -l | awk '$4 == "user" {print $9"->"$3}'
```

```
cs130@raspberrypi ~/dir1 18 cat filesls | awk '$4=="user" {print $9"->"$3}' | head -5
difffile->webuser
myfiles1->user
myfiles100->user
myfiles11->user
```

Again, please carefully follow the syntax. All quotes, parenthesis, braces, etc should match.

OK. That was good. Now let's do something better.
Let's print the list of users who cannot log in.

It used to be that on the Linux, users' account information was stored in the ***/etc/passwd*** file. Then some people realized, that the name of that file was revealing. Everyone would know that the passwords are stored in that file. Not good. So, the passwords were moved to a different file. And so that nobody could figure out what that file it was, it was named:

/etc/shadow

Now, of course everyone knows, that the passwords are stored in the ***/etc/shadow*** file.

> Security by obscurity is only secure until it's obscure. Which means, it cannot be relied upon to be reliably secure.

– Well said!
– Thank you!

But let's go back to our problem. We want to see list of users on a system, who cannot login. Here it is:

```
cat /etc/shadow | awk -F ':' '$2 == "*" {print $1", "$2}'
```

And I need to give some explanations here. Before we go into the details of the command, we need to know what input format we will be working with. That is first thing you do before you do a first thing. If you do not know the format of the data, you cannot work with the data.

A ***head*** is our friend. Exactly for that very purpose:

```
cs130@raspberrypi ~ 2 su -
Password:
root@raspberrypi:~# head /etc/shadow
```

First thing's first. You need to be a ***root*** to see that file. Why? You can take a look at the file permissions and you will see. Here is what we'll do. There is command ***su*** (for switch user). With no user name it will switch to the ***root***. You can provide any user name for which you have account on that machine, and switch between users as needed. Of course, you need to know the passwords for these users. Of course, if you want to switch to the ***root***, you need to know the ***root's*** password. Which means... You are the ***root***.

> You log in and you work on the system as a regular user, switching to a ***root*** only when necessary

> If you are the ***root***, you can switch to any user without password. You don't need it and will not be asked for a one.

> When you are done working as that user, use logout command to switch back to your session. Your session hangs and waits for your return.

Now let's look closely at the **su** command I typed. See the space and the minus sign? That tells to switch to that user and to load user's profile. Without that you will not become a fully profiled user (for example, some environmental variables may not be loaded). In our case, for that particular example, I did not really need that, because I only needed a ***root's*** credentials to read that file, but... I get used to that way. I don't want to guess whether I switched to a full-profiled user or not, every time something does not work as it should. Alright. That was a side comment, now let's see the format of the file.

```
root@raspberrypi:~# head /etc/shadow
root:$6$dgzFwcMP$AJXLNeumHhAQWdZDAJsEywbdvWsk30DcfCdMZOBrH1aOKHKZIkf
daemon:*:17352:0:99999:7:::
bin:*:17352:0:99999:7:::
sys:*:17352:0:99999:7:::
sync:*:17352:0:99999:7:::
games:*:17352:0:99999:7:::
man:*:17352:0:99999:7:::
```

Here is couple of things that we can gather:

1. Fields are separated by a colon (:), not by a space.
2. The password is in the second field. You can conclude that by looking at the first line with the ***root's*** password.
3. Did I say “couple”? Oh, well... The last thing, is that the invalid password is apparently an asterisk.

```
- The root's password!!! OMG!!! In the plain text file!!!
What do these people really think about??!!!
```

> The password on a Linux is stored in a plain text file. But that does not mean that, as in some other systems, the ***password*** is stored in a plain text. Password is stored as a one-way hash, and good luck to crack it. Besides... If you are not a ***root***, good luck to read the file first. And if you are the ***root***... Well, the whole system is yours, what are you complaining about?

That again underscores the importance of keeping the ***root's*** password secure...

OK, back to our problem. To solve that we need to print list of users from the ***shadow*** file, with second field matching a single asterisk

And here it is, repeating the command and the output (truncated)

```
cat /etc/shadow | awk -F ':' '$2 == "*" {print $1", "$2}'
```

```
root@raspberrypi:~# cat /etc/shadow | awk -F ':' '$2=="*" {print $1", "$2}' | head -5
daemon, *
bin, *
sys, *
sync, *
```

What are these users for? Why are they there? Why cannot … should not they login?
To function properly a system runs a lot of processes and services. Many of those processes and services need to be or to have a user set for them in the system to be able to run. That's why they are here. But just because technically those are users, it does not mean that any of them should be able to login. For example, if you setup a database on your computer, it is very likely, that a "***mysql***" or an "***oracle***" user would be added to the system, because they need to be able to run the database's services. But if you are not careful, and you set a real passwords for those users, thus, allowing them to login...

Attempt to login to a system using the system' users is one of the ways to test for a security holes to get into your system.

Your system should be well-guarded against such attempts.

But actually, let's reverse the task, and print only users with the ***valid*** passwords. That's easy. All we need to do is to reverse the match.

```
cat /etc/shadow | awk -F ':' '$2 != "*" {print $1", "$2}'
```

```
root@raspberrypi:~# cat /etc/shadow | awk -F ':' '$2 != "*" {print $1", "$2}' | head -5
root, $6$J0AZ0Xl4$O5b38oZ2zzpvqcrtqxmwLUgV5EZR0MgRh76QPxLMHkBnlre.SBytd34m0F0DX3JoGLqBMsBLeL6
0KZ1
libuuid, !
pi, $6$KGuv7OGb$iUAxuPt7CIweZ9DBmoXHa.SBiQU6ym7/9WjiHwVho2RV.FdkhwmdR8RrGAWeJIlgtabtGaWMKpeTv
F0
cs130, $6$mnGG4ji4$8AdEgNVaU3/pW6Wmfmy65l8yJAS2.KEnq/0gqj8yKvyG2KVjrpm23lOWIKCexrCXT4Rwz0FNRz
```

Then you examine that list, and if you find any user that is not supposed to be there... You know what to do.

- What?
- Didn't I tell you?
- Nope!

– Alright. We need to wait until the second half of the semester then; for the lecture about user management. As for now, I think I omitted one detail from the last two examples with the passwords.

By default, ***awk*** breaks input by the spaces. But of course you can change that. That what we needed to do to change field separator from space to a colon. And here is how we did that (-F for the input field separator):

```
cat /etc/shadow | awk -F ':' '$2 == "*" {print $1", "$2}'
```

Note, that I can combine different field separators in my pipe. From the example above, suppose (****suppose*;*** it is just for the example), suppose I want to print the part of the root's encrypted password before the first dot (Again, that is very artificial example, there may be no dot there, and besides, I do not see a valid practical reason for that; that is only given as the example and exercise). What would be our command?

```
cat /etc/shadow | awk -F ':' '$2 == "*" {print $1", "$2}' | awk -F '.' '{print $1}'
```

And now we print the first field, which would be everything from the output of the first ***awk*** command until the first dot.

- Alright. That was educational, but you said it is not a real example. Can you perhaps show us something more real?
- OK. Let's try this.

Suppose you have an XML log file from running some script. Like that:

```
cs130@raspberrypi ~ 6 cat somexmllog
<run1><time>1221</time><description>my descrition from first run</description></run1></script1>
<run2><time>1321</time><description>my descrition from the second attempt run</description></run2></script2>
<run3><time>1421</time><description>my descrition at the final run</description></run3></script3>
cs130@raspberrypi ~ 7
```

It shows run attempt, the run time, some free-text description, etc. You want to extract only description. Again, description can be arbitrary text and you cannot make any assumption of its length and composition. The problem is that you have a lot of XML tags there. Let's approach that one step at a time. Let's first convert the XML tags to the spaces:

```
cat somexmllog | tr '<,>' ' '
```

```
cs130@raspberrypi ~ 14 cat somexmllog | tr '<,>' ' '
 run1  time 1221 /time  description my descrition from first run /description  /run1  /script1
 run2  time 1321 /time  description my descrition from the second attempt run /description  /run2  /script2
 run3  time 1421 /time  description my descrition at the final run /description  /run3  /script3
```

Command ***tr*** translates characters in a first set to the second set. In this case I substitute two tags with the spaces. I can also delete characters in a first set with a (-d) parameter.

Let's note, that my verbose description goes after the first tag "***description***" (that used to be an XML tag just a moment ago). Let's use that knowledge to construct our first ***awk*** command:

```
cat somexmllog | tr '<,>' ' ' | awk -F 'description' '{print $2}'
```

```
cs130@raspberryp1 ~ 16 cat somexmllog | tr '<,>' ' ' | awk -F 'description' '{print $2}'
 my descrition from first run /
 my descrition from the second attempt run /
 my descrition at the final run /
```

Thus, I discarded everything before my free-text description, and everything after that. The only thing left to take care of is the forward slash, which is remnants of XML format. As always there are few ways of clearing that. I want to show a one (a yet another one) with the ***awk***:

awk breaks input into the field. We need to know the field number to be able to refer to it. In out case we need to refer to the last field. But our description is a free text, with arbitrary length, and we cannot predict that length, and, therefore the number of the last fields, which ***awk*** will deal with. What to do?

- Since ***awk*** breaks input into the separate fields, perhaps it can also keep track of the number of those fields?
- Actually, that's what it exactly does. After all, it enumerates those fields, therefore it should know these numbers!
- Can we...?
- Yes...

```
cat somexmllog | tr '<,>' ' ' | awk -F 'description' '{print $2}'| awk '{$NF=""} 1'
```

What I do in the last part here, I use a special ***awk***'s internal variable (*$NF*), that keeps track of the number of fields. Therefore, numeric value, kept in that variable, refers to the last field in that line. Then I set the field, referred by that variable to the empty (thus, essentially deleting it). Now I need to set a condition. That is a highlighted part. The ***1*** is always true. Thus, I tell to the ***awk*** to always print that line (with the deleted value in the last field). Here it is:

```
cs130@raspberryp1 ~ 24 cat somexmllog | tr '<,>' ' ' | awk -F 'description' '{print $2}' | awk '{$(NF-1)=""} {$NF=""} 1'
my descrition from first
my descrition from the second attempt
my descrition at the final
cs130@raspberryp1 ~ 25
```

And if you look closely, you will see, that I also deleted the second to the last field there. I did not mean to do that, I just misread the format. But I decided to leave that screen to show you that we can use the ***NF*** variable to refer the previous fields also.

So. There is always more than one way of doing something. I could probably achieve the same result using few other different approaches, but I wanted to show the one with the ***awk***'s ***NF***.

> When assembling a long pipeline, always do it step by step, controlling and testing each of the previous steps before proceeding to the next one.

4. wget and sort utilities

4.1. wget

The **wget** is very powerful command line tool to communicate with web server. You can talk to it, running session, submitting user name and passwords; you can download pages or data from the web server, including recursively... A lot of things. It is not the only tool to do that, but it is one of. Since it runs from the command line, as with everything, that runs on a command line, you can use it to build into your scripts a functionality to communicate with the web server. That is beauty of a command line. You can include a lot of various functionalities in the script just because everything is integrated through the ***shell***.

4.2. sort

It will not be a secret, if I say, that it sorts an input to self. Let's run few examples, they are so straightforward, I barely need to comment on them.

First, let's see what we are going to work with:

```
cs130@raspberrypi ~ 12 ls -l
total 168
drwxr-xr-x 2 cs130 cs130  4096 Sep  1 20:20 bin
drwxr-xr-x 2 cs130 cs130  4096 Sep  2 20:46 dir1
-rw-r--r-- 1 cs130 cs130 59530 Sep  1 23:10 error_file
-rw-r--r-- 1 cs130 cs130 80467 Sep  1 23:25 find_result
-rw-r--r-- 1 cs130 cs130  8112 Sep  2 12:19 histfile
-rw-r--r-- 1 cs130 cs130   220 Sep  2 10:29 myfile
-rw-r--r-- 1 cs130 cs130    48 Sep  2 12:49 myfile1
-rw-r--r-- 1 cs130 cs130   303 Sep  5 09:46 somexmllog
```

Let's sort this:

```
cs130@raspberrypi ~ 13 ls -l | sort
drwxr-xr-x 2 cs130 cs130  4096 Sep  1 20:20 bin
drwxr-xr-x 2 cs130 cs130  4096 Sep  2 20:46 dir1
-rw-r--r-- 1 cs130 cs130   220 Sep  2 10:29 myfile
-rw-r--r-- 1 cs130 cs130   303 Sep  5 09:46 somexmllog
-rw-r--r-- 1 cs130 cs130    48 Sep  2 12:49 myfile1
-rw-r--r-- 1 cs130 cs130 59530 Sep  1 23:10 error_file
-rw-r--r-- 1 cs130 cs130 80467 Sep  1 23:25 find_result
-rw-r--r-- 1 cs130 cs130  8112 Sep  2 12:19 histfile
total 168
```

It sorts by the entire line. Let's specify a field to sort. Say, let's sort by the files sizes (**ls** command has an option to sort by the file size, but we want to see how the **sort** command does that). It is fifth field, so:

```
cs130@raspberrypi ~ 14 ls -l | sort -k5
total 168
-rw-r--r-- 1 cs130 cs130   220 Sep  2 10:29 myfile
-rw-r--r-- 1 cs130 cs130   303 Sep  5 09:46 somexmllog
drwxr-xr-x 2 cs130 cs130  4096 Sep  1 20:20 bin
drwxr-xr-x 2 cs130 cs130  4096 Sep  2 20:46 dir1
-rw-r--r-- 1 cs130 cs130    48 Sep  2 12:49 myfile1
-rw-r--r-- 1 cs130 cs130 59530 Sep  1 23:10 error_file
-rw-r--r-- 1 cs130 cs130 80467 Sep  1 23:25 find_result
-rw-r--r-- 1 cs130 cs130  8112 Sep  2 12:19 histfile
```

We can notice that it sorts in lexicographical order. Let's do it numerically:

```
cs130@raspberrypi ~ 15 ls -l | sort -k5 -n
total 168
-rw-r--r-- 1 cs130 cs130    48 Sep  2 12:49 myfile1
-rw-r--r-- 1 cs130 cs130   220 Sep  2 10:29 myfile
-rw-r--r-- 1 cs130 cs130   303 Sep  5 09:46 somexmllog
drwxr-xr-x 2 cs130 cs130  4096 Sep  1 20:20 bin
drwxr-xr-x 2 cs130 cs130  4096 Sep  2 20:46 dir1
-rw-r--r-- 1 cs130 cs130  8112 Sep  2 12:19 histfile
-rw-r--r-- 1 cs130 cs130 59530 Sep  1 23:10 error_file
-rw-r--r-- 1 cs130 cs130 80467 Sep  1 23:25 find_result
```

We can reverse the sort:

```
cs130@raspberrypi ~ 16 ls -l | sort -k5 -nr
-rw-r--r-- 1 cs130 cs130 80467 Sep  1 23:25 find_result
-rw-r--r-- 1 cs130 cs130 59530 Sep  1 23:10 error_file
-rw-r--r-- 1 cs130 cs130  8112 Sep  2 12:19 histfile
drwxr-xr-x 2 cs130 cs130  4096 Sep  2 20:46 dir1
drwxr-xr-x 2 cs130 cs130  4096 Sep  1 20:20 bin
-rw-r--r-- 1 cs130 cs130   303 Sep  5 09:46 somexmllog
-rw-r--r-- 1 cs130 cs130   220 Sep  2 10:29 myfile
-rw-r--r-- 1 cs130 cs130    48 Sep  2 12:49 myfile1
```

And finally, and very useful option is to sort uniquely (using the -u parameter). I do not show the screen here, because these lines are already unique; but you will use this option often.

So. When your manager approaches your desk asking whether you can produce a report on a web log of ten largest files causing server crash, and commenting something on their best programmers asking for a day or two to write and test the program to do that... Your answer probably would be:

– Let me take a look

And by the time your manager reaches his/her desk (stopping to fill a cap of tea or coffee), you would already send the file generated by the command like that:

```
cat someweblog | awk '$(NF-1)==”500” {print $6” “$7}'| sort -u | sort -k1 -nr | head
```

(assuming that field #6 is the file size, field #7 is the file name, and the second to the last field is the status code)

Just... do not forget to test it first (as I did; forgetting it).

5. Summary and review.

Unnamed pipes, ***awk*** tool, ***head*** and ***tail*** utilities. ***/etc/passwd***, ***/etc/shadow***.

Commands:

xargs, wc, head, tail, awk, su, tr, sort, wget

Lecture 6. Introduction to pattern matching and regular expressions

- Really?.. I mean, why did I go to this field? Why did I take this class? What was not good in my life?
- I know... But... This is Linux.

1. Introduction to the problem

Last time we did couple of examples that probably left some questions, even if you did not ask. Let's look at this (found in the dusty old chest in the attic of a long abandoned house):

Let's note, that my verbose description goes after the first tag "***description***" (that used to be an XML tag just a moment ago). Let's use that knowledge to construct our first ***awk*** command:

```
cat somexmllog | tr '<,>' ' ' | awk -F 'description' '{print $2}'
```

```
cs130@raspberrypi ~ 16 cat somexmllog | tr '<,>' ' ' | awk -F 'description' '{print $2}'
 my descrition from first run /
 my descrition from the second attempt run /
 my descrition at the final run /
```

Thus, I discarded everything before my free-text description, and everything after that.

...While reading that manuscript, one question arises: What if there was a word "***description***" In the description field itself? Recall, that (from the same manuscript):

> *...our description is a free text, with arbitrary length, and we cannot predict...*

– OK, and what was the other problem?
– It was with the passwords. We wanted to filter out the invalid passwords based on some assumptions, but there was other kind of invalid password that we let in.

```
cat /etc/shadow | awk -F ':' '$2 != "*" {print $1", "$2}'
```

```
root@raspberrypi:~# cat /etc/shadow | awk -F ':' '$2 != "*" {print $1", "$2}' | head -5
root, $6$J0AZ0Xl4$O5b38oZ2zzpvqcrtqxmwLUgV5EZR0MgRh76QPxLMHkBnlre.SBytd34m0F0DX3JoGLqBMsBLeL6
0KZ1
libuuid, !
pi, $6$KGuv7OGb$iUAxuPt7CIweZ9DBmoXHa.SBiQU6ym7/9WjiHwVho2RV.FdkhwmdR8RrGAWeJIlgtabtGaWMKpeTv
F0
cs130, $6$mnGG4ji4$8AdEgNVaU3/pWGWmfmy65l8yJAS2.KEnq/0gqj8yKvyG2KVjrpm23lOWIKCexrCXT4Rwz0FNR
```

So, the problem is that when doing match, we can not always know or predict what ***is*** or what ***should be*** an exact match. Even our examples of matching for the word "***user***"... there can be some things there not completely defined, like what if later on a new group with the "***user***" as a part of its name would be added... and does that mean that we need to re-do all our scripts?

Thus, not always can we know the ***exact*** match conditions. But in much more often cases we may know (or figure out) the ***pattern*** of the match. And if we can figure out the ***pattern***, we can write a ***regular expression*** to match to that pattern.

You can think of the regular expressions as a "fuzzy" logic as opposed to the strict match, and because of that it gives us much more flexibility in writing and expressing the rules.

One other note. You may find the saying (I read it from one of the source which I cannot recall its origin, but nevertheless I try to give a fair credit to it): that the ***regular expression is more the art than a science***... And I fully and completely agree with that.

From that may follow, that you may write a regular expression (OK, it's time for that: ***RegEx***), but you may not always be able to ***read*** it... Your script, heavily loaded with the ***RegEx*** is pretty much one-time undertaking. You probably would no be able to (easily) maintain it unless the ***RegEx*** in there are fairly simple.

Let's start with some simple examples:

1.1. Some simple examples writing the *RegEx*

That invalid password problem re-visited. So our first approach did not really work the best as it could. Let's try a different method. Let's note, that all the valid passwords are long, and the invalid ones, are pretty short. With that observation, let's request that our filter would only allow long passwords. How long? We can pick an arbitrary number. Let it be 3. Anything shorter, we will consider an invalid. So. Here it is.

```
cat /etc/shadow | awk -F ':' '$2 ~ /.{3,}/ {print $1 ", " $2}'
```

We know everything here except the highlighted part. Here it is.

```
$2 ~ /.{3,}/
```

What it says is this: "Take the second field (`$2`) and ***do a match if*** (the tilde sign, `~`) there are at least three any characters in that field (`.{3,}`)". Now let's do a breakdown for that last part.

A single dot matches any possible character. Really any. It could be anything indeed, even un-printable ones, like the new line, carriage return... any.

Expression inside the braces: (`{3,}`) has general form: {***min***, ***max***}, where the first number is minimum number of characters to match, and the second number is, correspondingly the maximum number. If I omit any of them, as in my example, that means I do not request that condition. Thus, in my case I only request minimum three matches, and there is no upper limit. Which translates to the: "***At least three***".

If I placed that number differently, like that: `{,3}` I would request ***at most*** three matches.

And If I wrote that expression like that: `{3}` I would request ***exactly*** three matches.

All specifiers apply their condition to the character, immediately preceding them. In our case it was a single dot, which as we already know matches any character whatsoever (`.{3,}`) and the whole condition requires to have at least three characters in that place.

– Good. That was not difficult actually.
– Actually, not at all. People who created that wanted it to be useful. Which means … (did I hear the words "*smart*" and "*simple*"?). Thus, the only difficulty here is to memorize few syntax rules and few meanings. But, as we know, that is true for any language... And not only in the Computer Science.

One last part here. When we request an exact match we say:

```
$2 == "user"
```

Whereas for the ***RegEx*** we need to say:

```
$2 ~ /user/
```

Note the tilde and forward slashes. Again, that is syntax to tell to please do a ***RegEx*** here.

– So, what would the statement we just wrote a match to?
– It would match to any string, containing the word ***user***. It can be a ***webuser***, an ***oracleuser***, an ***sqluser***, or just the ***user,*** or ***users***. In that regard it works like **`grep`** with only difference that grep will still match the entire line, while with that our statement we request to apply the rule to the second field only. But, just as with **`grep`** on the entire line, the way we wrote our ***RegEx***, allowed the match to occur within the entire second field. Yes, we restricted it to be the second field only, but we allowed to match anywhere in that field.
– And if we did not want to?
– We have few options. Let's say we wanted to anchor the word "***user***" to be only at the beginning of the field. That would be like that:

```
$2 ~ /^user/
```

And with that condition we would have discarded all those ***webusers***, ***oracleusers***, and so on. If we wanted it to be anchored to the end of the field, we would use... guess what? A dollar sign. Remember, the thing, which other meaning indicates the end of something:

```
$2 ~ /user$/
```

– And if we wanted to place it somewhere in between?

– That would be more tricky. We will need to see what pattern there it is for that. Say, if we want that word to be exactly 10 characters before the end of the field, we could use that construct:

```
$2 ~ /user.{10}$/
```

And if we wanted it to be 10 characters apart from other word, for example "*group*", it would be like that:

```
$2 ~ /user.{10}group/
```

See, with each new added rule, the complexity of the ***RegEx*** increases. But... that is something to be expected, isn't it?

– Alright, I think I am starting grasping that. And what about our other example with extracting the description from the xml log?
– Before we go for that let me formalize few things a little.

2. RegEx syntax

Let me enumerate few considerations, both general, and specific to the ***RegEx***.

1. You write an expression for each character or string of characters you want to match
2. You often work not with the single characters, but with the ranges. For example, you want to match "*track*" or "*truck*", but not "*trick*"
3. Keep in mind case-sensitivity.
4. There are many characters with a special meaning (see the table below). If you want to match those, you need to escape those.
5. Keep in mind that what ***you*** think you wrote may not be what the ***shell*** thinks you wrote.
6. Always test and build your ***RegEx*** by small parts.
7. Many modern languages provide support to ***RegEx*** to some degree or another. In our discussion we will be using the ***awk***, the ***egrep***, and the ***perl***. These days ***perl*** is not as popular, as it used to be, but it was probably one of the first (if not the first) language with built-in support to the ***RegEx.*** It has probably one of the most complete and fullest support for them, and, generally can be considered as a keeper of a gold standard*. Note, that we will use the ***egrep***, instead of regular ***grep***. Regular ***grep*** has very limited support to the ***RegEx***. Thus, we will use it's extended version, ***egrep***. It has the same syntax and the same flags, as the regular ***grep*** has.

---

* Disclaimer: This is my personal opinion, not all people may agree with that.

Let's draw couple of tables, where I tried to summarize the ***RegEx***'s magic. I purposefully isolated

perl's syntax into the separate column. Let's start with the characters having a special meaning. That also means, that if you want to match that exact character, you need to escape its original meaning.

<table>
<tr><th>Character</th><th>Meaning</th><th>Example</th></tr>
<tr><td>Single dot (.)</td><td>Any possible character.</td><td>/tr.ck/</td></tr>
<tr><td>Caret (^)</td><td>Anchors to the beginning of the field</td><td>/^track/</td></tr>
<tr><td>Dollar sign ($)</td><td>Anchors to the end of the field</td><td>/track$/</td></tr>
<tr><td>Repetition</td><td></td><td></td></tr>
<tr><td>Question mark (?)</td><td>Zero or one occurrences of the previous character.</td><td>/words?/ (matches words or word)</td></tr>
<tr><td>Plus sign (+)</td><td>One or many occurrences of the previous character.</td><td>/ +/ (one or many spaces)</td></tr>
<tr><td>{min,max}</td><td>Between min (if defined), and max (if defined) occurrences of the previous character.</td><td>/.{3,}/ (At least three any characters)</td></tr>
<tr><td>Asterisk (*)</td><td>Do as many repetitions as needed to produce a match.</td><td>Hmmm. Kind of limited usage.</td></tr>
<tr><td>Ranges, grouping, and alternation</td><td></td><td></td></tr>
<tr><td>Pipe sign</td><td>Alternation</td><td>Often used in combination with parenthesis</td></tr>
<tr><td>Parenthesis ()</td><td>Used to grouping or alternation</td><td>/(this)|(that)/
/tr(a|u)ck/</td></tr>
<tr><td>Square bracket []</td><td>Used in alternation, ranges, and negation (with the caret sign)</td><td>/tr[au]ck/
/[0-9]/ (all digits)
/[^]/ not a space</td></tr>
<tr><td>Caret sign (^) within square brackets</td><td>Used for negation</td><td>/tr[^i]ck/ (Matches any character but i.</td></tr>
</table>

Ranges.

Range	**perl**	**egrep, awk, perl**
space	\s	' ' <== yes, that's space there
digits	\d	[0-9]
word characters	\w	all word characters, [a-zA-Z] etc
not space	\S	[^]

non-digit	\D	[^0-9]
non-word characters	\W	[^a-z]

As always, there is more than one way of writing the same ***RegEx***. For example, this form:

$1 ~ /(a|b|c|d|e)/

And this form

$1 ~ /[a-e]/

Are essentially the same, with the only difference, that the first form can extract the exact character from the match and save it in the special variable (a grouping function of parenthesis).

And... That's all you need to know to write the ***RegEx***! Well... almost, but not entirely. Still, let's jump to some examples (this time it will be many, so bear with me). We'll start with the ***very*** simple ones.

3. Some examples writing RegEx.

To not to unnecessary annoy you, my comments will be minimal. Only what's indeed necessary to understand. You will see, that actually most of them are pretty straightforward.

echo "text" | awk '$1 == "text"'

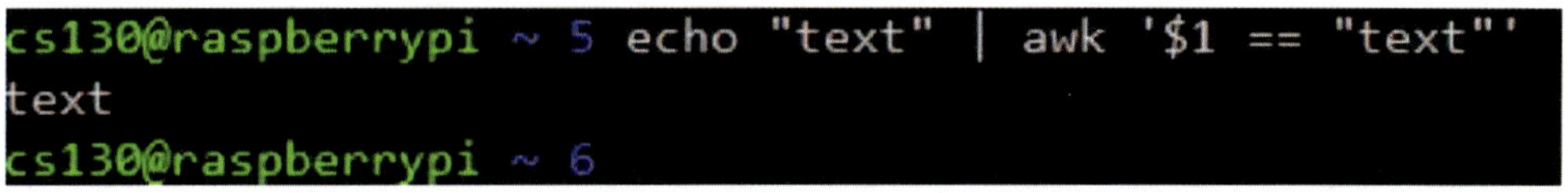

```
cs130@raspberrypi ~ 5 echo "text" | awk '$1 == "text"'
text
cs130@raspberrypi ~ 6
```

Matches. But:

echo "texts" | awk '$1 == "text"'

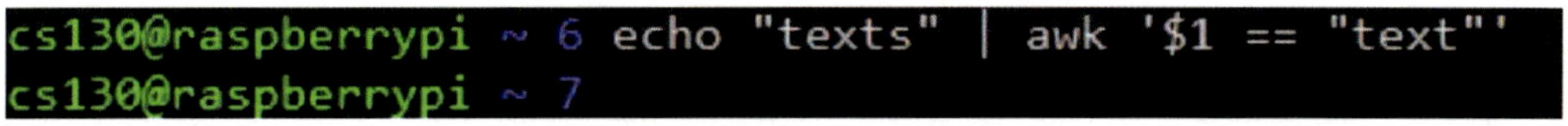

```
cs130@raspberrypi ~ 6 echo "texts" | awk '$1 == "text"'
cs130@raspberrypi ~ 7
```

Does not (note, that I requested the exact match). Whereas both,

echo "text" | awk '$1 ~ /text/'

and

echo "texts" | awk '$1 ~ /text/'

```
cs130@raspberrypi ~ 7 echo "text" | awk '$1 ~ /text/'
text
cs130@raspberrypi ~ 8
cs130@raspberrypi ~ 8 echo "texts" | awk '$1 ~ /text/'
texts
```

do match.

Anchoring to the beginning and to the end of the field:

```
cs130@raspberrypi ~ 9 echo "texts" | awk '$1 ~ /text$/'
cs130@raspberrypi ~ 10
cs130@raspberrypi ~ 10 echo "the texts" | awk '$1 ~ /^text/'
cs130@raspberrypi ~ 11
```

No match.

Case sensitivity:

```
cs130@raspberrypi ~ 11 echo "Text" | awk '$1 ~ /text/'
cs130@raspberrypi ~ 12
```

No match

Seems simple. Let's rack it up a little.

3.1. Racking up.

Suppose we have a web log file, and we want to extract all those records that have any of the 30x status code, i.e. we are interested in any redirections, or any other status codes for that matter. To prepare for that task let's try this:

```
cs130@raspberrypi ~ 18 echo '300' | awk '$1 ~ /30[0-9]/'
300
```

Hit.

```
cs130@raspberrypi ~ 19 echo '300' | awk '$1 ~ /30[2-4]/'
cs130@raspberrypi ~ 20
```

Miss. Explanation: I request the last digit to be within the range 2 – 4, i.e. to be either 2, 3, or 4. Obviously it will not match the last 0 from the input. Continuing.

```
cs130@raspberrypi ~ 20 echo '302' | awk '$1 ~ /30[2-4]/'
302
cs130@raspberrypi ~ 21 echo '303' | awk '$1 ~ /30[2-4]/'
303
cs130@raspberrypi ~ 22
```

Both match. See why? Next one. Here we request not a range, but alternation (see difference in syntax with the above example). We want either 2 or 4 to be on the last place.

```
cs130@raspberrypi ~ 22 echo '303' | awk '$1 ~ /30[24]/'
cs130@raspberrypi ~ 23 echo '304' | awk '$1 ~ /30[24]/'
304
```

The #22 does not match, whereas #23 does. See why? Next one.
Again, alternation, written differently.

```
cs130@raspberrypi ~ 25 echo '304' | awk '$1 ~ /30(2|4)/'
304
cs130@raspberrypi ~ 26
```

Result is the same as above. Hit.

Let's switch the tools and start using ***egrep***. Note the changes in the syntax. Also note, that I add negation to the already familiar alternation syntax:

```
cs130@raspberrypi ~ 27 echo '304' | egrep '30[^24]'
cs130@raspberrypi ~ 28
cs130@raspberrypi ~ 28 echo '303' | egrep '30[^24]'
303
```

#27: Miss, #28: Hit.

Alright. Now we are probably ready to the real things. Remember our web log?

3.2. Extracting data from the web log

We will apply exactly what we just did to the NASA's web log. Let's see first few lines with redirected requests. By now we should know that these could be either 302 or 304 status code (the second to the last field in the web log).

```
cs130@raspberrypi ~ 35 cat NASA_access_log_Aug95 | awk '$(NF-1) ~ /30[24]/ {print $7" "$(NF-1)}' | s
ort -u | sort -k7 | head
/. 302
/ 304
/base-ops/procurement/procurement.html 304
/biomed/vegetation 302
/cgi-bin/imagemap/astrohome?0,0 302
/cgi-bin/imagemap/astrohome?103,182 302
/cgi-bin/imagemap/astrohome?104,195 302
```

Everything should be familiar by now. Right? Do you see anything you do not understand? Should not be. Let's continue and do the same with the server side error codes. This time we don't know what they could be, so we allow for all ten digits to be present in the last third place of the code field.

```
cs130@raspberrypi ~ 36 cat NASA_access_log_Aug95 | awk '$(NF-1) ~ /50[0-9]/ {print $7" "$(NF-1)}' |
sort -u | sort -k7 | head
/history/apollo/./ 500
/images/./ 500
/images/getstats.gif 501
/images/launchmedium.gif 501
/ksc.html 501
```

Continuing with the 400th error codes:

```
cs130@raspberrypi ~ 37 cat NASA_access_log_Aug95 | awk '$(NF-1) ~ /40[0-9]/ {print $7" "$(NF-1)}' |
sort -u | sort -k7 | head
/100125,1305@compuserve.com 404
/11/history/apollo/image 404
/11/history/apollo/images 404
/11/history/apollo/images/ 404
/11/history/gemini/gemini-1/docs/ 404
/128.159.104.89/tvnet 404
/128.159.104.89/tv/tv.html 404
/%20history/apollo/apollo-13/apollo-13.html 404
.□2□□□□□□□□□□□.□□ □ 400
/%3A//spacelink.msfc.nasa.gov 404
```

And here I want to pause for a second and point your attention to the second to the last line. You see it? Can you read it?

As soon as your site is live on the world ***wide*** web, it is up to and against everything on the world ***wild*** web. I will return to that at the very end of this lecture. Now continuing.

BTW, instead of giving a range for the third position in the status code field, I could use a single dot (.) to match any character. But obviously, I could lose precision, since I would now allow for ***any*** character to be on that place.

3.3. Examples with repetitions

Let's consider repetitions. Just to remind:

Character	Meaning
+	Previous character (or group) can repeat one or more (many) times.
?	Previous character (or goup) can repeat zero (none) or one time. i.e. Exists or not exists.
*	Can repeat any number of times to produce match... Really.... I don't know. Basically it is a combination of + and ?
{min,max}	Between min and max. We talked about that several times already
{number}	Exactly that number of repetitions.

Let's see.

echo '302' | egrep '302+' //match
echo '302' | egrep '302?' //match
echo '302' | egrep '302{3}' //no match

```
cs130@raspberrypi ~ 38 echo '302' | egrep '302+'
302
cs130@raspberrypi ~ 39
cs130@raspberrypi ~ 39
cs130@raspberrypi ~ 39 echo '302' | egrep '302?'
302
cs130@raspberrypi ~ 40
cs130@raspberrypi ~ 40
cs130@raspberrypi ~ 40 echo '302' | egrep '302{3}'
cs130@raspberrypi ~ 41
```

And that's what we see here.

Good. We are mostly done with the learning examples. Now let's do something more interesting.

3.4. Our users example from last time re-visited

Last time we worked on matching the users trying to distinguish between just a *user*, a *webuser*, and the *sqluser*. And here is what was scribbled down in our notes from the last time:

Note, that I could achieve the same result with the ***grep***.

```
ls -1 | grep -v 'webuser' | grep -v 'sqluser'
```

No, no, we couldn't achieve the same results like that. Because I would not run the command like that.

What I ***would*** run, is that:

```
ls -1 | egrep -v '(webuser)|(sqluser)'
```

Note, that I use an extended version of a ***grep*** (***egrep***), and I use a pipe sign to alternate the input. Note, that I need to include the entire words into parenthesis, or only the characters surrounding the pipe will be alternating.

Let's start without the negation first (no -v flag):

```
cs130@raspberrypi ~ 12 echo webuser | egrep '(webuser)|(sqluser)'
webuser
cs130@raspberrypi ~ 13
```

Note, that since the "*user*" part is the same, I could alternate only the "*web*" or "*sql*" parts:

```
cs130@raspberrypi ~ 16 echo webuser | egrep '(web)|(sql)user'
webuser
```

But I liked coloring the entire word.

Alright. Now let's add that -v flag to negate the filter:

```
cs130@raspberrypi ~ 14 ^egrep^egrep -v^
echo sqluser | egrep -v '(webuser)|(sqluser)'
cs130@raspberrypi ~ 15
```

or

```
cs130@raspberrypi ~ 17 echo webuser | egrep -v '(web)|(sql)user'
cs130@raspberrypi ~ 18
```

– So... We can use alternation in the ***grep*** too!

– May be not in the regular ***grep***, but in the extended one (the ***egrep***), but yes...

3.5. Negation revisited.

Let's return to the negation. This is actually very useful feature. Let's recall our example from the last lecture where we tried to extract the description field from the XML log. What we did there, we used a combination of ***tr*** and ***awk*** tools:

```
cat somexmllog | tr '<,>' ' ' | awk -F 'description' '{print $2}'| awk '{$NF=""} 1'
```

The only two things that we know about description field, is that it can be any arbitrary text, of any length and composition, and that it is bordered by the opening and closing *<description>* tags. Let's use that fact and try to construct a ***RegEx*** to do the job:

<description>.+</description>

```
cs130@raspberrypi ~ 43 cat somexmllog | egrep '<description>.+</description>'
<run1><time>1221</time><description>my descrition from first run</description></run1></script1>
<run2><time>1321</time><description>my descrition from the second attempt run</description></run2></
script2>
<run3><time>1421</time><description>my descrition at the final run</description></run3></script3>
```

Aside from the fact, that match extended to the *<description>* tags itself, we seem to achieve what we wanted. After all, we can take care about those tags later.

But not that simple. Suppose we move the log from one machine to the different platform, and all the sudden our new line separator does not work anymore. So, everything is on a one single line. And now when we want to use our construct, it … it does not seem to work that well anymore.

```
cs130@raspberrypi ~ 49 cat somexmllog | tr -d '\n' > somexmllog_oneline
cs130@raspberrypi ~ 50
cs130@raspberrypi ~ 50 cat somexmllog_oneline | egrep '<description>.+</description>'
<run1><time>1221</time><description>my descrition from first run</description></run1></script1><run2
><time>1321</time><description>my descrition from the second attempt run</description></run2></scrip
t2><run3><time>1421</time><description>my descrition at the final run</description></run3></script3>
cs130@raspberrypi ~ 51
```

What we see now, is that match starts from the and including the first *<description>* tag (as it was before) and extends through the almost all the XML until the last *</description>* tag.

Not good. But... Why?

The ***RegEx*** uses a **greedy** match. That means it tries to start match as early, as it can, and extend it as far, as it can. Since we requested any number of any characters between the *<description>* tags, the ***RegEx*** happily obliged, treating the inner *</description>* tags as an "any" characters as well and only stopped on the outer ones.

– Not good. We need to fix that.
– But... how?

- We surely need to modify our ***RegEx***. It does not work as we want it to. But what shall we replace it with? There is really no any pattern in the description field. You say, that if we can find the pattern, we can write a ***RegEx***. But I can't find a pattern there.
- If we can't find a pattern ***inside*** the field, perhaps we can try to look ***outside***. And immediately outside the description field there is a closing XML tag. And we know that XML tags are defined by the left and right angle characters. ***And there should be no any of those inside the field or the XML will be malformed***, i.e. its format will be invalid.

With that new knowledge let's try to re-write our ***RegEx***.

<description>[^<]+

Here we request to match any number of any characters that are not an opening bracket of the XML tag. We use a caret to do negation, and because of that, the entire thing is in the square brackets. The last plus sign tells to use as many repetitions of such characters, as possible, which means, until the first opening bracket is met.

```
cs130@raspberrypi ~ 52 cat somexmllog_oneline | egrep '<description>[^<]+'
<run1><time>1221</time><description>my descrition from first run</description></run1></script1><run2
><time>1321</time><description>my description from the second attempt run</description></run2></scrip
t2><run3><time>1421</time><description>my description at the final run</description></run3></script3>
cs130@raspberrypi ~ 53
```

And this time it works as a charm, not only finding each individual description fields correctly, but also excluding the closing XML tag.

- But... Why in the very first time we did not have such problem?
- Because by default, if we did not request otherwise, match works on a single line.

Alright. We learnt how to find the match correctly. But that is only half of the deal. By itself that knowledge has a little value if we cannot extract the match to be used some place downstream.

And that is another big functionality and another big usage of the ***RegEx***.

4. Extracting the matches made by the RegEx

Alright. How to extract that match? Yes, we can use ***awk*** to extract fields, but for the purpose of this exercise, let's do that with the ***perl***.

As an ***awk***, the ***perl*** is a whole and complete stand-alone language. As an ***awk***, we can quickly run some commands from that from the command line. If you search online for the keywords "***perl*** *one liner*" or "***awk*** *one liner*", you will see an amazing collection of very useful and very functional utilities composed from the single or just very few their statements. We will use one of them.

We will use this form of the ***perl***'s one-liner:

perl -nE 'print $1 if /(pattern)/'

-nE flags tell ***perl*** not to look at the script file to execute (what it does by default), but instead run the command that follows on a command line. That command that follows is this:

print $1 if /(pattern)/

Which translates to the human language as this: Print the variable indexed by the number one, if there is pattern to match found. Where is that variable indexed by the number one created from? It is created from whatever there will be inside the parenthesis (that's why we need them) if the match is found.

Thus, our job is to construct the pattern and to not to forget to place the parenthesis around that pattern. Everything else will be the ***perl***'s job.

- Nice!
- Let's go for it! The argument to the command – is our XML log file.

```
cs130@raspberrypi ~ 66 perl -nE 'print "$1\n" if/description>([^<]+)<\/descr/' somexmllog
my descrition from first run
my descrition from the second attempt run
my descrition at the final run
cs130@raspberrypi ~ 67
```

Note, that we need to escape this forward slash, or the pattern matching syntax will be broken by an extra forward slash. There is also other way around that, but... we are probably a little bit too deep in this already.

And we see how it works.

5. Some other examples of RegEx at work

Now let's quickly and without much explanation run over few other examples. Just for the reasons of completeness, so you had some understanding of that. And we'll do that with different tools. We will consider some example “validating” email address and phone numbers and re-formatting the phone numbers. Validating of email addresses is a big problem for the Customer Service Departments, especially in large corporations. A lot of resources is spent for that. While it should be understood, that it is not possible to validate email addresses programmatically, what ***is*** possible, is to ***help*** avoiding obvious typos, and many (not all) honest mistakes.

Let's go.

5.1. Matching an IP address

For simplicity let's do it with the IPv4 addresses:

echo '192.168.0.254' | egrep '[0-9]{1,3}\.[0-9]{1,3}\.[0-9]{1,3}\.[0-9]{1,3}'

```
cs130@raspberrypi ~ 69 echo '192.168.0.254' | egrep '[0-9]{1,3}\.[0-9]{1,3}\.[0-9]{1,3}\.[0-9]{1,3}'
192.168.0.254
```

or

echo '192.168.0.254' | egrep '([0-9]{1,3}\.){3}[0-9]{1,3}'

```
cs130@raspberrypi ~ 70 echo '192.168.0.254' | egrep '([0-9]{1,3}\.){3}[0-9]{1,3}'
192.168.0.254
cs130@raspberrypi ~ 71
```

5.2. Matching an email addresses

Note, that full and reliable validation of the email address is impossible by the programming means, therefore what follows is not a comprehensive validation, but example for the purpose of illustration.

echo "abc123@some.com" | egrep '[a-z0-9_\-\.]+\@([a-z0-9_]+\.){1,}\.?com'

```
cs130@raspberrypi ~ 71 echo "abc123@some.com" | egrep '[a-z0-9_\-\.]+\@([a-z0-9_]+\.){1,}\.?com'
abc123@some.com
```

```
cs130@raspberrypi ~ 73 echo "abc123@some.other.com" | egrep '[a-z0-9_\-\.]+\@([a-z0-9_]+\.){1,}\.?co
m'
abc123@some.other.com
```

Note, that “edu” does not match in the next example:

```
cs130@raspberrypi ~ 76 echo "abc123some.edu" | egrep '[a-z0-9_\-\.]+\@([a-z0-9_]+\.){1,}\.?com'
cs130@raspberrypi ~ 77
```

But if we modify it like that:

```
cs130@raspberrypi ~ 75 echo "abc123@some.other.edu" | egrep '[a-z0-9_\-\.]+\@([a-z0-9_]+\.){1,}\.?(c
om|edu|net|org)'
abc123@some.other.edu
```

It'll match.

Extracting top level domain from the emails

echo "werr@mail.yahoo.com" | perl -ne 'print "\n$1" if /([^\.\@]+\.(com|edu|info))/'

```
cs130@raspberrypi ~ 102 echo "werr@mail.yahoo.com" | perl -ne 'print "\n$1\n" if /([^\n\.\@]+\.(com|
edu|info))/'

yahoo.com
```

5.3. Phone numbers

echo "+1 (760) 123-4567" | egrep \+1 \([0-9]{3}\) [0-9]{3}\-[0-9]{4}'

```
cs130@raspberrypi ~ 95 echo "+1 (760) 123-4567" | egrep '\+1 \([0-9]{3}\) [0-9]{3}\-[0-9]{4}'
+1 (760) 123-4567
cs130@raspberrypi ~ 96
```

```
cs130@raspberrypi ~ 96 cat > phones
+1 (760) 123-4356
+1 761.123.3456
762.123.3456
763-123-4567
(764) 123-3456
765 123 3456
+1.766.123.3456
+1-767-123-3245
cs130@raspberrypi ~ 97
```

Extracting area codes:

```
cs130@raspberrypi ~ 97 perl -ne 'print "\n$2" if /([\( \.\-]|)(\d\d\d)\D/' phones

760
761
762
763
764
765
766
767cs130@raspberrypi ~ 98
```

Phones re-formatting (with extensions) (we touched that last time):

```
+1 (760) 123-4356x333
+1 761.123.3456ext345
762.123.3456:567
763-123-4567
(764) 123-3456
765 123 3456
+1.766.123.3456
```

```
cs130@raspberrypi ~ 99 perl -ne 'print "\n($2) $3-$4 $6" if /([\( \.\-]|)(\d\d\d)\D+(\d{3})\D+(\d{4}
)(\D+(\d+))?/' phones_with_ext

(760) 123-4356 333
(761) 123-3456 345
(762) 123-3456 567
(763) 123-4567
(764) 123-3456
(765) 123-3456
(766) 123-3456 cs130@raspberrypi ~ 100
```

5.4. Finding repetitions in the string:

echo "kjlkjlkqweqweghghrtrt" | perl -ne 'print $1 if /(\w{3})\1/'

```
cs130@raspberrypi ~ 104 echo "kjlkjlkqweqweghghrtrt" | perl -ne 'print "$1\n" if /(\w{3})\1/'
kjl
cs130@raspberrypi ~ 105
```

Where (\1) is a backreference to the match (grouped in parenthesis) to be used in the R*egEx* itself.

5.5. In file (in place) substitution.

Suppose you want to update your web site and in the process you want to replace all occurrences of the images having the .gif extension to that one with .jpg. You don't need to go inside each and every file to manually change all those occurrences. It is just not practical. Instead, what you'd do is this:

perl -pi.back -e 's/\.gif/\.jpg/g' file* (or file file1 file2 etc)

```
cs130@raspberrypi ~ 105 cat > html1
img.gif
cs130@raspberrypi ~ 106 cp html1 html2
cs130@raspberrypi ~ 107 perl -pi.back -e 's/\.gif/\.jpg/g' html*
cs130@raspberrypi ~ 108 ls -lrt html
html1        html1.back   html2        html2.back
```

Note me not completing the last command, but hitting <*tab*> twice just to see the files.

```
cs130@raspberrypi ~ 1 cat html{1,2}
img.jpg
img.jpg
cs130@raspberrypi ~ 2
```

```
cs130@raspberrypi ~ 109 cat html{1,2}.back
img.gif
img.gif
cs130@raspberrypi ~ 110
```

So, here we not only can replace inplace (not opening the file, and creating the backup file), but can do it on a batch of files, without setting a loop or anything like that, and without manually opening and manually replacing in each file.

5.6. Removing unwanted characters (sanitizing the input)

When you run a customer-facing web site you never want to take the users' input from the web and use it directly in the downstream applications. You just don't want that. Look at that line from the NASA's web log. Some people will spend their time and energy constructing very smart and clever requests, trying to break into the *shell* and start doing their things. No, you do not want to take the input directly.

> When working with the input to your applications (any input), you should be cognizant of these things:
> - The input can be corrupted (for example because of interrupted connection);
> - There can be an honest mistake; or
> - There can be a malicious attempt.

Yes, people from all places across the globe can feed to your application any input they may think of.

But you can do something about that. And the simplest thing, you can filter out the special characters from there. And what could be the better tool to do that than the ***RegEx***?

echo 'lksjd!@#$%%&^*&(*)(wkerkw' | perl -pe 's/\W//g'

```
cs130@raspberrypi ~ 117 echo 'lksjd!@#$%%&^*&(*)(wkerkw' | perl -pe 's/\W//g' | xargs echo
lksjdwkerkw
cs130@raspberrypi ~ 118
```

Let's see. Here is that line again:

```
echo 'lksjd!@#$%%&^*&(*)(wkerkw' | perl -pe 's/\W//g'
```

Let's break that into parts.

```
echo 'lksjd!@#$%%&^*&(*)(wkerkw'
```

With the first part I output some number of special characters I randomly typed on a keyboard interlaced with the legitimate ones. We want to remove the former and leave only the later. Now let's take a look at the second part after the pipe:

```
perl -pe 's/\W//g'
```

Here I tell **`perl`** to take that input and do a substitution (the 's' flag before the ***RegEx*** starts).

Because we do not the regular match, but the substitution, we need to tell what we want to match and what we want to substitute that match with. We do that using this syntax:

```
/what to match is here/what substitute it with goes here/
```

> Remember our history substitute syntax? We did history substitute like that:
>
> **^string to find^string to replace^**
>
> You can see that the syntax is very similar.
>
> Good thing we have similar syntax for similar tasks. It helps in memorizing things

And, finally, we do not want to stop at the first substitution. We want to continue through the entire input. That we do using the 'g' flag for the "*global*" at the end:

```
///g
```

With that explanation, let's take a look at our ***RegEx*** again:

```
/\W//
```

I want to match any (and all) non-word characters. I do not know and I cannot know what those special characters would be. But I know that I don't want to accept any that are not the regular ones. So my first part in the ***RegEx*** is to match any and all non-word characters.

That was the first part. Now I need to tell **perl** what I want it to substitute them with. That would go to the second part of the ***RegEx***. What is in my second part of the ***RegEx***? Nothing. I want to substitute all those unwanted and unwelcome characters with ***nothing***, thus, essentially removing them from the input.

And that's it.

Alright. Today's lecture was loaded with lot of examples. But the good thing is that we are almost finished the hardest part of this course. We have some small topic to cover, then there will be one, maybe two boring lectures, and then, just sailing through the end of the semester.

And on that point, I will break until next time.

6. Summary and review.

Regular expression and pattern matching. Finding the patterns to match. Negating the match. Using ***RegEx*** for validation, extraction, re-formatting, substituting, and sanitizing the input. In-place substitution.

Lecture 7. Bash string substitution. Loops. Symbolic and hard links. Crude process scheduling. Running jobs on the background

We continue making our way in the world of Linux. I once said that every major topic we cover can be prefaced with the words "You cannot think about working with Linux without that...". Since there is more than one way of doing things, this time let me do it differently: "This is one of the lecture you do not want to miss".

Let's go.

1. Bash string substitution.

We spent quite a deal of time talking about Regular Expressions. Suppose we have a ***path*** to the file and we want to extract and use just a file name.

```
/home/bob/bin/ls → ls
```

Or, oppositely, we may want to extract the path itself.

```
/home/bob/bin/ls → /home/bob/bin/
```

If I asked you to do that, you'd probably say, that there is more than one way of doing that. And then to extract the file name, you'd probably write something like that:

```
echo '/home/bob/bin/ls' | awk -F '/' '{print $NF}'
```

Right?

And for the ***path***:

```
echo '/home/bob/bin/ls' | perl -pe 's/([^\/]+)$//g'
```

to show, that you can do ***RegEx*** too. Right?

Well. There is still more than one way of doing this. And I am going to show to you yet another one. ***Bash*** comes with a rich functionality to work with the string. The complete discussion of that functionality is not in the scope of this course. If you look online, you'd find out that there are chapters and chapters dedicated to that. If we wanted to cover this completely, that would probably be at least several weeks. Thus, I am going to show you just two quick examples to demonstrate the topic.

First, let's put it into the variable:

m=**/home/bob/bin/ls**

To extract a ***path*** from that string, that is what we'd do using ***bash***'s string substitution:

echo ${m%/*}

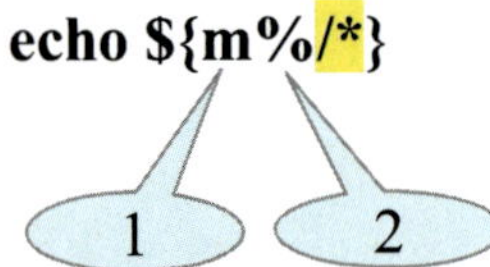

What I say here is to take the variable (1), and discard the first ***rightmost*** match, that defined after the *%* sign (2). What goes after the *%* sign? The highlighted part, which is translated as “The forward slash followed by any number of any characters (wild character)”, which is the file name. That discards the file name part leaving only the ***path***:

```
cs130@raspberrypi ~ 4 m=/home/bob/bin/ls
cs130@raspberrypi ~ 5 echo $m
/home/bob/bin/ls
cs130@raspberrypi ~ 6 echo ${m%/*}
/home/bob/bin
```

If, oppositely, we want to remove the ***path***, leaving only the file name, we would need to slightly modify that, by telling to discard everything on the ***left*** that matches the pattern.

echo ${m##*/}

```
cs130@raspberrypi ~ 8 echo ${m##*/}
ls
cs130@raspberrypi ~ 9
```

Thus, the difference between these two commands is this:

1. ***%*** sign vs ***#*** sign. On your keyboard former is located to the right of the later. Therefore, if you need to remove from the right, you use ***%,*** and if you need to remove from the left, you use a ***#***.
2. Single sign vs double sign. In first case it tells to remove just one (first) match, whereas the second instruction is to remove “*everything*” (like global flag for our ***RegEx***).

And that is actually quite useful feature.

Suppose you downloaded some good number of pictures from your camera. Or perhaps you come across your old photo archive. The problem is that you see all those pictures have capitalized extensions like that: .JPG. Since Linux is case-sensitive, your photo and picture applications do not recognize these files as the image files.

– Don't tell me that I need to manually rename all those hundreds of old files...
– No, I don't. And I am not going to either. Instead, if you asked me, I'd write this:

```
for i in `ls *.JPG`; do mv "$i" "${i%.JPG}.jpg"; done
```

- Hmmm. Show us!
- Alright.

```
cs130@raspberrypi ~/dir2 28 touch pic{1..50}.JPG
cs130@raspberrypi ~/dir2 29 ls
pic10.JPG  pic16.JPG  pic21.JPG  pic27.JPG  pic32.JPG  pic38.JPG  pic43.JPG  pic49.JPG  pic8.JPG
pic11.JPG  pic17.JPG  pic22.JPG  pic28.JPG  pic33.JPG  pic39.JPG  pic44.JPG  pic4.JPG   pic9.JPG
pic12.JPG  pic18.JPG  pic23.JPG  pic29.JPG  pic34.JPG  pic3.JPG   pic45.JPG  pic50.JPG
pic13.JPG  pic19.JPG  pic24.JPG  pic2.JPG   pic35.JPG  pic40.JPG  pic46.JPG  pic5.JPG
pic14.JPG  pic1.JPG   pic25.JPG  pic30.JPG  pic36.JPG  pic41.JPG  pic47.JPG  pic6.JPG
pic15.JPG  pic20.JPG  pic26.JPG  pic31.JPG  pic37.JPG  pic42.JPG  pic48.JPG  pic7.JPG
cs130@raspberrypi ~/dir2 30 for i in `ls *.JPG` ; do mv "$i" "${i%.JPG}.jpg"; done
cs130@raspberrypi ~/dir2 31 ls
pic10.jpg  pic16.jpg  pic21.jpg  pic27.jpg  pic32.jpg  pic38.jpg  pic43.jpg  pic49.jpg  pic8.jpg
pic11.jpg  pic17.jpg  pic22.jpg  pic28.jpg  pic33.jpg  pic39.jpg  pic44.jpg  pic4.jpg   pic9.jpg
pic12.jpg  pic18.jpg  pic23.jpg  pic29.jpg  pic34.jpg  pic3.jpg   pic45.jpg  pic50.jpg
pic13.jpg  pic19.jpg  pic24.jpg  pic2.jpg   pic35.jpg  pic40.jpg  pic46.jpg  pic5.jpg
pic14.jpg  pic1.jpg   pic25.jpg  pic30.jpg  pic36.jpg  pic41.jpg  pic47.jpg  pic6.jpg
pic15.jpg  pic20.jpg  pic26.jpg  pic31.jpg  pic37.jpg  pic42.jpg  pic48.jpg  pic7.jpg
cs130@raspberrypi ~/dir2 32
```

- Explain! Now!
- Alright.

As always, let's break that expression into parts. Here is our line, and let's look at the highlighted part.

```
for i in `ls *.JPG`; do mv "$i" "${i%.JPG}.jpg"; done
```

You see, I use a back-quotes. That means, whatever result of the command will be returned, I can get handle of it. Like that:

```
cs130@raspberrypi ~/dir2 33 myfiles=`ls *.jpg`
cs130@raspberrypi ~/dir2 34 echo $myfiles
pic10.jpg pic11.jpg pic12.jpg pic13.jpg pic14.jpg pic15.jpg pic16.jpg pic17.jpg pi
pic1.jpg pic20.jpg pic21.jpg pic22.jpg pic23.jpg pic24.jpg pic25.jpg pic26.jpg pic
ic29.jpg pic2.jpg pic30.jpg pic31.jpg pic32.jpg pic33.jpg pic34.jpg pic35.jpg pic
c38.jpg pic39.jpg pic3.jpg pic40.jpg pic41.jpg pic42.jpg pic43.jpg pic44.jpg pic4
47.jpg pic48.jpg pic49.jpg pic4.jpg pic50.jpg pic5.jpg pic6.jpg pic7.jpg pic8.jpg
cs130@raspberrypi ~/dir2 35
```

Now let's go to the left of that highlighted part:

```
for i in `ls *.JPG`;
```

I actually don't need to create an intermediate variable, like I made on the command prompt above. I can use the expression inside the back-quotes directly. That expression returns a list of file names (we know that). What I do next, I iterate through that list, i.e. go to each of its elements (which in our case are file names) and assign each of that file name to the (temporary) variable that I cleverly named ***i***.

Now let's go to the right of the above highlighted part:

```
do mv "$i" "${i%.JPG}.jpg"; done
```

You should recognize this command:

```
mv "$i" "${i%.JPG}.jpg"
```

It moves files. We also know, that this command renames the files. What it renames to what? We know that commands like that accept two parameters: The source and the destination. Where are they?

They are actually on their exact places where they are supposed to be.

Here is the source: The variable, cleverly named ***i,*** that will be replaced by the new file name on each iteration through the list of file names.

source

```
mv "$i" "${i%.JPG}.jpg"
```

destination

And here is the destination: That same variable, with removed extension in the caps, and replaced with that one in all small letter, using the ***bash***'s string substitution as we just did above.

The last part to explain, is this. Because we do everything in the loop, ***The Syntax*** requires us to follow some rules. We need to start the whole action with the keyword "***do***", and finish it with the keyword "***done***", separating each command with the semicolon. And as you can figure out, I can put more than one (actually any number of) commands between "***do***" and "***done***" there. For example, I can print the files names in the process, like that:

```
for i in `ls *.JPG`; do echo "$i"; mv "$i" "${i%.JPG}.jpg"; done
```

And that concludes our introduction to the ***bash***'s string substitution and loops.

2. Writing and testing a simple script

Suppose we want to find the files that take the most disk space. We will build a command for that. What would be that command?

```
find / -atime +30 -exec du -s '{}' \; 2>/dev/null | sort -n -r | head
```

Type that command, hit <***enter***> and while it runs (it will take some time to complete) let's look at that command, reading it left to right.

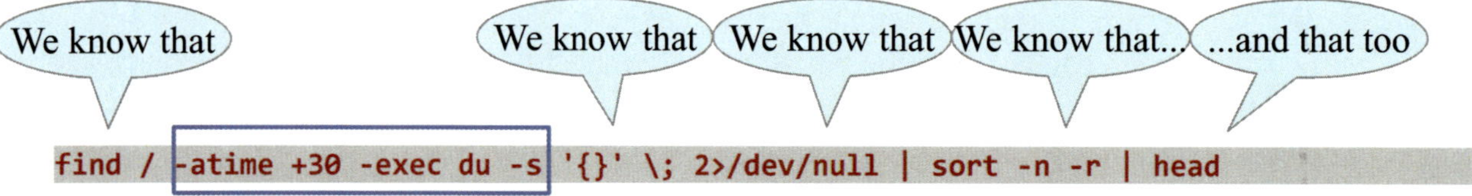

So, we know (or at least we should know) almost all parts of that command, with the exception of that in a blue box. What it tells to the ***find***, is to apply condition that access time should be greater than 30 days (***-atime*** + ***30***) and then execute the **du -s** command. The **du** command displays disk utilization by the directories. With the (-s) option, it will give summary for each of the directory.

Thus this command will find all the directories (we have a read access to) on the entire directory tree that were not accessed for the last 30 days, and then print out the 10 one, occupying largest space.

This is nice tool to report on the disk utilization status. But it is a housekeeping task. It is not something you would run daily (probably). And that is not something that requires your manual attention. It is a good tool to run in an unattended mode.

BTW, by that time it just completed its run and we can look at the result of its execution, just to see what it is:

```
cs130@raspberrypi ~ 1 find / -atime +30 -exec du -s '{}' \; 2>/dev/null | sort -n -r | head -5
4173018 /
2633672 /usr
1675076 /usr/lib
886768  /opt
812580  /usr/share
```

This is list of five of largest directories that have not been accessed for more than one month. Actually, probably listing of the ***root*** directory does not have much sense here, but let it be.

Alright, back to our discussion. Again, that is not something you would type yourself every day. You would put into the file, make a script and schedule it to run unattended; regardless, whether you are in the office or not, whether there is a holiday, or not, whether you went for a vacation, or not...

So, first thing's first. Perhaps we need to start creating a script out of that command.

```
cs130@raspberrypi ~ 17 cat > du_script
#!/bin/bash
find / -atime +30 -exec du -s '{}' \; 2>/dev/null | sort -n -r | head -5
cs130@raspberrypi ~ 18 ls -l du_script
-rw-r--r-- 1 cs130 cs130 85 Sep  8 14:39 du_script
cs130@raspberrypi ~ 19 chmod 755 du_script
cs130@raspberrypi ~ 20 ls -l du_script
-rwxr-xr-x 1 cs130 cs130 85 Sep  8 14:39 du_script
cs130@raspberrypi ~ 21
```

Here it is. We don't need a full-grade editor to add two lines to a file. What are these two lines? First one tells what ***shell*** will run that script. In the systems, with more than one ***shell***, that is important thing to specify. On other systems... Oh well, let's stick to the best practice. And the second is our command copied and pasted into the buffer. The whole thing terminated with the ***eof*** (**^D**) .

Then we need to run this:
#18. Checking that file exists and created

#19. Adding executable permissions to make it a running script
#20. Checking permissions.

We have our script. Before we use it, ***And especially*** before we run it in the unattended mode, we need to test it.

> Before you run something in unattended mode, you should always make sure that
> 1. The script runs correctly with all its commands, and
> 2. The scheduling is done correctly.

For now we want to verify that script is correct and produces correct results. There is only one way to do that. We need to re-run it. To run the script, you type the name of the script and hit <***enter***>. And to remind you our discussion about single dot, I will prep-end it with the single dot (since I did not save that change in my ***PATH***).

Alright. It completed. The output looks like we had on the command line, with the exception of the result for the root directory. And here we see, that it actually does not make sense to include the root directory into the search like that, for it can change even between the runs.

```
cs130@raspberrypi ~ 21 ./du_script
4173086 /
2633672 /usr
1675076 /usr/lib
886768  /opt
812580  /usr/share
cs130@raspberrypi ~ 22
```

> One of good test for your script is to compare output to the ones, generated before the changes/modifications/updates took place.

Let's modify the command in the script by adding this as the last element there:

```
find / -atime +30 -exec du -s '{}' \; 2>/dev/null | sort -n -r | head -5 | tail -4
```

And re-run it.

```
cs130@raspberrypi ~ 25 ./du_script
2633672 /usr
1675076 /usr/lib
886768  /opt
812580  /usr/share
cs130@raspberrypi ~ 26
```

Now it looks good. But before we can use it as a script in unattended mode, we need to take care about output. We discarded the errors. That is good. That is what you probably want to do in the most cases.

But we also need to redirect the ***stdout*** to the file. You need to do it for two reasons:

1. You want to have the result saved some place you can access.
2. You don't want your screen suddenly be flooded with some alien messages.

Thus, we need to modify our command line yet again:

```
find / -atime +30 -exec du -s '{}' \; 2>/dev/null | sort -n -r | head -5 | tail -4 >
/home/bob/myysearch.log
```

When we write script, we need to provide complete ***absolute path*** to all the files and tools, which we use inside the script. Otherwise our script may not be able to find them. So we use ***absolute path*** to the log file. Also, we may need to create the empty file and to give it a write permission.

touch /home/bob/mysearch.log

chmod 666 /home/bob/mysearch.log

And **now** we are ready to make our scheduling.

3. Crude process scheduling with cron directories

Linux provides a very (simple and) powerful tool to schedule your processes. You can schedule running them with one-minute granularity, or if you do not need such precision Linux also provides you ability to run them hourly, daily, weekly, or monthly in which case it is even easier to do. Let's take a look at the **/etc/cron*** directories. To see them, I typed:

```
/etc/cron<tab><tab>
```

```
cs130@raspberrypi ~ 26 ls /etc/cron
cron.d/       cron.daily/   cron.hourly/  cron.monthly/ crontab       cron.weekly/
cs130@raspberrypi ~ 26 ls /etc/cron
```

From these names, you probably can figure out, that the system will run everything in these directories with the specified periodicity.

Since these are under the */etc*, You need to be a ***root*** to do that. And here it probably be first time in our class, when we legitimately need to switch to the ***root***.

```
cs130@raspberrypi ~ 26 ls /etc/cron^C
cs130@raspberrypi ~ 26 su -
Password:
root@raspberrypi:~#
```

And we need to copy our script in one (or perhaps even not in one) of those directories. As a ***root***, I have access to any file of any user, so it is fine that the script was created under the different user. From the ***root***'s perspective, they all belong to him/her. Besides, the permissions I assigned, allow anyone to read that file, thus, to make a copies of it. So. We need to place file into some of those directories...

...Shall we copy it there or move it there? Copy or move?

If I move it there, it will be removed from its original location... Perhaps that is not convenient.

Shall I copy?

If I copy, I will have two copies of the same file in different places on the system.

> Every time you have more than one file in different places (unless they are backup copies), you create a maintenance nightmare.

Let's do it differently. Let's neither move nor copy, but create a symbolic link there.

4. Symbolic links

Symbolic (soft) link is not a file. You can think about it, as a pointer to the source file. Thus, you have just one physical file, and you can make any number of symbolic links to it in different places. The beauty of that approach, is not only in that it saves the disk space (although for large files it also can be a consideration), but, mostly, that if you need to update the file, you don't need to go around and update all those copies. You do that in just one place.

To create a symbolic link:

ln -s <source> <destination>

Ln command creates a link, and with (-s) flag you tell to make a symbolic link.

(Always: source → destination)

For example:

ln -s your_script /etc/cron.weekly/

you can also do

ln -s source_name /etc/cron.weekly/another_name

Note, that you can link directories also, not necessary the individual file.
One important thing. The source should exist, the destination should not exist. Unless you use the -f flag to enforce, attempt to create a link to the existing destination, will give you an error. Let's do.

```
cd /home/<user>; ln -s du_script /etc/cron.weekly/
```

```
cs130@raspberrypi ~ 2 su -
Password:
root@raspberrypi:~# cd /home/cs130/
root@raspberrypi:/home/cs130# ln -s du_script /etc/cron.weekly/
root@raspberrypi:/home/cs130# ls -lrt /etc/cron.weekly/
total 4
-rwxr-xr-x 1 root root 771 Jan  5  2015 man-db
lrwxrwxrwx 1 root root   9 Sep  8 17:10 du_script -> du_script
root@raspberrypi:/home/cs130#
```

Let's do an ***ls -l*** on the target directory. How to see if the entry is a link? Let's look at the leftmost character in the first field. (here) . A letter l (a small *el*) tells you that the entry is a link, not a regular file. Also you should see the arrow pointing to the actual file.

```
lrwxrwxrwx 1 root root   9 Sep  8 17:10 du_script -> du_script
```

On the left side of that arrow is source, and on the right side, is the destination. But you know what?... Something does not seem right here. It looks like the source and the destination are the same... Could it be that we created a circular reference? Let's run this check:

```
root@raspberrypi:~# find -L /etc/cron.weekly/ -type l
find: `/etc/cron.weekly/du_script': Too many levels of symbolic links
root@raspberrypi:~#
```

I asked the ***find*** command to find an entry of type link (***-type l***), that are broken (***-L***). And the returned message should give us some hints. Indeed, it looks like that we created a link pointing to... itself. Not good.

Why did that happen?

Remember our command?

```
ln -s du_script /etc/cron.weekly/
```

> **Always use an absolute paths when possible. That prevents you from making many mistakes.**

Let's fix it. But first, let's remove it. How? With the same ***rm*** command, as we did for the files. And then let's re-build our link using the absolute ***paths***.

```
root@raspberrypi:~# rm /etc/cron.weekly/du_script
root@raspberrypi:~# ln -s /home/cs130/du_script /etc/cron.weekly/
root@raspberrypi:~#
root@raspberrypi:~# ls -l /etc/cron.weekly/
total 4
lrwxrwxrwx 1 root root  21 Sep  8 17:40 du_script -> /home/cs130/du_script
-rwxr-xr-x 1 root root 771 Jan  5  2015 man-db
root@raspberrypi:~#
root@raspberrypi:~# find -L /etc/cron.weekly/ -type l
root@raspberrypi:~#
```

Now when we do a long listing, we see that the source on the left side of the arrow points to an existing file in the destination, and if we run our check with the ***find*** command, we see that this time there is no broken links detected.

Thus, we made a ***sym*** link. From that point it does not matter – whether we will be working with the original source file, or symbolic link, the changes will be reflected in all instances of that. Note that despite the link has full set of permissions, only the owner of the original file (or people allowed by the permissions in the original file) can do changes there.

5. Hard links

Opposite to the soft is hard. There is other type of link to the file. Unlike a "soft" link, this type is not a pointer to the file. It is... a file.

We cannot have two or more ***of the same file name in the same location***. But that does not mean we cannot have two or more ***of the same files***.

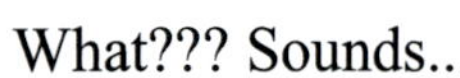

What??? Sounds...  weird.

When I do command ***cp file1 file2*** , I create a copy of the source file. We know that, and we get accustomed to that. We also accustomed to the fact that the destination file is a different file.

How can that be that the system allows to have more than one of ***the same files***?

Actually, nothing superstitious is here. Let's take a look at the disk.

When we create a file, we allocate a certain part of the disk. Like that.

But to ***access*** that file, we need a handle to it. Like that:

But no one said that we cannot have more than one ***handle*** to the same file. Like that:

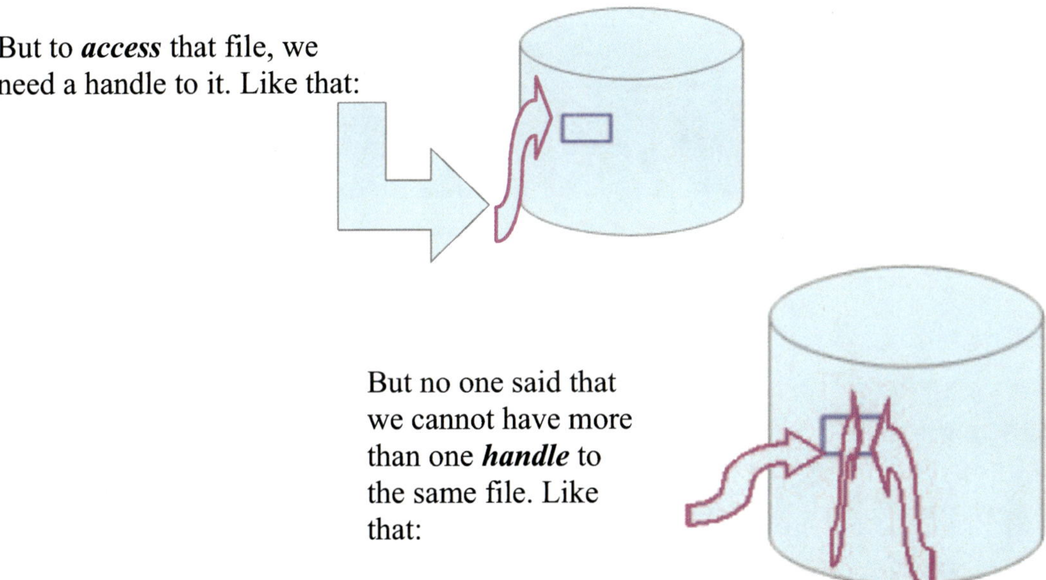

And finally, some of you may recall, that in some languages to delete the file there is command "***unlink***". Indeed, the file is accessible on the disk until there is at least one link to it exists.

Now let's run some examples.

1. Creating a file.

```
cs130@raspberrypi ~/dir3 42 touch myfile1
cs130@raspberrypi ~/dir3 43 ls -lt
total 12
-rw-r--r-- 1 cs130 cs130    0 Sep  9 11:23 myfile1
```

2. Making a hard link to that file (if the location is the same, the names have to be different... Yes there is still some rules). The same command we did for the soft link, but with no (-s) parameter.

```
cs130@raspberrypi ~/dir3 44 ln myfile1 myfile2
cs130@raspberrypi ~/dir3 45 ls -lti
total 12
34103 -rw-r--r-- 2 cs130 cs130    0 Sep  9 11:23 myfile1
34103 -rw-r--r-- 2 cs130 cs130    0 Sep  9 11:23 myfile2
```

We talked about the ***inode*** number. If two files are the same, their ***inode*** number should be the same. That's what we see here, with the (-i) flag to the ***ls*** command.

These two files are... it is a one file. It occupies the single space on a disk, and takes the singular size. From now on there is no distinction as to which file is which. Now let's take a look at something else. There was one field in our discussion of the long listing output that we left for the later. Now this "***later***" come to be. Let's compare these two screenshots:

```
cs130@raspberrypi ~/dir3 42 touch myfile1
cs130@raspberrypi ~/dir3 43 ls -lt
total 12
-rw-r--r-- 1 cs130 cs130     0 Sep  9 11:23 myfile1
```

And look at this number: here

The one ***before*** we created a hard link.

And ***after*** we made a hard link: here

```
cs130@raspberrypi ~/dir3 44 ln myfile1 myfile2
cs130@raspberrypi ~/dir3 45 ls -lti
total 12
34103 -rw-r--r-- 2 cs130 cs130     0 Sep  9 11:23 myfile1
34103 -rw-r--r-- 2 cs130 cs130     0 Sep  9 11:23 myfile2
```

That's how I know that the file has a …. has more than one hard links to it.

Let's move one of them to the home directory.

```
cs130@raspberrypi ~/dir3 47 mv myfile2 ~/
cs130@raspberrypi ~/dir3 48
```

And now we have a problem. From the long listing we see that the file has a “twin”. But... where is it? How to find them, if the names are different?

Remember our friend ***find***? Remember we used it to find a file by the ***inode*** number? We'll do this again. From the long listing we know the ***inode*** number to search for.

```
cs130@raspberrypi ~/dir3 50 find ~/ -inum 34103
/home/cs130/myfile2
/home/cs130/dir3/myfile1
```

And we see the twins found in both places. Let's run the same command a little differently and see a long listing on those twins, just to verify:

```
cs130@raspberrypi ~/dir3 52 find ~/ -inum 34103 -exec ls -li '{}' \;
34103 -rw-r--r-- 2 cs130 cs130 0 Sep  9 11:23 /home/cs130/myfile2
34103 -rw-r--r-- 2 cs130 cs130 0 Sep  9 11:23 /home/cs130/dir3/myfile1
cs130@raspberrypi ~/dir3 53 ^C
```

– That's all good and exciting, but what are the hard links used for?

– That's a good question. Unlike the ***sym*** links, that are used extensively, the usage for the hard links is pretty limited. If you search online, you would hardly see any usage of that besides a one. Because of its property, that it is the same file that does not occupy additional space on a disk, that is a nice option to make a backup copies without doubling up the disk space. However, it needs to be understood, that it is only guards against deletion of the file. If I modify the file, its twin will be modified as well without any notice. So. Let's see how that works.

5.1. Using hard links for backup copying of the files (as a guard against accidental deletion)

Let's create a simple directory structure with some files there.

```
cs130@raspberrypi ~/dir3 19 mkdir t1
cs130@raspberrypi ~/dir3 20 cat > t1/file1
sadfsdf
cs130@raspberrypi ~/dir3 21 cat > t1/file2
dfgdfgddfg
cs130@raspberrypi ~/dir3 22 mkdir t1/t2
cs130@raspberrypi ~/dir3 23 cat > t1/t2/file11
aaaaa
cs130@raspberrypi ~/dir3 24
```

Let's see what we have:

```
cs130@raspberrypi ~/dir3 24 tree
.
└── t1
    ├── file1
    ├── file2
    └── t2
        └── file11
```

Creating back up directory, and using **cp -a** command to make an archive copy (*-a*). After that, if you compare tree on the backup directory with the previous one, they should be the same.

```
cs130@raspberrypi ~/dir3 28 cp -al bk1 bk2
```

```
cs130@raspberrypi ~/dir3 25 mkdir bk1
cs130@raspberrypi ~/dir3 26 cp -a t1 bk1/t1
cs130@raspberrypi ~/dir3 27 tree bk1
bk1
└── t1
    ├── file1
    ├── file2
    └── t2
        └── file11
```

And now let's create another backup directory. This time like that:

```
cp -al bk1 bk2
```

This command in addition to making an archive copy (*-a* flag), that we used just before, also creates hard links (*-l, a small el*). Now let's check the ***inode*** numbers for these files, they are... the same.

```
cs130@raspberrypi ~/dir3 30 ls -li bk[12]/t1
bk1/t1:
total 12
43152 -rw-r--r-- 2 cs130 cs130    8 Sep  9 11:14 file1
43153 -rw-r--r-- 2 cs130 cs130   11 Sep  9 11:14 file2
48791 drwxr-xr-x 2 cs130 cs130 4096 Sep  9 11:15 t2

bk2/t1:
total 12
43152 -rw-r--r-- 2 cs130 cs130    8 Sep  9 11:14 file1
43153 -rw-r--r-- 2 cs130 cs130   11 Sep  9 11:14 file2
48794 drwxr-xr-x 2 cs130 cs130 4096 Sep  9 11:15 t2
cs130@raspberrypi ~/dir3 31 ^C
```

And now if I accidentally remove on of those files, I still have a handle of it. Actually, I only lose the file when there is no more handles to it available to me. That is nice. We will return to that topic again, when we will discuss the incremental backup. And it is then, when we will see a full power of the hard links to save space.

6. Running jobs in background

Suppose you have some job that takes a lot of time to complete. You don't want it to take your terminal such that you can do nothing during that time. You may open another terminal and run that job from that "dedicated" terminal, but that may not always be an option, and also... why? The better way would be to run the job on the background. It also may be better for the system, because your background job can be run with the lower priority. The reason behind that is: if it runs on the background, you are not really concerned about fastest execution time.

So, if you want to run your job on a background, simply append an ampersand to the command:

cmd &

```
cs130@raspberrypi - 14 sleep 20 &
[1] 2577
```

The job will be taken to the background and you can still use your terminal. When the jobs completes, there will be a message displayed.

You can also send to the background the job, you already started on the foreground. You need to suspend that job first with **ctrl-Z**

After that, you will see the list of stopped jobs. Find your job and type **bg <number>.** That will send the job to the background.

number

```
cs130@raspberrypi          sleep 20
^Z
[2]+  Stopped                    sleep 20
cs130@raspberrypi - 16 bg 2
[2]+ sleep 20 &
```

Note, that if you send the job on the background, you probably want to redirect the messages, otherwise they will be filling your screen.

If you start a job on a background and leave (close) the terminal your job will be terminated. If you want it to still run, use a **nohup** option.

```
cs130@raspberrypi - 17 nohup sleep 20 &
[1] 2579
cs130@raspberrypi - 18 nohup: ignoring input and appending output to 'nohup.out'
```

That is very useful if you want to run this overnight, but do not want to keep the terminal open.

When the job finishes, next time you type something on a terminal, the message will be displayed that the job is finished.

You are not limited by one background job. You can run as many jobs as you want to

```
cs130@raspberrypi ~ 18 sleep 20&
[2] 2580
cs130@raspberrypi ~ 19 sleep 20&
[3] 2581
cs130@raspberrypi ~ 20 sleep 20&
[4] 2582
```

You can check status of all jobs by using **jobs** command:

```
cs130@raspberrypi ~ 21 jobs
[1]   Running                 nohup sleep 20 &
[2]   Running                 sleep 20 &
[3]-  Running                 sleep 20 &
[4]+  Running                 sleep 20 &
```

It will show you what jobs are running, what are stopped etc with the numbers that correspond to these jobs.

```
cs130@raspberrypi ~ 27 jobs
[1]   Running                 sleep 20 &
[2]-  Running                 sleep 20 &
[3]+  Running                 sleep 20 &
```

From that list, you can bring any job to a foreground:

```
cs130@raspberrypi ~ 29 fg 2
sleep 20
[1]-  Done                    sleep 20
cs130@raspberrypi ~ 30
```

Thus, you can send any job to a foreground or to a background using ***fg*** or ***bg*** commands.

7. Summary and review.

Bash string substitution, /etc/cron* directories, symbolic links, hard links, running jobs in background.

Commands:

ln, jobs, fg, bg

Lecture 8. Text editors (Vi). Named pipes. Mail. Cron.

"If you are researcher on this book, ... you must have been gathering material on it."
"Well, I was able to extend the original entry a bit, yes."
"And what does it say now?"...
"Mostly harmless"

Douglas Adams, The Hitchhiker Guide To The Galaxy.

– Hmmm... Looks like we have some important things to discuss today.
– Yes, indeed. So let's begin.

And we will start with the ***vi***.

1. vi (vim)

As always, the question is: "Why?"

As always, the answer is: "Because it is a standard text editor across the distros, because questions about that are on the Linux exam, because on the interview you should expect questions about ***vi***, and also...".

Fresh out of college, I did something on the *pico*, when my boss said: "Close **that** *pico*, and...".

And the way he said "***that*** *pico*"... At that moment I knew, that the ***vi*** would be my editor from now on. Because apparently for the UNIX people, anything other than ***vi*** was not … ***cool***.

I'd been using the ***vi*** for... I don't want to tell, for how many years. Probably, I don't even know that myself. But the beauty of it is that from time to time I look at some sites like "tips and tricks with ***vi***" and I think: "Wow! I did not know that was possible!" There are apparently other people, who leave the same type of comments there.

Vi is very powerful editor. It was made by the programmers and for the programmers. The power that is gives to a programmer is such, that I preferred to write my code on the ***vi*** despite all those IDE (Integrated Development Environments) that have long been available.

As I said, it is a very powerful editor. But you perhaps will not want to use it to write a report or essay, or other text or office document, or an artistic novel. It is a tool to write a code. Or a script. Or make or edit configuration' changes. Because by default Linux opens various configurations in the ***vi***. With that, let's begin.

1.1. Getting started with vi. First simple commands.

Vi is a text editor that comes with every Linux distro. It may be very minimalist distro; it may not have anything else, but it will have ***vi***. If you have Linux, you have ***vi***. ***Vi*** is probably the oldest legacy editor, it is ubiquitously distributed. You may not know anything else about the Linux, but you need to know at least basic navigation around ***vi***. If your system requires entering into the rescue mode, everything there will be done through the ***vi***.

Obviously, the modern ***vi*** is not the same as what it was when the world was new and beautiful. Its official name now is ***vim*** (for ***vi*** modified). But you probably will not see the ***vi*** of the first days of UNIX. And the **`vi`** command will launch what your system is shipped with.

Vi is a live project. People write all sort of modules and plugins for that. Your distro may have version of ***vi*** that may be different from your friend's version. It is extremely configurable and adaptable, but... You need to be very friendly with all that scary super-human syntax.

The easiest way of learning and demonstrating the ***vi*** is by using it. I will use two different installations for my demonstration, so the windows will be different.

To start ***vi***:

vi <myvifile>. You may skip the file name, but you probably do not want to.

If the file exists, it will be opened, otherwise a new file will be created (after you write it). From the status message at the bottom, you can see, that I opened a new file. ***Vi*** opens full terminal screen, so if you want to be able to do anything else, you may want to have other terminal window open (which is always a very good idea when you work on a Linux).

There are two modes in ***vi***: command mode and insert mode. To switch to the command mode (which is the one the ***vi*** opens into), press ***<esc>*** key. To switch to the insert mode (to start inserting the text) press an '***i***'. You should see the *"insert"* at the bottom. Then you can start typing the text. When you type long enough to fill the line, it will appear that the text is wrapped. But it is not. Let's hit ***<esc>*** to switch back to the command mode and press

```
~
~
-- INSERT --                                  0,1            All
```

```
:
```

to open the ***vi***'s command prompt at the bottom left and type ***set nu*** there.

```
lkjkljlkjs lkdfjlkdsjfls asdklfjsadklfj sdl
dkfj sldkfjlskdf slkdjflskfjlskdjf
:set nu
```

Colon opens the command prompt.

> Bottom left of the ***vi*** window is where all your communications with the ***vi*** will take place.

`set nu` command will display the line numbers, and you will see, that everything we typed was still on the same line. It is because by default ***vi*** does not wrap the lines; remember, it was made to be an editor for the programmers; they don't want the lines to be wrapped by themselves.

```
1 sldkfjslkdjfs sldkfjslkdf sldkfjsldkf slkdfjs d
  fsldkfj slkd lskdjf lskd lkj
```

But you can change this.

```
:set wm=2
```

(Colon tells the ***vi*** that you are going to give it some command).

That will set wrapping 2 characters before the right margin, effectively enabling wrapping. Of course, you can use another number. Let's continue with the insert mode.

```
~
~
:set wm=2
```

There is quite a few number of commands to enter into the insert mode. You can open the line for insert above your current line, or below it; after the cursor, or at the end of the line. Or at the beginning of the line, etc, etc, etc. All this aids you to minimize scrolling and moving through the window. Let's see some of the commands to enter into the insert mode:

command	action	

O (big o)	opens a line above your current line	`3 slkdjf sldkf ls slkdfj sldk flskd slk`
		`4 `
		`5 lskd ls`
		(I was on the line #5 before)

o	opens a line below your current line	`3 slkdjf sldkf ls slkdfj sldk flskd slk`
		`4`
		`5 `
		`6 lskd ls`
		(I was on a line #4 before)

A	appends to your current line	`5`
		`6 lskd ls`
		(The line #6 opens for the insert at the end)

a	appends after the cursor	4 5 6 lskd ls (The line #6 opens for the insert at cursor)
$	goes to the end of the line (without opening it)	5 6 lskd ls
0 (zero)	goes to the beginning of the line (without opening it)	5 6 lskd ls
0i (zero-i)	opens beginning of the line for inserting the text.	5 6 lskd ls Example of combination of commands. Here is in one command I go to the beginning of the line (0), followed by opening for the insert (i).
x	deletes the character under cursor	
p	puts characters from the buffer at the cursor's position	
xp	reverses two characters	Again, combination of two commands. Very handy to fix the typo.
dd	deletes the current line and places it into the buffer	
3dd	deletes current line and two following lines and places them into the buffer	
p **(small)**	puts content of the buffer below the current line	Thus, I can delete one (or more) lines, then go to another place and insert that (them) there.
P	puts content of the buffer above the current line	

(cap)		
yy	yanks the line into the buffer	Similarly to the dd, without deleting the line(s).
3yy	yanks 3 lines into the buffer	General pattern: Command preceded by number
C (cap)	Changes line from the current position to the end of the line	5 slkdjf | 6 7 k ~ Deletes from the cursor to the end of line and opens line for the insert
D	Deletes the line from the current position to the end of the line	5 6 lskd ls ~ Similar to the above but does not open line.
dw	Deletes from the current position, to the end of the word	2 sldkfjlsd slkd lskdfjs lskdjf lsk 3 (I just deleted from the position of cursor to the end of the word)

How to navigate the screen:

Vi is a terminal text editor. Early people did not rely on a mouse to scroll the text. Besides, they wanted to type as fast and efficient, as they could, which did not assume wasting time to move hand to and from the mouse. People who know and use a lot of keyboard shortcuts will probably understand that very well.

So. If you place your right hand over the keys **hjkl** on the keyboar, then (all in the command mode)

command	action	
h	Moves cursor to the left	
l	Moves cursor to the right	
j	Moves cursor down	

k	Moves cursor up.	
G	Moves to the end of the file	
1G	Moves to the first line	Again, command preceded with the number
5G	Moves to the 5th line	Same comment as above
w	Moves along the text word by word	
b	Moves backwards word by word	
%	If you have parenthesis, square, curly brackets, moves to the matching ones. A very useful feature for the programmers.	

But of course you can use arrows keys too.

Some other commands:

command	action	
:set ai	To set an auto-indentation.	All **set** commands can be reverted with **set no...**, for example **:set noai** to remove the auto-indentation, or **:set nonu** to remove the line numbering etc.
:q	To exit ***vi***	If you did not save (write your file), the ***vi*** will give you the warning. You can force to exit without writing the file with **:q!** command.
:q!	To force exit without saving changes	Very useful if you do not want to make changes to your file. Just exit it forcefully.
:w	To write the changes	
:wq	To write the changes and exit	Again, combination of the commands

All the settings you made during the session, are lost when you exit the session. To make it permanent, write them into the ***vi*** configuration file:

~/.vimrc

Tips and tricks: You may find yourself that you created a lot of settings and configurations but for some particular file you don't want them. Instead of switching them off one by one, you can temporary rename the configuration file to something else, and then open your ***vi*** session. Without configuration file it will use the default settings.

1.2. Continue with vi. Going dipper.

All in the command mode.

command	action	
m<letter> **i.e. mc**	Sets the bookmark to the current line to the **<letter>** (i.e. **c**)	There are 26 letters in the alphabet available for you to make bookmarks. I don't know about you, but I can memorize positions of at most two of those, with second, giving me troubles.
'<letter> **(i.e. 'c)**	Jumps to that bookmark.	
set list	Shows special characters: end of line, tabs etc.	Say, you have a tab-delimited file. Is there a field or is there no a field? Or it is empty? Setting list will save you hours of frustration.
~	Toggles upper and lower cases.	
*	Searches file for the word under the cursor	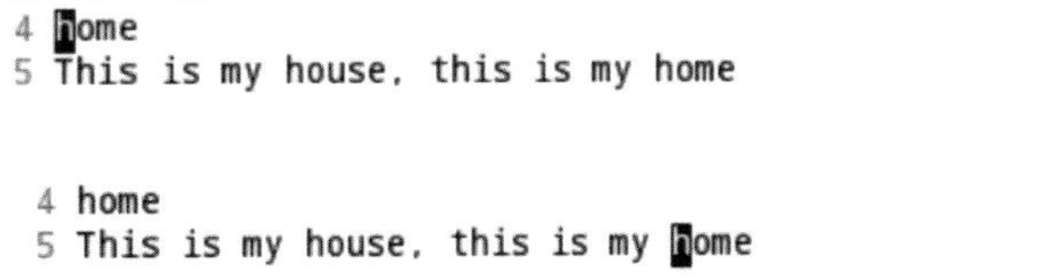 4 home 5 This is my house, this is my home 4 home 5 This is my house, this is my home
v	visual mark.	Yes, you can enter into the visual mode. You can select a word (w) and convert it to the upper case (U) or lower case (u), search, sort etc. You can also select a block of text. 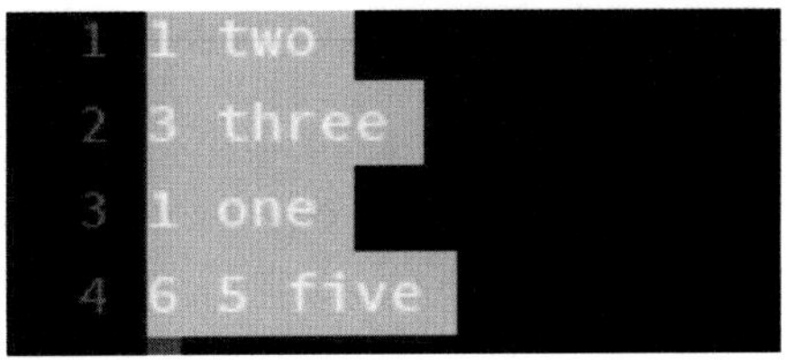 1 1 two 2 3 three 3 1 one 4 6 5 five

:sp
and
:vsp
 	
Also:
 	
Ctrl - w [s/v]
	How many text editors do allow you to work with different parts of text (or files) simultaneously? This command splits screen horizontally or vertically. Very useful feature for the programmer when you want to see some definitions which are usually on the top of the file, while you work somewhere in the middle. Or just moving blocks around. Or just editing in two places. Speaking about split windows. You can specify more than one file when starting ***vi***. **vi file1 file2**. Then you split the window and with :**b2** (second buffer) loading the second file. Very nice to work with two files in one window. If you want to open another file while you are already on ***vi***, split the window and **:e filename** To switch between screens **ctr-w w.** To close any window**: q**	`1 sldkfjslkdjfs sldkfjs`
		`lkdf sldkfjsldkf slkd`
		`fjs dfsldkfj slkd lsk`
		`djf lskd lkj`
		`2 sldkfjlsd slkd lskdfj`
		`s lskdjf lsk`
		`3`
		`4 home`
		`5 This is my house, thi`
		`s is my home`
		
		`1 sldkfjslkdjfs sldkfjs`
		`lkdf sldkfjsldkf slkd`
		`fjs dfsldkfj slkd lsk`
		`djf lskd lkj`
		`2 sldkfjlsd slkd lskdfj`
		`s lskdjf lsk`
		`3`
		`4 home`
		`5 This is my house, thi`
		`s is my home`
		`[No Name] [+] 5,30 All`
		`1 sldkfjslkdjfs sldkfjslkdf sldkfjsldkf slkdfjs d`
		`fsldkfj slkd lskdjf lskd lkj`
		`2 sldkfjlsd slkd lskdfjs lskdjf lsk`
		`3`
		`4 home`
		`5 This is my house, this is my home`
		`[No Name] [+] 5,30 All`

	Shell commands from ***vi***	Yes, you can run ***shell*** commands from the ***vi***, or even exit ***vi*** temporary to the ***shell*** and return back to the ***vi*** session when done.
:sh	Opens the shell. `Logout` returns to the editor. This is probably legacy from the earlier days; now you would just open another shell terminal. But with advent of the small mobile devices, where the screen real estate is again at value, that feature may be useful again. For example you write a script, and you want to test it without closing the ***vi.***	

<table>
<tr>
<td>:r! cmd</td>
<td>Inserts result of the shell command at the current position. The simplest example if you want to enter time stamp. :r! date. Another example – you want to generate a list of passwords and put it at the position of cursor. Without exiting, running the script, copying etc, you do – :r! for i in {1..9} ; do perl -le 'print map{(0..9,a..z)[rand 35]}1..8'; done . It places 9 random passwords in that position. Another example – :r! ifconfig | grep 'inet ' | awk '{print $2}' . Let's do one last example – you write the documentation and need to include directory listing – for example to show what should be present after installation of the software. Do :r! ls -l. You want to increase indentation of say 10 lines after the insert? 10>> will do. You want to replace your user name with something generic? 2,5s/user/nobody/g</td>
<td>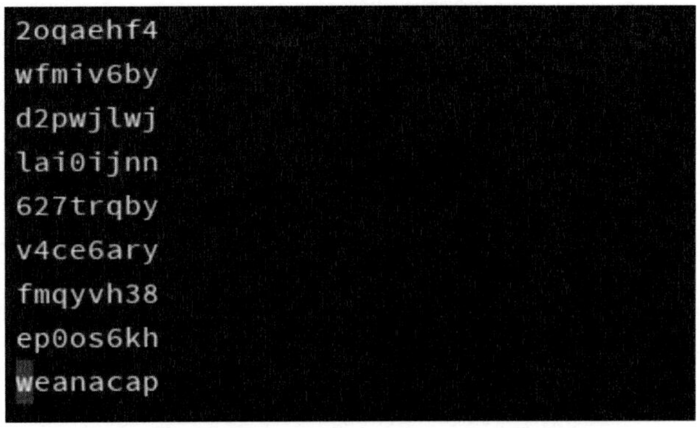
2oqaehf4
wfmiv6by
d2pwjlwj
lai0ijnn
627trqby
v4ce6ary
fmqyvh38
ep0os6kh
weanacap

addr:192.168.43.124
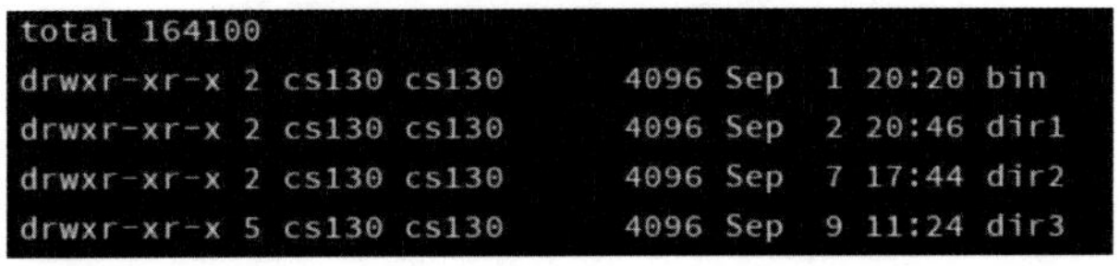
total 164100
drwxr-xr-x 2 cs130 cs130 4096 Sep 1 20:20 bin
drwxr-xr-x 2 cs130 cs130 4096 Sep 2 20:46 dir1
drwxr-xr-x 2 cs130 cs130 4096 Sep 7 17:44 dir2
drwxr-xr-x 5 cs130 cs130 4096 Sep 9 11:24 dir3
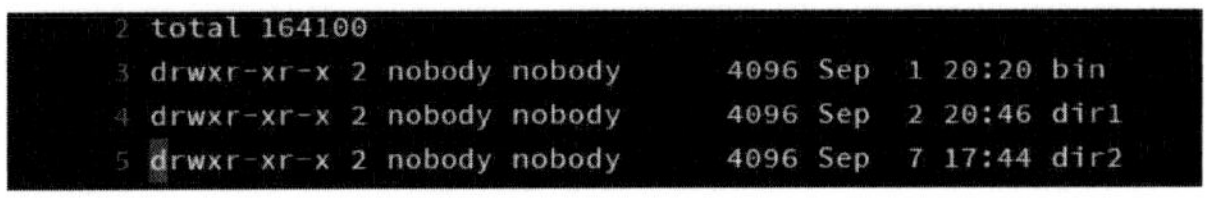
2 total 164100
3 drwxr-xr-x 2 nobody nobody 4096 Sep 1 20:20 bin
4 drwxr-xr-x 2 nobody nobody 4096 Sep 2 20:46 dir1
5 drwxr-xr-x 2 nobody nobody 4096 Sep 7 17:44 dir2</td>
</tr>
<tr>
<td>:r filename</td>
<td>Reads file filename and inserts it after the current line. Also very useful feature. If I wanted to append another file to the current one, I could do cat file2 >> file1. But this option allows me to insert the content of the file in any place of my current file. Also part of the file.</td>
<td>:r! head foo
Here I insert first ten lines.

:r! cat foo | awk 'NR>=10&&NR<=20'
And here I insert ten lines starting from the tenth line.
Tell me, which text editor allows you to insert part (or whole) another file into the current one with a stroke of a command?</td>
</tr>
<tr>
<td>:w</td>
<td>write. With the filename as parameter writes to that file ("Save as"). Also write part of the file (to another file)</td>
<td>:10,20 w filename
Here I write ten lines to the file <filename>
Tell me, which text editor allows you to save part of the file into the different file?</td>
</tr>
<tr>
<td>1,$s/str1/str2/g</td>
<td>Substitute strings in the entire file, or part of it (the g flag is optional)</td>
<td>We saw example of that just above.</td>
</tr>
</table>

<table>
<tr><td>. (single dot)</td><td>Repeats the last command</td><td></td></tr>
<tr><td>"r20yy</td><td>Yanks 20 lines to the register r. Then in other file: "rp to paste.</td><td>To exchange text between files</td></tr>
<tr><td>:1,x! sort</td><td>sort lines. Can use all options for the sort (field number etc). Ex:
:1,3!sort -k2 -r
(To sort first three lines on the second field in reverse order)</td><td> 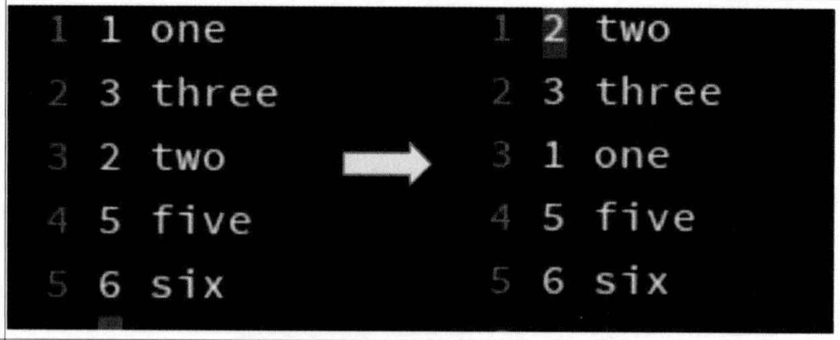1 1 one
2 3 three
3 2 two
4 5 five
5 6 six
→
1 2 two
2 3 three
3 1 one
4 5 five
5 6 six</td></tr>
<tr><td>:set all</td><td>To show all options</td><td></td></tr>
<tr><td>Ctrl-A / ctr-x</td><td>To increment/decrement the number.</td><td>Applies to the first number following the cursor on a current line 
1 9 two   1 1 two
<num> ctl-A (to increment by the <number>)</td></tr>
<tr><td></td><td>Example: Insert few lines at the line 4 and re-number the rest of the file:
:r! ls -l | head
4,$s/^\d\+//</b>
<b>4,$!awk '{print NR+4, $0}'</td><td> 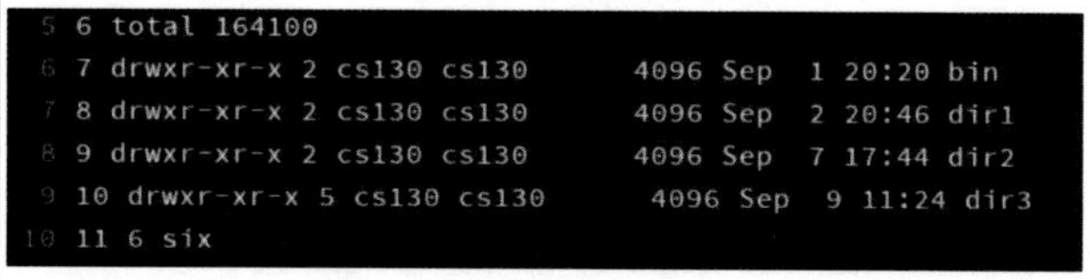5 6 total 164100
6 7 drwxr-xr-x 2 cs130 cs130 4096 Sep 1 20:20 bin
7 8 drwxr-xr-x 2 cs130 cs130 4096 Sep 2 20:46 dir1
8 9 drwxr-xr-x 2 cs130 cs130 4096 Sep 7 17:44 dir2
9 10 drwxr-xr-x 5 cs130 cs130 4096 Sep 9 11:24 dir3
10 11 6 six
Suppose we have a file with line numbers (that is part of the file, and not the ones that vi displays).
1. Inserting the listing.
2. Deleting the previous numbering
3. Re-numbering.
4. Show me any editor that can do that.</td></tr>
<tr><td></td><td>Abbreviations, mapping</td><td></td></tr>
<tr><td>ab str1 str2</td><td>When you type string str1 vi replaces it with str2</td><td> 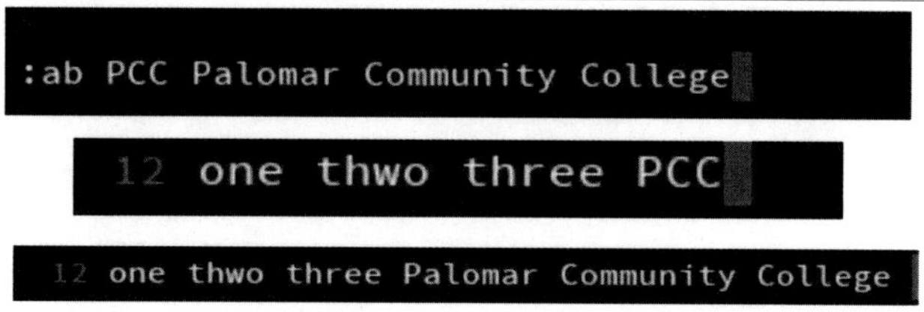:ab PCC Palomar Community College
12 one thwo three PCC
12 one thwo three Palomar Community College</td></tr>
</table>

1.3. Going even deeper.

My goal is obviously not to talk about everything, that ***vi*** can provide to you. I think, that nobody can. I'll perhaps mention just two or three of other things you can do, not necessarily giving examples. They are searching for the files and using the results of the search inside the ***vi***, ***RegEx*** withing ***vi***, and mapping.

- Searching from within vi.

You work on some project and you need to find reference for something, or use part of other file, or insert a quotation. You can do a grep-like search from within ***vi***. Actually, you can even do grep search, but it will be external tool from ***vi***. But ***vi*** comes with its own search – ***vimgrep***, or ***vim,*** which is probably more convenient to use.

In the command mode enter

:vim /<your text>/ <the files>

And let me stop here and not going to talk about how to work with the results. I just recalled, that this course is about Linux, not the ***vi***. We can easily spend weeks talking about the ***vi***, so let's proceed to our final example with that.

- Support for the ***RegEx.***

Yes, ***vi*** does support them. However that is tricky. For the fairly complex ones you will need a lot of escapes, which will complicate already unreadable syntax. Let's see a simple example how to switch first name and the last name in the file. As with everything else, you can find similar examples online.

And that's how I did that:

```
:15,18s/\([^,]*\), \(.*\)/\2 \1/
```

> Anyone can read that?

- And, finally, let's talk about mapping. We talked about abbreviations. The mapping is in some respect similar, but taken to the next lever.

For this example let's emulate the Ctrl-C and Ctrl-V keyboard shortcuts to make them work as the copy and paste (we can emulate other shortcuts too, let's limit ourselves by these two).

We will need to tell ***vi*** that we are going to type a special character (Ctrl-C). To tell that, we first press Ctrl-V combination, that makes ***vi*** to accept the following character, as a special one. For example, if you want to enter a new line into the ***vi***, you would do Ctrl-V followed by <***enter***>. You will see, that it is a special character, because it will be preceded with the caret sign and colored differently.

Thus, we enter into the command mode, and open the command prompt by hitting the colon. After which we enter the following combination of keys:

```
:map Ctrl-VC “ayy
```

The highlighted part says to yank (***yy***) a line into the named buffer ***a***. Yes, you can yank into the named buffers, we saw that in the table above.

Here it is. The command:

```
:map ^C "ayy
```

Now the pasting part. As we just learned, the Ctr-V is a special combination of keys in the ***vi***. Thus, we need to be little insistent to convince it to do what we want. We will repeat it twice. Just to be heard.

```
:map Ctrl-VCtrl-V “ap
```

The highlighted parts are the only difference with the previous command. The first one is, obviously the mapping of the Ctrl-V. And the second one says to paste (***p***) from the named buffer ***a***.

Again, you can see, that special characters are shown differently.

Let's see how it works. Here is my text:	And here it is after I copied and pasted the line:
15 Harry Potter 16 Robin Hood 17 Little John 18 Hermione Granger 19	15 Harry Potter 16 Robin Hood 17 Little John 18 Hermione Granger 19 20 21 Hermione Granger

1.4. Two most important commands in vi

And finally, I left two most important commands to the end. Although the one I already mentioned:

```
:q!
```

Quits your file without saving it. If you think you messed up somehow, don't try to fix that. The far better option is to force-quit.

And the last one (from the command mode)

```
u
```

Undo!

How can we live without being able to undo something what we did? ***Undo***, ***rollback***, ***Ctr-Z***... They all are such.... Back to the ***vi***. Here it is. It can undo as many changes, as it keeps in the history.

To summarize, ***vi*** is very rich and powerful editor. It is not the only Linux text editor. There are quite a number of other options. Some people (and I used to know some of them) write their own text editors, because nothing fit their taste. There is always a choice. But the ***vi*** is a standard one across the distros.

Some vi examples, used in this lecture were taken (with some modifications and adaptations) from various sources, like man pages, various boards, blogs, tutorials, guides etc.

2. Named Pipes

So far we passed data from one utility to another one by piping them together into the pipeline. We also did examples where two different processes communicated using the files. And, speaking of that, the file may be used not only to exchange the data; it may be used to pass some certain information or signals. What would be an easiest way to signal that certain resources are locked and should not be accessed for some period? The mere presence or not presence of some (even empty) file would be a good flag for that. And here we can see another important usage of the **touch** command to quickly create a file. But back to our discussion.

What if we want to read the data from the file, but the producer keeps writing data there? Do we wait until the producer is finished? What if the producer runs as a demon keeping writing and writing data? Will it finish? Shall we wait? Will the file become too large to fill up the disk while we wait? What if we want to use data while it's being generated; for example to write customers records to the database?

Furthermore, when we pipe two processes, we ***tie*** those two processes, and we tie ***those*** two processes. Sometimes we may want two or even more different processes to communicate with each other without being tied together.

So we have couple of problems here: one is scheduling problem – when the consumer process should run? Should it wait until the producer is finished? And if so, then how to know when that happens.

Second problem is limiting our communication channel to two processes.

As you can recall, we solved some of these problems by using a temporary unnamed pipes. We know that that pipe will be gone when the job will be completed.

But Linux allows us to create a more persistent pipe as means of communication. And because of its persistence, it should have a name. Thus, we have a ***named pipes*** (as opposed to the unnamed ones).

Unlike an unnamed pipes, that connect two specific processes, the named pipe is not bound to any one. Any process can write to, or read from that pipe. Because of that, and because any process can attach itself to the named pipe, some people view this a security issue. I personally think that it is pretty much the same as writing to and reading from the regular file. If you have access to it, you can read and write to it. So it should be no more security risk than using regular files, or shared files.

There is no requirement that producer and consumer connect to the named pipe at the same time. If producer sends the data, but there is no consumer to take it, producer is ***blocked*** in the ***wait*** status. Similarly, if consumer connects to the named pipe that has no data written to it, the consumer is ***blocked*** into the ***wait*** status. Named pipe is ***asynchronous*** blocking process. Also, it operates in the "First come, first served" order, or as a queue (FIFO, First in, first out). I can have more than one consumer, but only one gets the data, I can have more than one producer, but the data will be sent in the first in, first out order.
Let's see, how it works.

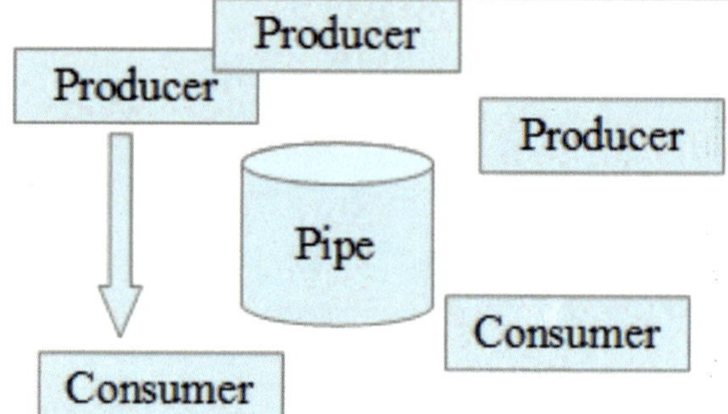

To create a named pipe, you do:

mkfifo <name_of_pipe>

Which is: "make FIFO". FIFO, of course is "First in, First out", i.e., again, "First come, first served".

For example

```
mkfifo myfifo
```

When you do **ls -l**, you will see the new entry in the listing – **myfifo.** Note the leftmost character there.

```
cs130@raspberrypi ~/dir1 9 mkfifo myfifo
cs130@raspberrypi ~/dir1 10 ls -lt
total 0
prw-r--r-- 1 cs130 cs130 0 Oct  7 14:19 myfifo
```

That's how you know that it is not a regular file, but a pipe. Other thing, note that the size of the pipe is zero.

After you have this pipe, anyone, who has a permission to that directory, can write to that pipe, and, likewise, can read from that pipe.

Let's see how it works.

Let's open three terminals (three? OMG what's going to happen here?). On one terminal let's do:

```
echo "some long line of data" > myfifo
```

```
cs130@raspberrypi ~ 1 echo "some long line of data" > dir1/myfifo
```

Note that after we hit "enter" the process enters into the wait state, because pipe is a blocking process. I.e. it blocks processing, until the reading/writing is done.

On the second terminal:

```
cat myfifo
```

cs130@raspberrypi ~/dir1 12
cs130@raspberrypi ~/dir1 12 cat myfifo
some long line of data
cs130@raspberrypi ~ 2 echo "some long line of data" > dir1/myfifo
cs130@raspberrypi ~ 3
ESC
CTRL
ALT
here
here

We should see the text we entered on the first terminal, and we note that the first process is finished.

Let's try this other way around. On the "left" window let's enter:

```
less -f myfifo
```

We need to use **-f** flag, because otherwise ***less*** will complain that **myfifo** is not a regular file.

```
cs130@raspberrypi ~/dir1 4 less -f myfifo
```

On the "right" window repeat previous command to send data to the pipe, and see that data read by the ***less*** on the left.

```
some long line of data
myfifo (END)
```

Press **Shift-F** on the ***less*** window, and it enters into the waiting mode.

```
~
some long line of data
Waiting for data... (interrupt to abort)
```

That mode of the ***less*** is very useful if you want to monitor something in the real time, for example you want to monitor some log in the real time. (Did I say "***very*** useful?")

On the first terminal start repeating the **echo** command, and you see that on the window with the ***less*** open, the text appears line by line.

```
~
~
some long line of data
some long line of data1
some long line of data2
some long line of data3
```

```
cs130@raspberrypi ~ 3 echo "some long line of data" > dir1/myfifo
cs130@raspberrypi ~ 4 echo "some long line of data1" > dir1/myfifo
cs130@raspberrypi ~ 5 echo "some long line of data2" > dir1/myfifo
cs130@raspberrypi ~ 6 echo "some long line of data3" > dir1/myfifo
cs130@raspberrypi ~ 7
ESC    CTRL    ALT
```

Let's not stop there.

Let me connect to the machine from yet another terminal (I promised to do three terminals, didn't I?).

```
cs130@raspberrypi ~ 1 ./myotherraspberry
cs130@192.168.1.1's password:

The programs included with the Debian GNU/Linux system are free software;
the exact distribution terms for each program are described in the
individual files in /usr/share/doc/*/copyright.

Debian GNU/Linux comes with ABSOLUTELY NO WARRANTY, to the extent
permitted by applicable law.
Last login: Wed Oct  7 14:37:36 2020 from 192.168.43.224
cs130@raspberrypi ~ 1
```

...and send data to the pipe from there:

```
cs130@raspberrypi ~ 1 echo "here is the line from the other raspberry" > dir1/myfifo
cs130@raspberrypi ~ 2
```

...and sure enough, here it is, on the “left” window of the first computer, with the **less** faithfully accepting it:

here

```
some long line of data
some long line of data1
some long line of data2
some long line of data3
here is the line from the other raspberry
Waiting for data... (interrupt to abort)
```

(See, I even had to switch networks to be able to do that demo; that's how motivated I am) 

We can do many more interesting experiments here, but let's do a last one. From the first terminal let's send the text to the pipe on the background.

```
cs130@raspberrypi ~ 7 echo "some long line of data3" > dir1/myfifo &
[1] 9867
cs130@raspberrypi ~ 8
```

Let's send the text (different text) on the “left” terminal:

```
cs130@raspberrypi ~/dir1 5 echo "text from the left ter
minal" > myfifo &
[1] 9882
cs130@raspberrypi ~/dir1 6
```

Now read the pipe:

```
text from the left terminal
some long line of data3
myfifo (END)
```

Again, no matter who the sender was, “*the winner takes it all**”.

---

* Not a mine copyright

Alright. That was educational. How to remove the pipe? Just as a regular file: **rm**

```
cs130@raspberrypi ~/dir1 9 rm myfifo
cs130@raspberrypi ~/dir1 10 ls
cs130@raspberrypi ~/dir1 11
```

There are couple of peculiarities to keep in mind:

1. If one process had sent data to a pipe, and I deleted the pipe before the data was collected, the first process hangs on wait on a broken pipe. Remember it is a blocking call. I will need to kill it with the Ctr-C.

2. I may send the data to the pipe, which does not exist. The process will hang on the wait status. After that I can create a pipe, and first process will happily send the data to the newly created pipe.

Finally, however weird it may sound, you can create a symbolic link to a named pipe.

3. Mail

Linux comes with the mail utility. Different distros may have different email utilities, but they work similarly. The mail utilities are pretty simple, straightforward, and easy to use. Since they all integrated into the shell, you can easily embed the whole email capabilities into your script. One thing you should note, that they are fully compliant with the ***smtp*** (simple mail transfer protocol), and therefore

```
The following demonstration is for educational purposes only. As
with all lectures in this course, all the examples are for your
education. You should not use or abuse these examples to do any
harm whether intentionally or not. The instructor is not liable for
any consequences that may arise should you do otherwise.
```

To send email:

mail <username if on a local system> or complete email address, if outside, but the mail should be configured to SMTP relay.

For example, in its simplest form (I have only two users on this system, so I will do demonstration exchanging emails between them):

mail <user>

Enter subject, type the message, Ctrl-D to finish.

Some system may want you to end the message with the single dot on a line.

```
cs130@raspberrypi ~ 2 mail newuser
Cc:
Subject: Hi from me
This is my very important message.
.
cs130@raspberrypi ~ 3
```

You can also use (-s) flag for subject, in which case you won't be asked for a one in the mail window.

mail -s "Hello" root

Well, I did not need to be a ***root*** here, but I wanted to demonstrate that you can send and receive messages from the ***root***. I repeat it again, you work as a regular user, switching to a ***root*** only when needed. Alright.

You can do everything completely on the command line:

echo "<your message>" | mail -s "<your subject>" <recipient>

```
root@raspberrypi:~# echo "msg from root" | mail -s "from root" cs130
root@raspberrypi:~# logout
You have new mail in /var/mail/cs130
cs130@raspberrypi ~ 14
```

Note, that notification of a new email is given to me on the terminal. To see the emails, I'll do:

mail

This command opens the mail and displays list of your emails.

```
cs130@raspberrypi ~ 14 mail
"/var/mail/cs130": 1 message 1 new
>N   1 root@raspberrypi   Wed Oct  7 16:43  15/485   from root
?
```

> All your emails are kept in the mail file. That makes it possible, if necessary, parse that file to read the email or extract whatever data you need to outside of the mail program (read: from the script)

To read message from your email program, from the list of emails, you do:

t (type) or **p** (print) **[number]**

For example: **t 1** to read the first message.

```
? t 1
Return-path: <root@raspberrypi>
Envelope-to: cs130@raspberrypi
Delivery-date: Wed, 07 Oct 2020 16:43:42 -0700
Received: from root by raspberrypi with local (Exim 4.84_2)
        (envelope-from <root@raspberrypi>)
        id 1kQJ5x-0003Qj-Fj
        for cs130@raspberrypi; Wed, 07 Oct 2020 16:43:41 -0700
Subject: from root
To: <cs130@raspberrypi>
X-Mailer: mail (GNU Mailutils 2.99.98)
Message-Id: <E1kQJ5x-0003Qj-Fj@raspberrypi>
From: root@raspberrypi
Date: Wed, 07 Oct 2020 16:43:41 -0700

msg from root
```

When in the email message, type

n

to read next message.

Type

h

to return to the list of headers.

d [number] or range

deletes that email or range.

q

Quits the mail

```
? q
Saved 1 message in /home/cs130/mbox
Held 0 messages in /var/mail/cs130
cs130@raspberrypi ~ 15
```

And you can see the locations of the read messages and unread messages.

Since mail client compatible with the ***smtp*** email protocol, when sending an email, you can specify a return address:

echo "Party tonight?" | mail -s "Hi there" root -rJohn

```
cs130@raspberrypi ~ $ echo "Party tonight?" | mail -s "Hi there" root -rJohn
```

The root:

```
You have new mail in /var/mail/root
root@raspberrypi:~# mail
"/var/mail/root": 2 messages 2 unread
>U   1 cs130@raspberrypi  Wed Oct  7 16:42  19/514   hi
 U   2 John@raspberrypi   Wed Oct  7 16:46  17/502   Hi there
```

Note, that in the above window the email is shown as coming from John. Let's open that

Look very carefully at the message's header.

```
? t 2
Return-path: <John@raspberrypi>
Envelope-to: root@raspberrypi
Delivery-date: Wed, 07 Oct 2020 16:46:48 -0700
Received: from cs130 by raspberrypi with local (Exim 4.84_2)
        (envelope-from <John@raspberrypi>)
        id 1kQJ8x-0003Qw-Cd
        for root@raspberrypi; Wed, 07 Oct 2020 16:46:48 -0700
Subject: Hi there
To: <root@raspberrypi>
X-Mailer: mail (GNU Mailutils 2.99.98)
Message-Id: <E1kQJ8x-0003Qw-Cd@raspberrypi>
From: John@raspberrypi
Date: Wed, 07 Oct 2020 16:46:47 -0700
Status: 0
X-UID: 2

Party tonight?
?
```

Here:

here

That is the only place, that shows you that the sender was not a John as shown here:

here

and here:

here

Some tools will additionally show you the authentication warning, but again, that would be a single line on the message's header.

That is again, to be fully compatible with the ***smtp*** specifications.

You surely have experience receiving messages like that.

Or like that:

echo "Please login with your user name and password" | mail -s "Message from your bank" root -rcustomerservice@<name_of_your_bank_here>.com

```
cs130@raspberrypi ~ 18 echo "Please login with your user name and password" | mail -s "Message from your bank" root -rcustomerseric
e@nameofyourbankhere.com
```

```
You have new mail in /var/mail/root
root@raspberrypi:~# mail
"/var/mail/root": 3 messages 3 unread
>U   1 cs130@raspberrypi  Wed Oct  7 16:42  19/514   hi
 U   2 John@raspberrypi   Wed Oct  7 16:46  17/502   Hi there
 U   3 customerserice@nam Wed Oct  7 16:53  17/610   Message from your bank
?
```

When you see messages like that like that ur mailbox, the three things that you never do:

1. You never click on that message to open it
2. If you did #1 above, you probably see a very realistic login page or link to the login page. Second thing you never do is to click on any link or any button inside that email. Even on the link that offers you the option to "unsubscribe" or "stop receiving the mails". I repeat, **you do not click on any links or buttons, including those**.
3. Last thing you never do if you still did the two above, you never login to that page with your real user name and password. Please be very cognizant: Those people are very resourceful. You may be in the relaxed mode and loose your guards. That's what these people want.

So... after those words.... this is how that message looks like:

```
? t 3
Return-path: <customerserice@nameofyourbankhere.com>
Envelope-to: root@raspberrypi
Delivery-date: Wed, 07 Oct 2020 16:53:50 -0700
Received: from cs130 by raspberrypi with local (Exim 4.84_2)
        (envelope-from <customerserice@nameofyourbankhere.com>)
        id 1kQJFm-0003Tq-7U
        for root@raspberrypi; Wed, 07 Oct 2020 16:53:50 -0700
Subject: Message from your bank
To: <root@raspberrypi>
X-Mailer: mail (GNU Mailutils 2.99.98)
Message-Id: <E1kQJFm-0003Tq-7U@raspberrypi>
From: customerserice@nameofyourbankhere.com
Date: Wed, 07 Oct 2020 16:53:50 -0700
Status: O
X-UID: 3

Please login with your user name and password
?
```

… And that's what you do:

```
? d 1 - 3
? q
Held 0 messages in /var/mail/root
root@raspberrypi:~#
```

We will touch that topic again in the lecture about the networking. For now, to wrap it up, since, as I already said, the email is fully integrated with the shell, you can pipe it to the whatever commands you want to. For example the one, that we already did last time:

```
find / -atime +30 -exec du -s '{}' \;  2>/dev/null | sort -n -r | head -5 | tail -4
> /home/bob/myysearch.log
```

Instead of writing the file, results can be sent to the email instead:

```
find / -atime +30 -exec du -s '{}' \; 2>/dev/null | sort -n -r | head -5 | tail -4 |
mail -s "disk usage" user
```

That is very useful option if you want to send some alert to expedite response. You can even configure the alert to be sent to the text message on the phone for even higher level of urgency.

... Well. Not result of ***that*** command, perhaps...

4. Cron

We already saw, that we can schedule processes to run at certain intervals: hourly, daily, weekly... by simply placing our script (a link to our script) to special directories under the */etc*. This is good for many purposes, but may not be good enough. Linux provides much more refined tool for scheduling jobs, that gives you much more granularity and control, than those pre-defined scheduling options.

In Linux and UNIX, scheduling is mostly done with the ***cron*** utility.

Cron is the daemon; that means it runs infinitely and checks for certain conditions to happen. There is file that ***cron*** reads; that file specifies what job and at which interval it should run. For each user, there is separate file, located in the ***spool*** directory (same directory, where users' email files are located). That is one of few files that you do not edit directly. Instead you use the tool:

crontab -e

The reason for that, the tool is also checks for the basic syntax before installing a new ***cron*** job for you. If that validation failed, you will see some sort of the message when you exit the ***crontab*** editor. Otherwise, the new ***cron*** will be installed. Obviously, when you install a new ***cron***, you want to make sure your script works correctly, and that your ***cron*** schedule is correct too. You also want to make sure that your script runs under the ***cron*** correctly, which is different from your script is correct, runs correctly, and your schedule is correct. Thus, you may want to run few iterations of your script, scheduling it for every minute or other appropriate intervals just to see that everything is good and well.

Alright, that was general consideration. Now we are at the ***crontab*** file. First time you open that file (and if you have not added anything to that), the file will be empty. Otherwise you'll see the previously scheduled jobs, so that you can edit them, modify, or delete. Let's add a new ***cron*** job.

crontab -e

```
cs130@raspberrypi ~ $ crontab -e
no crontab for cs130 - using an empty one

Select an editor.  To change later, run 'select-editor'.
  1. /bin/ed
  2. /bin/nano        <---- easiest
  3. /usr/bin/vim.tiny
```

Hmmm. But thank you, Raspberry, for suggesting me the easiest one anyways. With your permissions:

```
Choose 1-3 [2]: 3
```

An empty file opens (because I have not scheduled anything for the ***cron*** yet). Look at the bottom of it.

```
"/tmp/crontab.6BogWt/crontab" 24L, 924C
```

From its status, you'll see, that it is not a ***crontab*** file directly, but a temporary file. The new ***crontab*** will be installed after and if your command passes validation.

Let's add something there. Unlike scheduling with the directories, where we had to have scripts there, for a ***cron*** we have additional option of entering a raw command. Why do we need to write a script for something that can be executed with one or two statements?

To schedule job with the ***cron*** we provide five parameters separated by a space. These parameters are:

minutes, hours, days, months, days of weeks.

And it is nice to see, that Raspberry gives a hints:

```
# m h  dom mon dow   command
```

Let's add a command to execute every minute:

*** * * * * echo "remember the time `date`" >> /home/cs130/timelog**

```
* * * * * echo "remember the time `date`" >> /home/cs130/timelog
```

Remember, we need to use the absolute path names in things like that!

Save and quit ***vi***, wait for a minute (let me type few lines here), and now let's look at the directory:

```
-rw-r--r-- 1 cs130 cs130       188 Oct  8 19:03 timelog
You have mail in /var/mail/cs130
```

We see that file. Let's check it:

```
cs130@raspberrypi ~ 17 tail timelog
remember the time Thu Oct  8 19:00:01 PDT 2020
remember the time Thu Oct  8 19:01:01 PDT 2020
remember the time Thu Oct  8 19:02:01 PDT 2020
remember the time Thu Oct  8 19:03:01 PDT 2020
```

Note also the message notifying me on a new emails. By default ***cron*** notifies me about jobs by the email. We can disable that option by setting

MAILTO = ""

At the beginning of our ***crontab*** file.

Back to our ***crontab***. With the settings we used, we scheduled our command to run for every minute. We know it because all fields are marked with asterisks.

If you want to run it hourly, set the minutes to 0.

If you want to run it daily, set the minutes and hours to 0.
If you want to specify certain time of day to run, for example at 2:45 am, you would do:

45 2 * * * command

For 2:45 pm:

45 14 * * * command

If you want to run the command every 5 minutes:

0,5,19,15,20,25,30,35,40,45,50,55 * * * * command

Hmmm.... Too much typing. That is obviously awkward. Let's do a shortcut:

/5 * * * * command

This is much nicer, but not all systems may support that.

How would we set the time execution of every Monday at 8 am?

0 8 * * 1 command >> /home/user/log

And again, the "***command***" there can be a script, or just a command as we did above.

Let's do something... interesting

0 8 31 12 1 command >> /home/user/log

That command should run at 8:00 am on Jan, 31, if it is Monday. In other words, it will run once in every 7 years not counting the leap years, if I am correct here.

There are also few special forms

@reboot

@yearly, and all common types: hourly, monthly etc., but you also can do that without ***cron***, by placing the script to the corresponding directories, as we did at the beginning.

5. Summary

Vi, named pipes, mail, cron.

Commands: ***vi, mail, mkfifo, crontab***

Lecture 9. Some system utilities.

He reached out and pressed an invitingly large red button... The panel lit up with the words "Please do not press this button again"

Douglas Adams, The Hitchhiker Guide To The Galaxy.

Today we will talk about process management, user management, and Linux's messaging. Let's begin. As with all my lectures, there is one condition.

```
Do no harm!
```

```
As with all lectures in this course, all the examples are for your
education. You should not use or abuse these examples to do any
harm whether intentionally or not. The instructor is not liable for
any consequences that may arise should you do otherwise.
```

1. Process management

Without saying anything at all to the effect of how important this functionality is, let's just begin. You will probably see the importance of that as we go. There are number of utilities on a command line, that provide process management.

1.1. top.

`top` shows information about top running processes and their and system's status: memory, status of processes (running, sleeping, zombies etc), uptime, system utilization etc. Much like windows task monitor, or should I say, windows task monitor is much like the ***top***.

```
top - 13:12:34 up 5 days,  2:37,  3 users,  load average: 0.00, 0.00, 0.00
Tasks: 154 total,   1 running, 153 sleeping,   0 stopped,   0 zombie
%Cpu(s):  0.2 us,  0.2 sy,  0.0 ni, 99.7 id,  0.0 wa,  0.0 hi,  0.0 si,  0.0 st
KiB Mem:    945512 total,   622188 used,   323324 free,   192920 buffers
KiB Swap:   102396 total,        0 used,   102396 free.   204124 cached Mem

  PID USER      PR  NI    VIRT    RES    SHR S  %CPU %MEM     TIME+ COMMAND
25715 cs130     20   0    5108   2536   2148 R   1.0  0.3   0:00.13 top
    7 root      20   0       0      0      0 S   0.3  0.0   0:38.51 rcu_sched
    1 root      20   0   22792   3864   2732 S   0.0  0.4   1:15.74 systemd
    2 root      20   0       0      0      0 S   0.0  0.0   0:00.34 kthreadd
    3 root      20   0       0      0      0 S   0.0  0.0   0:03.98 ksoftirqd/0
```

When you start it, it will take your entire window and will run, updating and refreshing itself automatically every few seconds, until you terminate it by pressing the ***q*** key on a keyboard. You can also launch it providing the number of iterations, after completing which it will terminate. We will see that in a bit.

The fields, displayed by default are *PID, user, priority, nice-ness,* few *memory* fields, *status of the process, % cpu, % memory, total cpu time,* and the *command.*

There are few options to customize the display:

f – field management

r – reverse sort.

You can press the ***h*** for help.

From within the **top** you can kill a process:

press '***k***'

```
top - 13:14:36 up 5 days,  2:40,  3 users,  load average: 0.00, 0.00, 0.00
Tasks: 154 total,   1 running, 153 sleeping,   0 stopped,   0 zombie
%Cpu(s):  0.2 us,  0.2 sy,  0.0 ni, 99.7 id,  0.0 wa,  0.0 hi,  0.0 si,  0.0 st
KiB Mem:    945512 total,   622360 used,   323152 free,   192924 buffers
KiB Swap:   102396 total,        0 used,   102396 free.   204124 cached Mem
PID to signal/kill [default pid = 25716]
```

The **top** will ask you for the ***ID*** of the process you want to kill. By default it will display the first one from the list. Supposedly, it is done to let you easily kill the run-away (and hence, the ***top***) process.

After you provide the process's ***ID***, the **top** will ask you what signal you want to send to that process. And here let me sidetrack a little.

1.1.1. Signals.

The ***OS*** communicates with the processes by sending (and receiving) some signals. There are quite a few signals exist that allow you to send various requests or exchange information. From our previous discussions you can probably recall, that we already used that functionality. We did that to suspend process before sending it to the background (...yes? Remember that Ctrl-Z?) We also used an interrupt signal (Ctrl-C) for number of occasions. For our today's discussion we are interested in the signals that terminate the process.

And since we already used the ***SIGTERM***, let's talk about the other one. The ***SIGKILL*** signal is the strongest signal to unconditionally kill the process. It cannot be intercepted or ignored. When the process receives it, it has no choice, but to immediately oblige. What do I mean when say "intercepted or ignored"? When process receives a signal to exit, a well-behaved one ought to do some housekeeping and cleaning up after itself. It has to release back to the system all the resources it borrowed and used, close all the file descriptors, all connections, remove all temporary files, etc.... Pretty much as with every rent, when it terminates, the tenant shall return property back in the same condition as it was at the beginning of the rent. Well... at least it supposed to. And that is the purpose of the allowance to still being able to execute some code after the signal is received. A processes that are the good citizens, understand and follow that. However... Have you had a situation that you want to terminate some job only to see that after the moment it pops back again on the process's monitor? Some applications can be coded in such a way, that after they receive a terminating signal, they... ignore it. You did ***not*** hear me saying the word "malicious", did you? Sometimes that could be just a programmers' mistake. Or, may be omission. Or, maybe intention... Alright, we are not here to discuss that. So. There is a signal to terminate that cannot be intercepted or ignored. And that signal is... surprisingly, ***SIGKILL***. We'll continue with that in a little while. For now let's look at the screen, and note, that by default the **top** suggests to send a ***SIGTERM***, and if you look closely you will see the number 15 there. That's because signals have numerical values, and the ***SIGTERM*** has a numeric equivalent of 15.

```
top - 13:14:36 up 5 days,  2:40,  3 users,  load average: 0.00, 0.00, 0.00
Tasks: 154 total,   1 running, 153 sleeping,   0 stopped,   0 zombie
%Cpu(s):  0.2 us,  0.2 sy,  0.0 ni, 99.7 id,  0.0 wa,  0.0 hi,  0.0 si,  0.0 st
KiB Mem:    945512 total,   622360 used,   323152 free,   192924 buffers
KiB Swap:   102396 total,        0 used,   102396 free.   204124 cached Mem
Send pid 25716 signal [15/sigterm]
  PID USER      PR  NI    VIRT    RES    SHR S  %CPU %MEM     TIME+ COMMAND
```

Now back to our discussion about the **top**.

From the **top**'s window, by pressing the '*r*' key, you can re-nice the process (to change its level of priority):

When starting the **top,** you can ask it to show the processes for a specific user:

```
top -u <user>
```

```
cs130@raspberrypi ~ ? top -u cs130
```

And you see, that it lists my processes there:

```
top - 13:17:47 up 5 days,  2:43,  3 users,  load average: 0.00, 0.00, 0.00
Tasks: 153 total,   1 running, 152 sleeping,   0 stopped,   0 zombie
%Cpu(s):  0.2 us,  0.1 sy,  0.0 ni, 99.7 id,  0.0 wa,  0.0 hi,  0.1 si,  0.0 st
KiB Mem:    945512 total,   622832 used,   322680 free,   192936 buffers
KiB Swap:   102396 total,        0 used,   102396 free.   204128 cached Mem

  PID USER      PR  NI    VIRT    RES    SHR S  %CPU %MEM     TIME+ COMMAND
25738 cs130     20   0    5108   2472   2076 R   0.7  0.3   0:00.12 top
25688 cs130     20   0    5116   3296   2892 S   0.0  0.3   0:00.03 systemd
25691 cs130     20   0   24220   1240     16 S   0.0  0.1   0:00.00 (sd-pam)
25694 cs130     20   0   12284   3552   2860 S   0.0  0.4   0:00.12 sshd
25696 cs130     20   0    6480   4444   2868 S   0.0  0.5   0:00.32 bash
```

Or, processes with given ***PID***:

```
top -p <PID>
```

```
cs130@raspberrypi ~ 10 top -p 25696
```

```
top - 13:19:51 up 5 days,  2:45,  3 users,  load average: 0.00, 0.00, 0.00
Tasks:   1 total,   0 running,   1 sleeping,   0 stopped,   0 zombie
%Cpu(s):  0.2 us,  0.0 sy,  0.0 ni, 99.8 id,  0.0 wa,  0.0 hi,  0.0 si,  0.0 st
KiB Mem:    945512 total,   622748 used,   322764 free,   192940 buffers
KiB Swap:   102396 total,        0 used,   102396 free.   204132 cached Mem

  PID USER      PR  NI    VIRT    RES    SHR S  %CPU %MEM     TIME+ COMMAND
25696 cs130     20   0    6480   4444   2868 S   0.0  0.5   0:00.35 bash
```

At the beginning, I mentioned, that you can request only certain number of iterations (as opposed to infinite by default):

```
top -n <number>
```

But if I run this command:

top -n 1

I will not be able to see anything, because the top will launch and immediately close. I don't know about you, but my eyes will not be able to catch even slightest glimpse of that.

In such case, why is that needed?

This is very useful if you want to output the result of **top** to the file or if you want to query the status of the system from the script. Suppose you want to monitor the cpu utilization or memory utilization, or both, and you want to create a log file with time stamps, perhaps to troubleshoot a performance issues. If you need something, it is very likely you can do that something. Let's do that:

```
top -b -n 1
```

```
cs130@raspberrypi ~ 4 top -b -n1 | head
top - 02:30:30 up  5:28,  1 user,  load average: 0.07, 0.08, 0.09
Tasks:  63 total,   1 running,  62 sleeping,   0 stopped,   0 zombie
%Cpu(s):  4.8 us,  1.5 sy,  0.0 ni, 93.6 id,  0.1 wa,  0.0 hi,  0.0 si,  0.0 st
KiB Mem:    448736 total,   107472 used,   341264 free,    18244 buffers
KiB Swap:   102396 total,        0 used,   102396 free,    57296 cached

  PID USER      PR  NI  VIRT  RES  SHR S  %CPU %MEM    TIME+  COMMAND
 2291 lightdm   20   0 91856  11m 9252 S  11.3  2.6   7:36.63 lightdm-gtk-gre
 9076 cs130     20   0  4528 1216  944 R  11.3  0.3   0:00.06 top
 2108 root      20   0 15544 6044 3048 S   5.7  1.3   3:30.81 Xorg
cs130@raspberrypi ~ 5
```

Where the *-b* flag tells **`top`** to run in a batch mode.

1.2. ps

Another very useful utility is **`ps`** (for ***process status***).

Unlike **`top`**, the **`ps`** displays status of processes at the time of the command. It shows user, who runs the process, the ***PID*** of the process, ***PID*** of the parent of that process, and the command. Command is shown with complete argument, so if you run database script and provide all connection information including the password as an argument on the command line, be aware, that anyone on the system can see your entire command arguments with the **`ps -ef`**.

```
ps -ef
```

```
cs130@raspberrypi ~ 18 ps -ef | head
UID        PID  PPID  C STIME TTY          TIME CMD
root         1     0  0 Sep09 ?        00:01:15 /sbin/init splash
root         2     0  0 Sep09 ?        00:00:00 [kthreadd]
root         3     2  0 Sep09 ?        00:00:03 [ksoftirqd/0]
root         5     2  0 Sep09 ?        00:00:00 [kworker/0:0H]
root         7     2  0 Sep09 ?        00:00:38 [rcu_sched]
```

That will show processes from all users on all terminals. You can ***grep*** it to see some specific processes. For example if I want to see what is the ***apache's*** status (whether the ***httpd*** runs or not), I would do :

```
ps -ef | grep httpd
```

Or to check whether the ***sshd*** is running or not,

```
ps -ef | grep sshd
```

```
cs130@raspberrypi ~ 19 ps -ef | grep httpd
cs130    25775 25696  0 13:24 pts/0    00:00:00 grep --color=auto httpd
cs130@raspberrypi ~ 20 ^httpd^sshd^
ps -ef | grep sshd
root       544     1  0 Sep09 ?        00:00:00 /usr/sbin/sshd -D
root     25683   544  0 13:11 ?        00:00:00 sshd: cs130 [priv]
cs130    25694 25683  0 13:11 ?        00:00:00 sshd: cs130@pts/0
cs130    25778 25696  0 13:25 pts/0    00:00:00 grep --color=auto sshd
cs130@raspberrypi ~ 21
```

And I see, that at the time of the command, there is no ***httpd*** running, but there is ***sshd***. I said that **`ps`** shows you the processes from all users from all terminals. Let's see it.

I will open the new ***bash*** session, launch some process there to run on a background (with the ***nohup*** option allowing the process to still run when the session is closed), and exit the session. I will not be able to see that background process with the **jobs** command on my old session. But I can see it (and manage it) with the **ps**. Here is the screen:

```
cs130@raspberrypi ~ 22 bash
cs130@raspberrypi ~ 1 nohup sleep 300&
[1] 25874
cs130@raspberrypi ~ 2 nohup: ignoring input and appending output to 'nohup.out'

cs130@raspberrypi ~ 2 jobs
[1]+  Running                 nohup sleep 300 &
cs130@raspberrypi ~ 3 exit
exit
cs130@raspberrypi ~ 23 jobs
cs130@raspberrypi ~ 24 ps -ef | grep cs130 | grep sleep
cs130     25874     1  0 13:26 pts/0    00:00:00 sleep 300
cs130     25877 25696  0 13:27 pts/0    00:00:00 grep --color=auto sleep
cs130@raspberrypi ~ 25
```

While **top** provides a general snapshot of the system's status in a "real time", the **ps** is probably more suitable to hand-managing the processes. Let's see the example.

Suppose I have an active process:

sleep 300

On an active terminal, I can interrupt it with Ctrl-C. But if I am on another terminal, or if the process runs on the background, I cannot interrupt it like that.

> I cannot interrupt a background process with the Ctrl-C

What we'll do in such a case is this:

ps -ef | grep <your process>

Find out the process's ***id***, which is in the second column,

```
cs130@raspberrypi ~ 26 ps -ef | grep cs130 | grep sleep
cs130     25883 25696  0 13:28 pts/0    00:00:00 grep --color=auto sleep
cs130@raspberrypi ~ 27
```

And then

kill -9 <process id>

Number 9 is the numeric value for the ***SIGKILL***. As I said above, it is a signal to immediately terminate the process. It cannot be intercepted or ignored.

You may read the opinion that you should be cautious sending the ***SIGKILL***, because you may make a mistake sending it to the wrong process, and for that reason you should send the ***SIGTERM*** instead.

I don't think that is a solid argument. ***SIGTERM*** is also a terminating signal. Once you hit the <***enter***>, there is no undo, meaning you've sent the signal. So... You want to check if the process a well-behaved, or you want to terminate it? Sometimes you need to act, and you need to act quickly, leaving all arguments for a later. If you decide you need to kill the process... you have a signal to do that.

In my live classes I demonstrated how with the very simple script I can quickly bring a system to an unresponsive state. I will not provide this code here in the printed paper format. Instead, I will do other example, which, while is not ***that*** telling, still should give you some ideas about what I am saying:

```
cs130@raspberrypi ~ 4 for i in {1..100}; do sleep 300 &
> done
```

```
[105]   Running                 sleep 300 &
[106]   Running                 sleep 300 &
[107]   Running                 sleep 300 &
[108]   Running                 sleep 300 &
[109]-  Running                 sleep 300 &
[110]+  Running                 sleep 300 &
```

I launched hundred of jobs. Hmmm. Maybe I made a mistake. Can I... I mean, can I get rid of them before the ***root*** noticed anything? I certainly do not want to receive a communication from the ***root*** to that regard.

What are my options? To go one by one sending them to the foreground and Ctrl-C?

It is... It is a little too many for that. And the time is pressing.

We need to do it differently.

```
ps -ef | grep sleep | awk '{print $2}' | xargs kill -9
```

```
cs130@raspberrypi ~ 8 ps -ef | grep sleep | awk '{print $2}' | xargs kill -9
```

And we cleared it. Let's check the processes:

```
ps -ef | grep sleep | wc -l
```

```
cs130@raspberrypi ~ 8 ps -ef | grep sleep | wc -l
1
cs130@raspberrypi ~ 9 ps -ef | grep sleep
cs130      1448  1273  0 14:19 pts/1    00:00:00 grep --color=auto sleep
cs130@raspberrypi ~ 10
```

We see none of them. So, we cleared them. And we did that with just one command.

You could also use ***killall*** command:

killall sleep

Be careful here, because you are killing all such jobs; there may be legitimate jobs, they also will be killed. Because of that I think it is always better to kill processes by specifying the ***pid***.

But the point is, sometimes you need to move fast. Other time, before you kill a process, try to contact the user first and see what is that user doing. Because killing a process although may look like as a protection of the system, on the other hand may interrupt an important business process – for example database loading with lot of data at the end of month. So do it responsibly, because with the power comes responsibility.

But, as I mentioned, when user's action lead to the system becoming non-responsive, you may need to move fast first, and then discuss with the users their actions and approaches later.

1.2.1. Some system's resources.

Why the system may become unresponsive?

All systems have finite resources. It is just by the nature. If you have something in the hardware box, that box is finite. Thus, anything you can fit into that box (however large it can be) is finite.

> That's why you cannot fix program that leaks resources by upgrading the hardware. By so doing, you just extend the time before failure... Although... If all you care about is to be able to run that software for 24 hours, after which you can afford to reboot the system.... All the decisions are based on the particular situations.

To run processes, system needs to have available threads, and available process ***ID***s

We can check them with the command:

```
ulimit -a
```

```
cs130@raspberrypi ~ 10 ulimit -a
core file size          (blocks, -c) 0
data seg size           (kbytes, -d) unlimited
scheduling priority             (-e) 0
file size               (blocks, -f) unlimited
pending signals                 (-i) 7314
max locked memory       (kbytes, -l) 64
max memory size         (kbytes, -m) unlimited
open files                      (-n) 65536
pipe size            (512 bytes, -p) 8
POSIX message queues     (bytes, -q) 819200
real-time priority              (-r) 2
stack size              (kbytes, -s) 8192
cpu time               (seconds, -t) unlimited
max user processes              (-u) 7314
virtual memory          (kbytes, -v) unlimited
file locks                      (-x) unlimited
cs130@raspberrypi ~ 11
```

Which shows us quite some information, including number of open files, stack size, max number of user processes etc.

How many roads.... I mean... How many threads can one user have?

```
ulimit -u
```

```
cs130@raspberrypi ~ 11 ulimit -u
7314
cs130@raspberrypi ~ 12
```

What is the maximum number of processes can there be on the system?

```
cat /proc/sys/kernel/pid_max
```

```
cs130@raspberrypi ~ 12 cat /proc/sys/kernel/pid_max
32768
cs130@raspberrypi ~ 13
```

And threads?

```
cat /proc/sys/kernel/threads-max
```

```
cs130@raspberrypi ~ 13 cat /proc/sys/kernel/threads-max
14629
cs130@raspberrypi ~ 14
```

So. The resources are finite. And sometimes we need to act quickly and with resolve.

2. Continue with process management

We left our discussion that sometimes we need to move fast and kill number of processes in batch.

Let's return back to the killing process. We have these jobs:

```
sleep 300&
sleep 300&
sleep 300&
…....
hundreds of them.
```

Now let's go to the other terminal (we want to have two terminals open for this example), and do:

```
ps -ef | grep sleep | wc -l
```

```
cs130@raspberrypi ~ 2 ps -ef | grep sleep | wc -l
101
cs130@raspberrypi ~ 3
```

Let's look closely. And particularly, let's look at the third field, showing the process's parent ***PID***:

```
cs130@raspberrypi ~ 15 ps -ef | grep sleep | head
cs130       1463  1273  0 14:22 pts/1    00:00:00 sleep 300
cs130       1464  1273  0 14:22 pts/1    00:00:00 sleep 300
cs130       1465  1273  0 14:22 pts/1    00:00:00 sleep 300
cs130       1466  1273  0 14:22 pts/1    00:00:00 sleep 300
```

Looks like that all our processes are spawned from the same parent. So. Instead of killing all those individual jobs can we perhaps instantly kill them all by killing the parent's process? It would be the easiest thing, right? Looks like it is a good idea.

> I do not advise you to run the next example on your home computer. While it should not damage your system, the instructor is not liable for the consequences it may have on it if you chose to do so.

Let's get the parent's ***PID***, which is the number in the third column in that table, and do:

```
kill -9 <parent PID>
```

OOPS!!! We just killed our bash!!!. Not a good move.

Bash is a very resilient ***shell***. It is very hard to crash it, you really need to put an effort to do that. It withstands incorrect parsing of the parameters, special characters... it withstands many things that usually may crash the regular program. In all my career I probably managed to crash ***bash*** only one or two times. But you can. Here is one example. And when you do that, you have no options, but to close that terminal and to move to another one, because with ***bash*** killed... Well, we talked that the ***shell*** is your interface to the ***OS*** right? You just cannot do anything if you have no interface. You need to close that one and move to another session.

> And that is yet another reason why you want to have more than one terminals open at the same time... If you work in a multi-terminal environment, of course.

> And that is yet another reason why you work (and particularly run all these examples) as a regular user, not as a ***root.***

But what happens with those sleeps? Did they go away? Let's find that out.

```
ps -ef | grep sleep
```

```
cs130@raspberrypi ~ 3 ps -ef | grep sleep | head
cs130      1463     1  0 14:22 ?        00:00:00 sleep 300
cs130      1464     1  0 14:22 ?        00:00:00 sleep 300
cs130      1465     1  0 14:22 ?        00:00:00 sleep 300
cs130      1466     1  0 14:22 ?        00:00:00 sleep 300
```

No. They are still there. But look at their parent's ***PID***. It changed. Now it shows ***PID*** 1. That is an ***init*** 1's level (system's level) ***PID*** (we'll talk about ***init*** levels soon), and what happened, we just created the orphans. Orphans are the processes which parent was terminated without waiting for the child to exit. When that happens, child of such process is automatically moved to the system's level and now it is the system, that owns these processes. In case of other way around, if child exits while parent did not collect its status, the child becomes a zombie, and you can see such zombie processes with the **`top`** command. We should not worry too much about zombies, because eventually they should be gone, although they still have entries in the process table and theoretically can deplete the process' ***ID*** pool. But let's not worry about zombies. Let's see how to find out about orphans.

One possible way would be:

```
ps -ef | grep -v root | awk '$3 == “1”'
```

(Remember, the default action of ***awk*** is print, right?)

```
cs130@raspberrypi ~ 7 ps -ef | grep -v root | awk '$3 == "1"' | more
```

```
avahi         461      1  0 14:02 ?          00:00:00 avahi-daemon
message+      468      1  0 14:02 ?          00:00:00 /usr/bin/dbu
ion
nobody        540      1  0 14:02 ?          00:00:00 /usr/sbin/th
ocket --pidfile /var/run/thd.pid --user nobody /dev/input/ev
ntp           587      1  0 14:02 ?          00:00:00 /usr/sbin/nt
pi            640      1  0 14:02 ?          00:00:00 /lib/systemd
pi            792      1  0 14:02 ?          00:00:00 /usr/bin/dbu
pi            793      1  0 14:02 ?          00:00:00 /usr/bin/dbu
pi            806      1  0 14:02 ?          00:00:00 /usr/lib/gvf
pi            810      1  0 14:02 ?          00:00:00 /usr/lib/gvf
pi           1018      1  0 14:02 ?          00:00:00 /usr/bin/ssh
pi           1070      1  0 14:02 ?          00:00:00 /usr/lib/gvf
rtkit        1092      1  0 14:02 ?          00:00:00 /usr/lib/rtk
pi           1104      1  0 14:02 ?          00:00:00 /usr/lib/gvf
pi           1109      1  0 14:02 ?          00:00:00 /usr/lib/gvf
pi           1113      1  0 14:02 ?          00:00:00 /usr/lib/gvf
pi           1118      1  0 14:02 ?          00:00:00 /usr/lib/gvf
pi           1125      1  0 14:02 ?          00:00:00 /bin/sh /usr
pi           1129      1  0 14:02 ?          00:00:00 /usr/lib/men
pi           1135      1  0 14:02 ?          00:00:00 /usr/lib/gvf
cs130        1229      1  0 14:05 ?          00:00:00 /lib/systemd
cs130        1463      1  0 14:22 ?          00:00:00 sleep 300
cs130        1464      1  0 14:22 ?          00:00:00 sleep 300
cs130        1465      1  0 14:22 ?          00:00:00 sleep 300
```

We need to filter out the ***root's*** processes (***root*** runs its processes with the parent ***PID*** 1). Then we print only those, which parent's ***PID*** is 1. After that very carefully examine the result. After we made the first mistake like that, we don't want just go around terminating processes we don't know anything about.

So, what should we do to avoid mistakes like that? When we found out the parent's ***PID***, instead of going and terminate it, do one additional step:

```
ps -ef | grep <that process PID>
```

And you should see the line that says what the process it is. In our case if we did that, we would see, that this is a ***bash shell***. And at that point you would probably realize that what you wanted to do just a minute ago, may not be such a good idea after all.

We could also use another command, which gives you a visual tree structure:

```
pstree -anph
```

Where (-***h***) highlights your processes, (-***a***) gives you command line, (-***p***) shows ***PID,*** and (-***n***) sorts by the ***PID:***

```
|-sshd,542 -D
|   |-sshd,1224
|   |   `-sshd,1235
|   |       `-bash,1237
|   `-sshd,1571
|       `-sshd,1577
|           `-bash,1579
|               |-sleep,1823 300
|               |-sleep,1824 300
|               |-sleep,1825 300
|               |-sleep,1826 300
|               |-sleep,1827 300
```

And you would immediately see, that the parent is a ***bash***, which you don't want to kill.

Now, obviously you can kill only processes that you own. You cannot kill other users processes, or system processes, or ***root's*** processes. The ***root*** can obviously kill any process. I mentioned, that in my live classes I used to run some script to demonstrate the concept. In the situation like that, the ***root*** would probably kill that my script. After that, ***root*** would probably suspend my account until clarifying with my manager few questions regarding the legitimate use of the system.

3. Messaging

(Login as a (different) user(s) on two terminals, and switch to a *root* on one)

So. The ***root*** apparently caught me playing all these games with the system....

The root:

```
who -u
```

```
oot@raspberrypi:~# who -u
i        :0           2020-09-14 13:17   ?          646 (:0)
i        tty1         2020-09-14 13:17 01:16        764
s130     pts/0        2020-09-14 14:05 00:28       1224 (192.168.1.64)
s130     pts/1        2020-09-14 14:32   .         1944 (192.168.1.64)
s130     pts/2        2020-09-14 14:23 00:02       1571 (192.168.43.224)
```

(sees me, my *pts* (pseudo-terminal), time)

```
write <user>
```

(cannot write)

```
mesg
```

(check if can write)

It said that can not (that's by default, that's what you want)

```
mesg y
```

```
root@raspberrypi:~# mesg
is n
root@raspberrypi:~# mesg y
root@raspberrypi:~#
```

Now can write

```
write <user>
```

(The write prompt opens). Typing to the user:

```
"Hello, I hope you are fine. Can you please provide a little details as to what that script that you are running on the system? Thank you and have a good day."
```

Hitting <*enter*>, sending the *EOF*, and the user on his/her terminal receives the message from the ***root***:

```
cs130@raspberrypi ~ 1
Message from pi@raspberrypi on pts/1 at 15:56 ...
Mesg from root: What are you doing with the system, dude?
EOF
```

> Note that on this my raspberry, the message shown as coming out from the regular user. On different systems it may be shown as coming directly from the ***root***.

When you receive a message from the ***root***, you reply to it. And you want to reply fast.
User:

```
write root
```

And... It says that you cannot write to the ***root***, because... the ***root*** is not logged in!!!

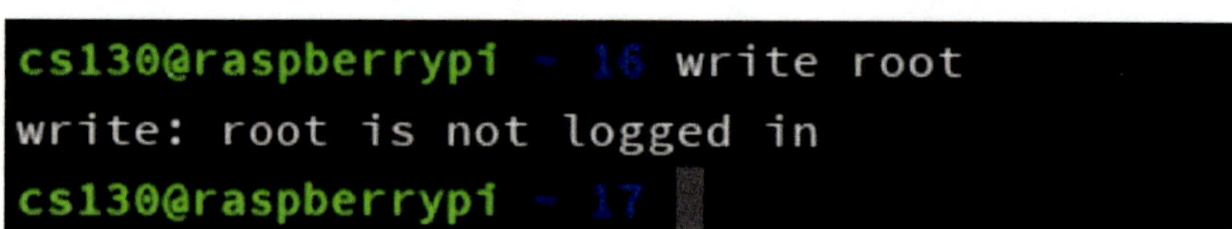

OK, for that particular raspberry, that is probably not very telling, but for the systems that show the message coming out of the ***root's*** account?.. That can be super confusing... Whereas the ***root*** is waiting.

> That is one of the several reasons you do not log in as a ***root***. At more than several occasions I told you to log in and do most of the work as a regular user, switching to the ***root*** only when necessary.
>
> So. Can you see the ***root***?.. But the ***root*** is there. 

But you received a message from the ***root***. And ***root*** is waiting for your reply. Patiently. And you don't want the ***root*** to wait for your reply for too long period of time.

Let's look again to the message we received:

```
cs130@raspberrypi ~ 1
Message from pi@raspberrypi on pts/1 at 15:56 ...
Mesg from root: What are you doing with the system, dude?
EOF
```

Look at the terminal (pts, *pseudo-terminal*) number on the message here

And reply back to that ***pts***:

```
cs130@raspberrypi ~ 1 mesg y
cs130@raspberrypi ~ 2 write pi pts/1
I need to run that script to save the world. Really important!
cs130@raspberrypi ~ 3
```

The ***root*** (after sending the message to us, immediately logging out):

```
root@raspberrypi:~# logout
cs130@raspberrypi ~ 2
Message from cs130@raspberrypi on pts/2 at 14:55 ...
I need to run this to save the world. Really important!
EOF
```

Root reads the message, and, satisfied, returns back to his regular activities: ~~Drinking tea/coffee and chatting with the friends.~~

Now. Let's look again at the first message, that we supposedly received from the ***root***.

```
cs130@raspberrypi ~ 1
Message from pi@raspberrypi on pts/1 at 15:56 ...
Mesg from root: What are you doing with the system, dude?
EOF
```

that

How can we know that it was indeed a ***root***, who sent it to us? We will not just trust to that part of the message in the blue box, will we?

No,we will not. But with messaging turned off (remember, we had to turn it on before sending a message to the ***root***): Like that

```
cs130@raspberrypi ~ 1 mesg y
cs130@raspberrypi ~ 2 write pi pts/1
I need to run that script to save the world. Really important!
cs130@raspberrypi ~ 3
```

.... With messaging, turned off, only the real ***root*** could send us the message. Thus, even without that preface we knew we needed to reply there – fast and convincing, exactly as we did.

Before we proceed, I cannot pass on the opportunity to just mention that that messaging system was in place long before all the now popular chats came around...

There is another command to send messages:

```
wall
```

That commands sends broadcast to all users on a system. And because of that and unless you are the ***root***, and have something very important to tell to the ***Urbi et Orbi***, you probably will never use it ... at all, although you may see the messages broadcast using that system... which we will see next.

4. Shutting down the system

Linux can run forever without noticeable degradation in performance. Still, you may want to shut it down. When you do, one thing you don't do is to shut it down by pulling the power cord. No system likes it, and the Linux is no exception. If your system runs GUI, you can click on that power button from the shutdown/logout menu. Otherwise you type the command at the root's prompt (you need to be a root to shutdown the system).

As you can expect, the command to shutdown the system is... ***shutdown*** . There are couple of options that you will use: **(*-h*)** to halt the system and **(*-r*)** to reboot it. Be careful with the ***-h*** option, because you will need a physical access to the box to power it back on. And that very well may not always be the case. Really! When you think "Linux", you probably think "the server". And when you think "the server", you may also think "a remote". It also may very well be that no one can readily physically locate the box... people may recall that it should be... errrr.... what was that data center on the East Coast.... we visited last year, do you remember?...

And that is not a joke. I've seen that before.

So, be careful halting down the system. Of course, if you run it from your laptop, that does not apply to you.

So, the command:

```
shutdown -h|r [<time> or "now"] "broadcast message"
```

Where the "broadcast message" is the message you provide to broadcast across the entire system.

You need to specify the time of shutdown, or type the word "now" for the immediate shutdown. When you choose that, the system will... immediately enter the shutdown, kicking everyone currently logged in without giving a chance to complete or save their work.

And, since we went from right to the left, the first argument on the left is flag, specifying whether you want it to halt, or to reboot.

Let's see. We will have two terminals. One for a regular user, and one for the ***root***. On his terminal the ***root*** enters the command:

```
shutdown -r 2 "rebooting in two minutes"
```

or

```
shutdown -h 5 "The system will be brought down in five minutes"
```

```
root@raspberrypi:~# shutdown -h 5 "System will be brought down in five minutes and I don't care"
Shutdown scheduled for Wed 2020-09-16 11:27:17 PDT, use 'shutdown -c' to cancel.
root@raspberrypi:~#
Broadcast message from root@raspberrypi (Wed 2020-09-16 11:22:18 PDT):

System will be brought down in five minutes and I don't care
The system is going down for power-off at Wed 2020-09-16 11:27:17 PDT!
```

When ***root*** enters that command, the broadcast message will appear on all open terminal windows, including the one for the ***root*** (no exceptions here). Thus, the same message will appear on the other terminal for the user:

```
cs130@raspberrypi ~ 2
Broadcast message from root@raspberrypi (Wed 2020-09-16 11:22:18 PDT):

System will be brought down in five minutes and I don't care
The system is going down for power-off at Wed 2020-09-16 11:27:17 PDT!
```

That message will be repeated regularly, and beginning from (I think) 5 minutes before the shutdown it will repeat every minute.

```
The system is going down for power-off at Wed 2020-09-16 11:27:17 PDT!
```

Since you can specify a time, you can schedule a shutdown well in advance. In that case the first message will appear to the user upon his/her log in.

Just because the ***root*** scheduled the shutdown, it does not necessarily mean that the shutdown will take place. Any time before the scheduled time the root can cancel it with:

```
shutdown -c
```

```
root@raspberrypi:~# shutdown -c

Broadcast message from root@raspberrypi (Wed 2020-09-16 11:24:08 PDT):

The system shutdown has been cancelled at Wed 2020-09-16 11:25:08 PDT!

root@raspberrypi:~#
```

And again, that the same message will be shown on all open terminals:

```
Broadcast message from root@raspberrypi (Wed 2020-09-16 11:24:08 PDT):

The system shutdown has been cancelled at Wed 2020-09-16 11:25:08 PDT!
```

As I mentioned, you can shutdown machine immediately:

```
shutdown -h now
```

In that case there is no need to supply broadcast message: No one would have a chance to read it anyways. Actually, you don't have to give the broadcast message on a scheduled shutdown either, it is optional, and is a courtesy to the users

So, next time you finish working on your laptop, you don't have to search for that logout menu. Just enter a command.

```
shutdown -h now
```

5. User management (removing or modifying user account)

When you install the system, there will be a ***root***, and there will be at least one regular user that you have to create. Even if you build system for yourself, you need to have a regular user. That again highlights my point I've been making all along. You do your routine work on a system as a regular user, switching to a ***root*** only when necessary.

Let's talk about how to manage existing users first. We will see how to add a new user in a bit. Obviously, you need to be a ***root*** to be able to do all that.

5. 1. Locking user's account.

There are several tools available to modify user's account, which you can use to lock the user out of system. Let's start with the simple one. We will lock user by modifying a password file in certain way. Previously we touched that subject already, so let's do this:

```
passwd -l <user>
```

```
root@raspberrypi:~# passwd -l cs130
passwd: password expiry information changed.
root@raspberrypi:~#
```

That changes entry in the ***/etc/shadow*** file by placing the '*' or '!' character at the beginning of user's password. From our prior discussion you probably remember the format of the shadow file. By adding a single character to the password field, all login attempts will be rendered invalid:

```
grep <user> /etc/shadow
```

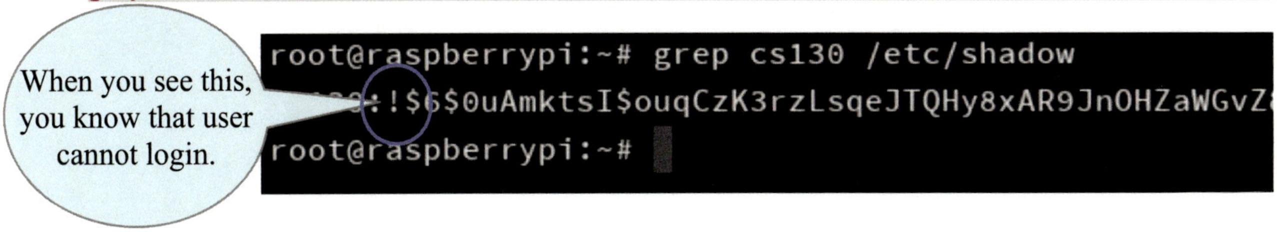

When you see this, you know that user cannot login.

```
root@raspberrypi:~# grep cs130 /etc/shadow
:!$6$0uAmktsI$ouqCzK3rzLsqeJTQHy8xAR9JnOHZaWGvZ
root@raspberrypi:~#
```

If user is currently on the system, the changes do not take effect immediately. In such case, the user still can be there and work there until user's authentications tokens need to be re-read. But if user logged out and wants to login back, the permission will be denied. We can quickly see it (no need to logout and login):

```
su - <user>
```

```
newuser@raspberrypi:~ $ su - cs130
Password:
su: Authentication failure
newuser@raspberrypi:~ $
```

Note, that no reason is given as for why. If you cannot login, you don't need to be provided with the reason.

To unlock the account:

```
passwd -u <user>
```

That removes the '!' character from the password field. Let's check the shadow file:

```
grep <user> /etc/shadow
```

```
root@raspberrypi:~# passwd -u cs130
passwd: password expiry information changed.
root@raspberrypi:~# grep cs130 /etc/shadow
cs130:$6$0uAmktsI$ouqCzK3rzLsqeJTQHy8xAR9JnOHZaWGvZ837Lvz5
root@raspberrypi:~#
```

...and we see that the password field is restored. Let's try from another terminal (where a different user is logged in. Remember, the ***root*** does not need a password to switch to any other user).

```
su - <user>
```

```
newuser@raspberrypi:~ $ su - cs130
Password:
cs130@raspberrypi ~ 1
```

...and now we can login. The **passwd** command is probably mostly known to be used to change the user's password. You can change your password with that command. The ***root*** can change password for any user, in which case a user name is provided as an argument. Here we used that command to lock/unlock the user's account by modifying the password.

Another way of locking user could be by using a command to modify user's account.

```
usermod --lock <username>
```

```
root@raspberrypi:~# usermod --lock cs130
root@raspberrypi:~# grep cs130 /etc/shadow
cs130:!$6$0uAmktsI$ouqCzK3rzLsqeJTQHy8xAR9JnOHZaWGvZ837Lvz5jFir
root@raspberrypi:~#
```

That also modifies the shadow file in the similar way, causing user not being able to login to the system.

There is yet another way. If you **grep** the */etc/passwd* file (the one where the passwords used to be stored) for your user name, you would see the ***path*** to your ***shell*** as a last entry on your line. That is needed to know which ***shell*** to be used. However, if you scroll through that file you'd see quite a number of accounts with the word ***nologin*** there.

```
grep nologin /etc/passwd
```

```
root@raspberrypi:~# grep nologin /etc/passwd
daemon:x:1:1:daemon:/usr/sbin:/usr/sbin/nologin
bin:x:2:2:bin:/bin:/usr/sbin/nologin
sys:x:3:3:sys:/dev:/usr/sbin/nologin
games:x:5:60:games:/usr/games:/usr/sbin/nologin
```

Remember our discussion about users on a system, that should not login? By risking to state the obvious, with ***nologin shell***, user cannot login to the ***shell.***

We can use that to disable the user's account by making it ***nologin*** with the command

```
usermod -s /usr/sbin/nologin <user>
```

```
root@raspberrypi:~# which nologin
/usr/sbin/nologin
root@raspberrypi:~# usermod -s /usr/sbin/nologin cs130
root@raspberrypi:~#
```

Note, that on your system the path to ***nologin*** may be different.

And if we check the ***passwd*** file:

```
grep <user> /etc/passwd
```

```
root@raspberrypi:~# grep cs130 /etc/passwd
cs130:x:1001:1001::/home/cs130:/usr/sbin/nologin
root@raspberrypi:~#
```

We should see the ***nologin*** for the user's account.

What happens if user tries to log in?.. It just can not.

To restore the account back, you would provide path to the real ***shell***:

```
usermod -s /bin/bash <user>
```

```
grep <user> /etc/passwd
```

```
root@raspberrypi:~# usermod -s /bin/bash cs130
root@raspberrypi:~# grep cs130 /etc/passwd
cs130:x:1001:1001::/home/cs130:/bin/bash
root@raspberrypi:~#
```

And we see that user's login ***shell*** is ***bash***.

So the user's control can be done with different mechanisms

We can also modify the user's account and set user's account to expire (in a future date, or in the past) by the command:

```
usermod -e yyyy-mm-dd <user>
```

If I run this command to set the expiration date, for example 2020-12-31 for the user ***cs130***, and if I look at the second to the last field in the ***shadow*** file, I'd see some number there. That number controls the expiration date:

```
root@raspberrypi:~# grep cs130 /etc/shadow | awk -F ':' '{print $(NF-1)}'
18627
root@raspberrypi:~#
```

I can remove the expiration date as well by providing an empty string for the above command, in which case that field will be cleared:

cleared

```
root@raspberrypi:~# usermod -e "" cs130
root@raspberrypi:~# grep cs130 /etc/shadow | awk -F ':' '{print $(NF-1)}'

root@raspberrypi:~#
```

Or, more visually:

```
5og0:18502:0:99999:7:::
j70y1:18521:0:99999:7:::
```

Finally, the ***root*** can completely remove the user's account:

```
userdel <user>
```

and if you also want to delete the user's home directory:

```
userdel -r <user>
```

```
root@raspberrypi:~# userdel newuser
root@raspberrypi:~# grep newuser /etc/passwd
root@raspberrypi:~# ls -l /home/
total 12
drwxr-xr-x  6 cs130 cs130 4096 Sep 15 16:58 cs130
drwxr-xr-x  2  1002  1002 4096 Sep 16 13:48 newuser
drwxr-xr-x 21 pi    pi    4096 Sep 14 13:17 pi
root@raspberrypi:~#
```

Note, that here I deleted the user, but still keep the home directory (with all the files). That's probably a prudent way to do, depending of course of the situations.

Just as before, the changes will not take place immediately. User can still stay on the system while no authentication tokens are needed to be read. User will not be able to log in, but the user will stay on the system. Because of that, you may want to force user out of system effective immediately.

Remember our discussion about whether you want to use ***SIGKILL*** or ***SIGTERM***? If you decided you need to forcefully remove user from the system, you probably do not want to think about that twice. So.

```
pkill -9 -u <user>
```

```
root@raspberrypi:~# pkill -9 -u newuser
root@raspberrypi:~#
```

That should kick user from the system immediately (by killing all the users' processes, which includes the ***bash*** session; so user just literally kicked out...)

```
newuser@raspberrypi:~ $ Connection to 192.168.1.1 closed by remote host.
Connection to 192.168.1.1 closed.
cs130@raspberrypi ~ 3
```

And then you can do

```
userdel <user>
```

Finally, I'll mention yet another tool to check or change the account login information for the user:

```
chage -l <user>
```

```
root@raspberrypi:~# chage -l cs130
Last password change                                    : Aug 28, 2020
Password expires                                        : never
Password inactive                                       : never
Account expires                                         : never
Minimum number of days between password change          : 0
Maximum number of days between password change          : 99999
Number of days of warning before password expires       : 7
root@raspberrypi:~#
```

5.2. Adding user.

Alright. We extensively reviewed how to disable user's account and how to remove user's account. But how to add a user's account? When you build a system, it asks you to add at least one regular user besides the root. But how to add a regular user to the existing system?

There are couple of tools for that. Let's start with the one that is often dubbed as a low-level utility because it leaves some of the steps to the manual processing.

Process of creating user's account involves few steps. The entries in the ***passwd***, ***shadow***, and ***group*** files are updated, the password is setup, and the home directory is created, and profile skeleton files are copied there.

Depending on the system the "low" level utility can do all the above steps except the password setup, or you may need to additionally create a home directory and copy the skeleton files there.

Why in that case use it still?

"Low level" also means it gives to you fine granularity control over the process, which may be particularly valuable if you do it in the script.

I will demonstrate the one, that does everything besides setting up password, because I also want to show you how to change a password.

It should not be a surprise, the command to add a user is:

```
useradd <user>
```

after that you should create a password for the user (although technically not required):

```
passwd <user>
```

That is the same command you use if you want to change your own password. In that case just type

```
passwd
```

Without giving user name.

Only ***root*** can change other user's password with the **passwd** ***<username>*** command. Regular user can only change his/her own password (that means typing it without ***<username>***. If you need to reset your password, the ***root*** will have to set a new one for you, which you then can change. We discussed, that the password is stored in one-way hash, there is no way to retrieve the plain text password from that file. But you will not bother the ***root*** with the forgotten passwords, right?

Back to the creating user. When the user is created with default options, the default login shell is assigned, and default home directory is created. We can change both these options.

To change the default home directory

```
useradd -d <dir> <user>
```

Other options: -u <user-id>, -g <group-id> or -G<group1, group2, ...>

-M creates user without home directory. In that case user will be logged to the root of the file system.

You can create temporary user by setting the expiration date – similarly how we modified an existing user by adding expiration date. We can do that when we create a new user with the (-e) flag.

We mentioned the skeleton files. These files are copied from the ***/etc/skel*** directory. Let's do

```
ls -la /etc/skel
```

And we see ***.bash*** profile files there which are used to create a basic skeleton profile.

```
root@raspberrypi:~# ls -la /etc/skel/
total 20
drwxr-xr-x   2 root root 4096 Jul  5  2017 .
drwxr-xr-x 111 root root 4096 Sep 16 11:19 ..
-rw-r--r--   1 root root  220 Jan 14  2017 .bash_logout
-rw-r--r--   1 root root 3512 Jul  5  2017 .bashrc
-rw-r--r--   1 root root  675 Jan 14  2017 .profile
root@raspberrypi:~#
```

That was a **useradd** , which we say (they say) is a pretty low-level utility. There is another, more integrated tool to add a user.

```
adduser <username>
```

It handles many of the jobs automatically, including adding a password.

Also you can use it to add new user to the group, including to the sudo group:

```
adduser <username> <group>
```

Finally we can create a user with no login shell, and user will not be able to login to the system with **-s /sbin/nologin** just as we did to modify the user above.

So... we have two utilities with very distinct names (***useradd*** and ***adduser***). If you do long listing of them, on some systems you may see that one is just a ***sym*** link to another. Apparently, they decided there is no sense to keep and maintain both of them, but for compatibility reasons they still provide an option to use and run both.
And now after that discussion, let's finally see how the other one works. The one, which is opposite to the "low level".

```
adduser <username>
```

```
root@raspberrypi:~# adduser newuser
Adding user `newuser' ...
Adding new group `newuser' (1002) ...
Adding new user `newuser' (1002) with group `newuser' ...
Creating home directory `/home/newuser' ...
Copying files from `/etc/skel' ...
```

Up to that point all steps are done automatically. Continuing with password setup. Here you need to type a password.

```
Enter new UNIX password:
Retype new UNIX password:
passwd: password updated successfully
Changing the user information for newuser
Enter the new value, or press ENTER for the default
        Full Name []:
        Room Number []:
        Work Phone []:
        Home Phone []:
        Other []:
Is the information correct? [Y/n] Y
root@raspberrypi:~#
```

Let's check the home directory for a new user:

```
root@raspberrypi:~# ls -l /home/
total 12
drwxr-xr-x  6 cs130   cs130   4096 Sep 15 16:58 cs130
drwxr-xr-x  2 newuser newuser 4096 Sep 15 20:07 newuser
drwxr-xr-x 21 pi      pi      4096 Sep 14 13:17 pi
root@raspberrypi:~#
```

Yes, it's there. Let's see the profile files:

```
root@raspberrypi:~# ls -la /home/newuser/
total 20
drwxr-xr-x 2 newuser newuser 4096 Sep 15 20:07 .
drwxr-xr-x 5 root    root    4096 Sep 15 20:07 ..
-rw-r--r-- 1 newuser newuser  220 Sep 15 20:07 .bash_logout
-rw-r--r-- 1 newuser newuser 3512 Sep 15 20:07 .bashrc
-rw-r--r-- 1 newuser newuser  675 Sep 15 20:07 .profile
root@raspberrypi:~#
```

Yes. So. This is how it works.

5.3. Adding user to the sudo list

The ***root*** has a complete and full ownership of the system. The job of the ***root*** is to be above all daily annoyances. Yet, there are times when people bug the ***root*** with some dull requests: they need to update this or that package, they need to install (system-wide) this or that software, they need to... they need to...

But... they can do that themselves. After all, they know what software they need, or packages they want, or configuration they would be happy with.

So, instead of annoying the ***root*** with something they could do, would not be it a good idea to delegate some power and authority to the users so they would be able to do this by their own?

Seems like a good idea. The ***root*** does not want to be distracted from ~~drinking coffee and chatting with friends~~ doing important job only root can do.

But how to do that?

To give them the ***root's*** password?

Absolutely not. You do not give your password to anyone. I mean ***anyone***. Your best friend, your manager, a President of the Galaxy...

None of them do have a business of knowing your password.

And also... as soon as you give out your password to anyone... It's just like giving out the keys from your house. As soon as you handled them to someone you do not know anymore where they were and what happened during that time... Was a copy made? Anything else?

So, you do not give the password to anyone.

But how in that case solve that problem of ***root*** not to be distracted from.... the important activities?

Is there a way to give to the user a ***root's*** privileges, without the ***root's*** logins?

Let's enable user to temporarily acquire the elevated privileges for a very short duration of time, and without ***root's*** credentials.

There are few configuration files that you do not edit directly, but through the special tools, that are intended to do a first level validation of your changes. Among those files is a **/etc/sudoers,** the file, that controls, who can stand together with the ***root***. That file has a read-only permission even for the ***root*** *(*but we know how to overwrite that restriction in ***vi)***. Anyways, it is not supposed to be edited directly. To edit that file, you use command (as a root):

```
visudo
```

Go to the end of the file (shift-G), then search backwards for the 'root' – you need to find a line that gives ***root's*** privileges to a … ***root*** .

```
# User privilege specification
root    ALL=(ALL:ALL) ALL
```

See that? that

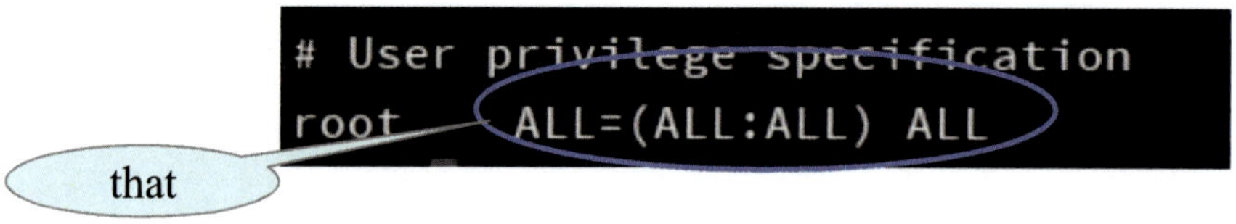

That's right. That's why the ***root*** has the ***root's*** privileges (that line probably specifies that ***root*** has ***ALL*** privileges). OK. Now what we'll do, we'll just copy that line, paste it immediately below and change it by replacing the ***root*** with the user name (We do not want to do much typing, especially here)

```
# User privilege specification
root    ALL=(ALL:ALL) ALL
cs130   ALL=(ALL:ALL) ALL
```

Save the file with **:w**, note that it first is saved to the temp file, and only then it is moved to the original.

Now as a user (on another terminal) try :

```
sudo whoami
```

```
cs130@raspberrypi ~ 2 whoami
cs130
cs130@raspberrypi ~ 3 sudo whoami

We trust you have received the usual lecture from the local System
Administrator. It usually boils down to these three things:

    #1) Respect the privacy of others.
    #2) Think before you type.
    #3) With great power comes great responsibility.

[sudo] password for cs130:
```

If you do **sudo** command for the first time, it will show you the time-honored message about your power and responsibility.

One of the three lines there reads:

```
Think before you type.
```

You always should know what you are doing!

Alright. You did **sudo**, and it asks you for ***your*** password. **I repeat, it will ask for *your* password, not the root's one!**

> If you are added to the ***sudoers*** list, your responsibility to keep your account secure and your password strong elevates radically. Because now your password can be a key to the entire system. You will probably be asked to sign few IT forms. Read them, understand them, and take them seriously.

Note, that in some systems changes may not take effect immediately; you may be required to re-authenticate yourself.

What happens if you try to do **sudo** while you are not on the ***sudoers*** list? Nothing special. You will just see that nice friendly message like below:

```
cs130@raspberrypi ~ 10 sudo whoami
cs130 is not in the sudoers file.  This incident will be reported.
cs130@raspberrypi ~ 11
```

… And, of course, the ***root*** will also see that....
But suppose everything is good and perfect. In which case you'd see the result of running your command as a ***root***:

```
cs130@raspberrypi ~ 9 sudo whoami

We trust you have received the usual lecture from the local System
Administrator. It usually boils down to these three things:

    #1) Respect the privacy of others.
    #2) Think before you type.
    #3) With great power comes great responsibility.

[sudo] password for cs130:
root
```

And you know, that you have a ***sudo*** privileges.

But it is not convenient to add each user to that file individually. Let's go back to the ***sudoers*** file and remove that user we just added. Now let's create a special ***sudo*** group. We will manage list of ***sudo*** users by managing the users in that group instead.

> Note, that on your system you may have a special group like "sudogroup" already built. You may see that group already in the ***sudoers*** file. But we will use that opportunity to see how to add a new group to the system.

```
groupadd sudoer
```

Check that the group exists:

```
tail /etc/group
```

```
root@raspberrypi:~# groupadd sudoer
root@raspberrypi:~# tail -2 /etc/group
newuser:x:1002:
sudoer:x:1003:
root@raspberrypi:~#
```

Do **visudo** again, go to the end of the file, and add that new group to the list with **%sudousers**

```
# Allow members of group sudo to execute any command
%sudo   ALL=(ALL:ALL) ALL
%sudoer ALL=(ALL:ALL) ALL
```

And again, we don't type all that ourselves. We copy and paste, changing only the group name.

Now let's add user to that group

```
usermod -aG sudoer <user>
```

```
root@raspberrypi:~# usermod -aG sudoer cs130
```

Let's check the users in the ***sudousers*** group:

```
cat /etc/group | awk -F ':' '$1~/sudo/ {print $4}'
```

```
root@raspberrypi:~# cat /etc/group | awk -F ':' '$1~/sudo/ {print $4}'
pi
cs130
root@raspberrypi:~#
```

Now switch to that user and do :

```
sudo whoami
```

```
cs130@raspberrypi ~ 2 sudo whoami
[sudo] password for cs130:
root
cs130@raspberrypi ~ 3
```

Good. Finally, to remove user from the group:

```
gpasswd -d <user> <group>
```

```
root@raspberrypi:~# gpasswd -d cs130 sudoer
Removing user cs130 from group sudoer
```

Again, the change may not take effect immediately. But when it does, we will again see that same friendly message:

```
cs130@raspberrypi ~ 10 sudo whoami
cs130 is not in the sudoers file.  This incident will be reported.
cs130@raspberrypi ~ 11
```

5.4. Couple important concluding points for this topic.

1. **Always know who you are on the system. It is usually thought that *sudo* allows you to run one command. However, there may be cases when *sudo* gives you a time slot. Before running a command following the *sudo*, it is a good idea to pause for a second and re-verify who are you before proceeding. Particularly be careful with this construct:**

```
sudo cmd1; cmd2
```

2. Note that the command:

```
sudo su -
```

Switches you to the *root* without asking for a *root* password, and probably without even

asking for *your* password. If you are on a *sudoers* list, do not step out of your workstation without locking it. Even for just a minute. We all know, that "even for just a minute" can turn out to be five or ten minutes or more. Sufficient time for someone to change the root's password.

6. Summary and review

Process management, user management, messaging.

Commands: top, ps, msg, write, kill, nice, useradd, adduser, passwd, usermod, sudo, groupadd, shutdown

Lecture 10. Some system utilities (contd). Init levels.

> *"The history of every major Galactic Civilization... pass through three distinct... phases..., otherwise known as the* ***How, Why, and Where****"*
>
> *Douglas Adams, The Restaurant at the End of the Universe.*

Those are good questions. But we'll rearrange them. Today we'll talk about "*Why*, *How*, and *Where*".

Today we will talk about the feature that.... I was about to say about the feature, that makes Linux Linux, but I realized, that everything we looked at so far can be attributed that way. Thus, I'll simply say, that today we will talk about Linux's ***init*** levels.

But since, as you already know, I cannot just jump into new subject, we will wrap up with some systems' utilities that we did not cover last time, because last time it was already a lot.

1. Wrapping up the review of system's utilities

1.1. Memory status.

Last time we talked about the **top** and **ps** tools. And we noticed, that both of them, although primarily made as a handle to the processes, also display some system information, for example, the status of the memory. Let's continue on that. We don't need anything fancy. If we want to check the status of the memory, there is a dedicated tool for that.

```
free
```

```
cs130@raspberrypi ~ $ free
             total       used       free     shared    buffers     cached
Mem:        945512     325644     619868      13772      65868     165540
-/+ buffers/cache:      94236     851276
Swap:       102396          0     102396
```

Similarly to the **top** and **ps** the **free** utility gives information about memory. It gives a breakdown so you can see a total memory, free, used in cache, etc. You can display a total with ***-t*** flag.

```
free -t
```

```
cs130@raspberrypi ~ 2 free -t
             total       used       free     shared    buffers     cached
Mem:        945512     565644     379868      25596     162816     179688
-/+ buffers/cache:     223140     722372
Swap:       102396          0     102396
Total:     1047908     565644     482264
```

The output format of that utility is very convenient if you want to use it in the script monitoring the memory status; you need to do much less work to parse its output, which is good (less work is always good).

- All these tools... they need to get the information about the memory status from somewhere, right
- Right. There is a file **/proc/meminfo** that you can query directly in case you may need it. It keeps the full information about the memory status.

```
cs130@raspberrypi ~ 3 cat /proc/meminfo | head
MemTotal:         945512 kB
MemFree:          619556 kB
MemAvailable:     797608 kB
Buffers:           65904 kB
Cached:           165540 kB
```

Since the system is a living thing, always busy with something, the content of that file is very dynamic, regularly updated. Let's run some experiment here.

First, let's take a snapshot of that file:

```
cat /proc/meminfo > meminfo.1
```

Now let me run some job on a system. Since I am a mere human, I will need some time, perhaps a minute or so to type the command and to correct all the numerous typos I'll make in the process. Let's determine what can give me that minute. Let me run this command:

```
cs130@raspberrypi ~ 9 date; for i in {1..1000000}; do echo "hi" > /dev/null; done; date
Sat Sep 19 04:35:32 PDT 2020
Sat Sep 19 04:36:33 PDT 2020
cs130@raspberrypi ~ 10
```

Looks like the million repetitions of simple word "hi" should give me the time I want. Note, that I did not use the `sleep`, which we used extensively. That's because I want system to do some actual work.

Now we are ready for our experiment.

I will repeat the same command (without time stamps), with the difference, I'll send the entire job to the background. I will need a terminal available. Of course we can do that on two terminals too, but since we know how to run jobs on the background, we have a power.

```
cs130@raspberrypi ~ 13 for i in {1..1000000}; do echo "hi" > /dev/null ; done &
[3] 3508
```

And then, soon after I started that job I enter this command.

```
cs130@raspberrypi ~ 14 sleep 15; cat /proc/meminfo > meminfo.2
cs130@raspberrypi ~ 15
```

The reason I want a slight delay is to give to my background's job a time to start utilizing the systems' resources.

When the second job completes (I don't need to wait for the completion of the first one), I will compare content of two files having memory snapshot data.

You need to find the difference between two files?

Run this command:

```
diff file1 file2
```

```
cs130@raspberrypi ~ 15 diff meminfo.1 meminfo.2 | more
```

And here is first few lines of the output, showing changes (the '*c*' character) on lines between 2 to 5:

```
2,5c2,5
< MemFree:          710032 kB
< MemAvailable:     806808 kB
< Buffers:           19532 kB
< Cached:           125624 kB
---
> MemFree:          519364 kB
> MemAvailable:     616304 kB
> Buffers:           19676 kB
> Cached:           125664 kB
```

On the top is the content of the first file, and the corresponding lines for the second file are at the bottom. We see, that amount of free memory decreased during running of our command, just as the amount of available memory. So, content of that file it is indeed a dynamic data.

And now since I touched the **/proc** directory, let's spend a minute talking about that.

1.2. The /proc file system

If we do

```
ls -l /proc
```

```
cs130@raspberrypi ~ 6 ls -l /proc | head
total 0
dr-xr-xr-x    8 root        root          0 Dec 31  1969 1
dr-xr-xr-x    8 root        root          0 Sep 17 16:17 10
dr-xr-xr-x    8 pi          pi            0 Sep 18 21:08 1001
dr-xr-xr-x    8 pi          pi            0 Sep 18 21:08 1013
dr-xr-xr-x    8 pi          pi            0 Sep 17 16:17 1016
```

we will see a number of directories and files there. We'll also see that almost all of the files have zero size. We'll also see directories with names as... numbers. That is a special file system, which sometimes called "*virtual*". Its purpose is to give interface to the kernel, and sometimes to change the kernel's parameters. Although you probably do not want to go directly and start editing files there...

Let's do :

```
sleep 300 &
```

```
cs130@raspberrypi ~ 7 sleep 300&
[1] 20148
```

and note the PID (20148)

Now:

```
ls -l /proc
```

and look for the directory with that number.

```
cs130@raspberrypi ~ 10 ls -l /proc/ | grep 20148
dr-xr-xr-x    8 cs130       cs130         0 Sep 18 21:13 20148
cs130@raspberrypi ~ 11
```

We should see, that there is a new directory in the **/proc** file system, which corresponds to that our PID.

Let's do

```
ls -l /proc/<PID>
```

to look what's inside that directory. We should see that there are number of files that have information about the process and its status. We see links to the command (**exe**), working directory (**cwd**), status, etc. In short (repeating myself), the entries in that directory give complete information about the process. There are quite a number of files there.

```
cs130@raspberrypi ~ 13 ls /proc/25689/
autogroup   comm             exe      latency    mountinfo   oom_adj        projid_map  smaps   syscall
auxv        coredump_filter  fd       limits     mounts      oom_score      root        stack   task
cgroup      cpuset           fdinfo   map_files  mountstats  oom_score_adj  sched       stat    timerslack_ns
clear_refs  cwd              gid_map  maps       net         pagemap        schedstat   statm   uid_map
cmdline     environ          io       mem        ns          personality    setgroups   status  wchan
cs130@raspberrypi ~ 14
```

(Note, that the PID has changed, because... in the process my sleep job completed and, along with that, the entire directory with that PID no longer exists on the */proc*. Therefore, I needed to start a new one.)

...So, you see, there are quite a few files there. Want to see what's in the ***exe*** ?

```
ls -l /proc/<PID>/exe
```

```
cs130@raspberrypi ~ 16 ls -l /proc/25689/exe
lrwxrwxrwx 1 cs130 cs130 0 Sep 22 16:21 /proc/25689/exe -> /bin/sleep
cs130@raspberrypi ~ 17
```

It is a link to the command we run! See another usage of the link? Very smart!

What else? What is that ***fd*** directory right next to the ***exe***? That name.... ***fd***.... kind of familiar.

```
ls -l /proc/<PID>/fd
```

```
cs130@raspberrypi ~ 15 ls -l /proc/25689/fd
total 0
lrwx------ 1 cs130 cs130 64 Sep 22 16:23 0 -> /dev/pts/0
lrwx------ 1 cs130 cs130 64 Sep 22 16:23 1 -> /dev/pts/0
lrwx------ 1 cs130 cs130 64 Sep 22 16:23 2 -> /dev/pts/0
```

… Looks like the file descriptors that point to the *pseudo-terminal*. To which *pseudo-terminal*?

```
tty
```

```
cs130@raspberrypi ~ 17 tty
/dev/pts/0
```

It's us! 

Really? Let's see.

```
cs130@raspberrypi ~ 18 sleep 300 2 > /dev/null &
[1] 26598
cs130@raspberrypi ~ 19 ls -l /proc/26598/fd
total 0
lrwx------ 1 cs130 cs130 64 Sep 22 16:46 0 -> /dev/pts/0
l-wx------ 1 cs130 cs130 64 Sep 22 16:46 1 -> /dev/null
lrwx------ 1 cs130 cs130 64 Sep 22 16:46 2 -> /dev/pts/0
cs130@raspberrypi ~ 20
```

– But... in the command we redirected the second file descriptor, and on the picture we see the number one which is redirected.... I am confused.

– Programmers are special people. They do everything differently from other people. Thus, they count things starting from zero. Therefore in their world, the ***second*** element has the count ***one.***

– I just cannot believe it. Everything in a Linux is a file?.. Alright, please no more discoveries. Can we do something less exciting? Please!

OK. Let's check the status of the process. It should be pretty dull.

```
less /proc/<PID>/status
```

```
cs130@raspberrypi ~ 12 less /proc/25689/status
```

```
Name:   sleep
Umask:  0022
State:  S (sleeping)
Tgid:   25689
Ngid:   0
Pid:    25689
PPid:   25625
TracerPid:      0
Uid:    1001    1001    1001    1001
Gid:    1001    1001    1001    1001
```

Looks like all our friends are there!

Now, it seems that some time passed while I've been doing all those screens. Let me repeat the last command:

```
less /proc/<PID>/status
```

```
cs130@raspberrypi ~ 12 ls -l /proc/20148/status
ls: cannot access /proc/20148/status: No such file or directory
[1]+  Done                    sleep 300
```

(Note the PID is different, I re-used the screen from the first one... The Linux people are... yes). And

```
cs130@raspberrypi ~ 13 ls -l /proc/ | grep 20148
cs130@raspberrypi ~ 14
```

As soon as job finishes, the entire directory is gone. That's what I said a half page above.

So, again, the process is described by the directory under the */**proc*** file system with the name of its PID. That's one of the reason, why the number of PID is finite, and why there should be PIDs available to start a new process.

1.3. A nice utility.

When we talked about the ***top***, we mentioned, that with that interface you can change the priority level of the process (obviously you should have sufficient rights for that). That is something called "*renice*" . We "*renice*" the process so it would give more priority to other (supposedly more important) processes.

But we also can "*renice*" the process using the ***nice*** utility.

nice - schedules or reschedules priority of the process. If you run your process from the schedule (for example from the *cron*), or you may run your job overnight, you know that your job may take a lot of time to complete, you may want to be nice to other people or processes, and schedule your process with lower priority:

```
nice -n <number> <your process command>
```

Numbers are in the range -20..20 with -20 is the highest and 20 is the lowest. Do not schedule the highest priority. Use ***nice*** only to lower priority, not to elevate it.

For the illustration, let's see the priorities and nice-ness level of first five jobs from the ***top*** monitor. We don't need all that *top's* header information, we can skip directly to the process table. To do that I will run ***top*** in a batch mode with just one iteration, and grep result for the first line in the table, with five lines following that header (flag -A + 5 for the grep):

```
cs130@raspberrypi ~ 16 top -b -n1 | grep -A +5 PID
  PID USER      PR  NI    VIRT    RES    SHR S  %CPU %MEM     TIME+ COMMAND
20881 cs130     20   0    5104   2340   2020 R  11.4  0.2   0:00.05 top
    1 root      20   0   22904   3984   2788 S   0.0  0.4   0:20.83 systemd
    2 root      20   0       0      0      0 S   0.0  0.0   0:00.09 kthreadd
    3 root      20   0       0      0      0 S   0.0  0.0   0:01.01 ksoftirqd/0
    5 root       0 -20       0      0      0 S   0.0  0.0   0:00.00 kworker/0:0H
cs130@raspberrypi ~ 17
```

We see one process ran by the root with the highest level of priority. And just for a comparison, here is all my processes on a system. They all run with the priority of 20 and nice-ness level of 0. And that is because I am such a nice person!

```
cs130@raspberrypi ~ 18 top -b -n1 -u cs130 | grep -A +10 PID
  PID USER      PR  NI    VIRT    RES    SHR S  %CPU %MEM     TIME+ COMMAND
20886 cs130     20   0    5104   2464   2140 R  11.5  0.3   0:00.05 top
19753 cs130     20   0    5116   3260   2860 S   0.0  0.3   0:00.03 systemd
19756 cs130     20   0   24332   1304     16 S   0.0  0.1   0:00.00 (sd-pam)
19759 cs130     20   0   12284   3636   2940 S   0.0  0.4   0:00.17 sshd
19761 cs130     20   0    6516   4644   2976 S   0.0  0.5   0:00.94 bash
20887 cs130     20   0    4272   1884   1756 S   0.0  0.2   0:00.00 grep
cs130@raspberrypi ~ 19
```

If you have a running process (which means that it has a ***pid***), and you want to re-nice it, you can do it by

```
renice -n <number> -p <pid>
```

And we know, how to get a pid of the process, (**ps** … | **grep** ….) or just ***pgrep<>*** or just ***pidof*** <>

Alright. Moving on to the next topic. It is a big one, but it is very interesting. I love it.

2. init levels in Linux

Let me recall the part in the first lecture where I said that you can run Linux in various modes: in graphical mode, and in terminal mode. When you run it in a terminal mode, you spare a lot of resources: CPU, memory, which you dedicate to the tasks, not to the graphical interface (which is very resource hungry). At several occasions I mentioned, that when you think "Linux", you probably think "server". And when you run system as a server, it is not very likely that you need to access it often or do some other work on it. You probably will dedicate it as that server. But in that case and if no one works there (or rarely works there), why would you want to waste the resources to run the GUI? Not productive.

So, you built the system, you configured it, installed your server, database, loaded with scripts, configured scripts, set the scheduling, now your server is ready. You put the box in some location in the corner, and you do not need to physically access it any more. All you really need is the network cable(s) and the power cord. That's it. No monitor, no mouse, no keyboard. So. What would be the last command you execute there before you disconnect all those devices?

> Disclaimer. I do not advise you to run the examples in this and following sections of this lecture on your home computer, unless it is a virtual machine that can be easily brought back to its original state. You can render system not bootable. *Instructor is not liable* for anything that can go wrong as result.

So. What would be that command?

> **The next command may not work on all distros. Again, I do not advise you running next examples.**

- **Alright. So. What would be that command?**

Your ***init*** schema may be different.

- ***What. Is. That. Command?!!*** 

```
init 3
```

You obviously need to be a root to do that.

You will see (but not from my screens, because I will not be able to really show that), that system logs you (and everyone else) out, and switches to the terminal-only mode. What if you want to restore the GUI back?

You will login to that terminal, and as a root type:

```
init 5
```

And it will start your familiar GUI (you will need to log in back again).

That's good. The only problem (as with many other examples we saw), that this setting only persists for the session. If you reboot the computer, it will start in the default configuration, and if that default configuration was an *init* level 5 (GUI), it will start that. You may say "not a big deal, we can always switch back to the *init* level 3". Yes, but why? What if system was rebooted overnight, or when you were on vacation in Yosemite?

Let's see how we can set the system to boot to the level we want to (say, *init* level 3).

But first, let's talk a little about all those *init* levels.

There are various ***init*** levels at which Linux runs. The one, which we used so far was level 5, which is multi-user, GUI mode. The one we switched to, the level 3, is also multi-user level, but runs in a terminal mode. There are other levels: level 1 is for a single user mode, which is what you use if you need to do maintenance on a system and don't want any other user to login during that time, some other are for multi-user without network file system, if you don't have a network, level 4 is not used, there is also level 0 and level 6. I need to mention, that in different distributions the levels designation may differ, but in general it follows the original design, which comes from Berkley Unix System V. The idea is very clever. Let's think about that – what defines an operating system? Collection of scripts, tools, and software that runs on a hardware. If I take a bundle of a scripts and tools and replace it with another bundle, I can get a different system. Replace windows components with the Linux components, and you have a Linux. The same is true for the levels that Linux runs on. What defines levels? Set of services, which are different on different levels. Remove some services, add another and you go from one level to another.

Lets draw a table to visualize all the *init* levels (again, different distros may have different schema, but the standard one is the following):

Level 0	shutdown
Level 1	single user mode no networking (for maintenance)
Level 2	multi user, no Network file system (we will talk about NFS very soon)
Level 3	full multi user mode, full network, no X server
Level 4	typically unused
Level 5	full multi user mode, full network, X server (X-11) – this is default mode, that you (probably) have on your computer
Level 6	reboot.

Today we will discuss two levels: level 3 and level 5. We already know, that the main difference between these levels is that level 5 runs GUI (X-server, X-windows, X-11 – you may see different designations). X server – is a Linux graphical interface.

So, when we did this command:

init 3

That stopped the X server on a machine and switched to the level 3. Note, that it is different from the **ctr-alt-backspace** command, that restarts X-server for an individual user.

Now the interesting question would be: How to find out what level I am running at? You may say "If you see a GUI, that's level 5, what's the problem?" Yes. But what if you are connected to the machine remotely? I repeat what I probably say every other lecture: "More likely than not, you will work with the Linux remotely". And in such case the situation becomes a little more interesting. Say you work on a remote machine and want to start some graphical application, say a browser. Or a graphical debugger. You can do that, if both your machines – the local and the remote ones run on a *init* level 5. How to find that out?

```
who -r
```

```
cs130@raspberrypi ~ 1 who -r
         run-level 5  2020-09-22 19:17
```

That will show the current level. And if that command shows *init* level 3... You probably may forget about starting those graphical tools.

So I mentioned levels 3 and level 5. What about level 0 and level 6? One is power off, and another is reboot. Thus, instead of using command that we did last time:

```
shutdown -r now
```

You could also use command

```
init 6
```

Which will reboot the system. Remember, there is always more than one way of doing things.

If you want to shutdown the system, you can do:

```
init 0
```

Unlike the **shutdown** command, which requires time argument, switching between run levels are instantaneous. When we power on the machine, we are back to the current default level.

Now let's talk about how to change the default ***init*** level so it would boot into there.

Since Berkley Unix System V the running level was defined in the file ***/etc/inittab***. More specifically, it was a small file, and there was just one line that defined running level, that system should boot into. So, if you wanted to change run level from 5 to 3, you would change one digit on one line in one file. Nothing could be easier.

I would guess, many... some distros still use that file from System V, but few years ago RedHat (what we have installed in the CS labs, and Raspberry, what I use for these lectures) switched to a different system. Just to make a point, that the system administration may not always be **that** easy, I'd guess.

If you open the ***/etc/inittab*** file under the RedHat, you will probably see the message that changes in that file no longer affect the run level. Nice. Not only that, they also provide an explanation what to do to switch run levels. Nice care about users. As for the Raspberry... They just removed that file entirely. That's what you do, when you disable something, right?

So, how to do that on a RedHat (I know, it works on a RedHat, but I'll do demonstrations on Raspberry)? Here is the command that the RedHat provides:

ln -sf /lib/systemd/system/<target name>.target /etc/systemd/system/default.target

But before we try that, first, let's take a look at the **/lib/systemd/system** directory – what are these ***runlevels***?

```
ls -l /lib/systemd/system/runlevel*
```

Let's do even better:

```
ls -l /lib/systemd/system/runlevel[0-9].target
```

```
cs130@raspberrypi ~ 1 ls -l /lib/systemd/system/runlevel[0-9].target
lrwxrwxrwx 1 root root 15 May  7  2017 /lib/systemd/system/runlevel0.target -> poweroff.target
lrwxrwxrwx 1 root root 13 May  7  2017 /lib/systemd/system/runlevel1.target -> rescue.target
lrwxrwxrwx 1 root root 17 May  7  2017 /lib/systemd/system/runlevel2.target -> multi-user.target
lrwxrwxrwx 1 root root 17 May  7  2017 /lib/systemd/system/runlevel3.target -> multi-user.target
lrwxrwxrwx 1 root root 17 May  7  2017 /lib/systemd/system/runlevel4.target -> multi-user.target
lrwxrwxrwx 1 root root 16 May  7  2017 /lib/systemd/system/runlevel5.target -> graphical.target
lrwxrwxrwx 1 root root 13 May  7  2017 /lib/systemd/system/runlevel6.target -> reboot.target
cs130@raspberrypi ~ 2
```

We should see that these are ***sym*** links, and each link specifies a run level. From their name we can gather that level 0 is power off, level 1 – is a single-mode rescue levels, 2 to 4 are multi-user terminal level, level 5 is a graphical level, and level 6 is reboot. That is the level the system enters to when the shutdown command is issued.

Now let's also check out the target (the level system boots into):

```
ls -l /etc/systemd/system/default.target
```

```
cs130@raspberrypi ~ 2 ls -l /etc/systemd/system/default.target
lrwxrwxrwx 1 root root 36 Jul  5  2017 /etc/systemd/system/default.target -> /lib/systemd/system/graphical.target
cs130@raspberrypi ~ 3
```

and we will see that the default target is a graphical target.

Thus, we need to make a link to a ***runlevel*** we want to, i.e. level 3, but they want to use ***name*** of the target instead of the number. We know how to make a ***symlinks***:

```
ln -sf /lib/systemd/system/multi-user.target /etc/systemd/system/default.target
```

Or, we can use a smart command for that:

```
systemctl set-default multi-user.target
```

```
root@raspberrypi:~# systemctl set-default multi-user.target
Removed symlink /etc/systemd/system/default.target.
Created symlink from /etc/systemd/system/default.target to /lib/systemd/system/multi-user.target.
root@raspberrypi:~#
```

(That's what you probably want to do on a Raspberry instead of `init 3`; but that will not take effect until reboot). Let's do `ls -l` again. We should see new link. Now let's reboot.

```
root@raspberrypi:~# ls -l /etc/systemd/system/default.target
lrwxrwxrwx 1 root root 37 Sep 22 20:45 /etc/systemd/system/default.target -> /lib/systemd/system/multi-user.target
root@raspberrypi:~#
```

```
shutdown -r now
```

```
root@raspberrypi:~# shutdown -r now
```

Let me refill my evening cup of tea in the meantime...

And if you log in from the box with the display and keyboard attached, you should notice, that login screen has changed. And you should also notice, that after the login you don't see any GUI. Just the terminal. But if you still need additional proof, you can always verify that with the command we already saw:

```
who -r
```

```
cs130@raspberrypi ~ 1 who -r
         run-level 3  2020-09-22 20:50
cs130@raspberrypi ~ 2
```

Now, let's take another look at those links.

```
ls -l /lib/systemd/system/runlevel[0-9].target
```

```
cs130@raspberrypi ~ 2 ls -l /lib/systemd/system/runlevel[0-9].target
lrwxrwxrwx 1 root root 15 May  7  2017 /lib/systemd/system/runlevel0.target -> poweroff.target
lrwxrwxrwx 1 root root 13 May  7  2017 /lib/systemd/system/runlevel1.target -> rescue.target
lrwxrwxrwx 1 root root 17 May  7  2017 /lib/systemd/system/runlevel2.target -> multi-user.target
lrwxrwxrwx 1 root root 17 May  7  2017 /lib/systemd/system/runlevel3.target -> multi-user.target
lrwxrwxrwx 1 root root 17 May  7  2017 /lib/systemd/system/runlevel4.target -> multi-user.target
lrwxrwxrwx 1 root root 16 May  7  2017 /lib/systemd/system/runlevel5.target -> graphical.target
lrwxrwxrwx 1 root root 13 May  7  2017 /lib/systemd/system/runlevel6.target -> reboot.target
```

This one

You see, the **named** entry is actually linked to the **number** level. Because it is difficult to remember the exact name (and also giving the ambiguity for the multi-user target), and is much easier (at least for me) to operate in the terms of run levels as numbers, let's try something different to restore back the graphical target. And this time we need a run level 5:

Ready? Let's type this line:

```
ln -sf /lib/systemd/system/runlevel5.target /etc/systemd/system/default.target
```

```
root@raspberrypi:~# ln -sf /lib/systemd/system/runlevel5.target /etc/systemd/system/default.target
```

Let's do ***ls*** on the link (always verify!):

```
ls -l /etc/systemd/system/default.target
```

```
root@raspberrypi:~# ls -l /etc/systemd/system/default.target
lrwxrwxrwx 1 root root 36 Sep 22 21:01 /etc/systemd/system/default.target -> /lib/systemd/system/runlevel5.target
root@raspberrypi:~#
```

We should see that the link is created. Now let's reboot:

```
shutdown -r now
```

By the way, since there is no X-server interface, we only can reboot it with the command as we don't have the graphical buttons. And we obviously do not want to use a hardware buttons to do a hard power off.

And... 

.... And it seems that we know how to make a ***symlinks*** because here we are, at the run level 5, which is graphical interface. But since I connect to the machine remotely from the client that does not support GUI at all, all I can do is to check the run level by running this command.

```
cs130@raspberrypi ~ 1 who -r
           run-level 5  2020-09-22 21:03
cs130@raspberrypi ~ 2
```

> As you can expect, probably 80% of all my typing in the above examples consisted of hitting the <***tab***> key. That is the best kept secret of a Linux's user.

– You told us that if the Linux runs remotely, there is no need for the X-server. Why would ***you*** run it at that level?
– Not exactly. Say, if that is a development machine, you may probably want to run it at level 5 to enable IDE (Integrated Development Environment), so that people could run graphical debuggers. Thus, it depends on what kind of server it is. As for me... I set that Raspberry to convert the old TV into the "smart" one. So I did need it to run the X-server.

> Again, I do not advise you to run all these examples on your home computer, unless it is a virtual machine that can be easily brought back to its original state. Your system may be different, there is too much typing, and cost of mistake as a root can be hefty. You can render system not bootable. *Instructor is not liable* for anything that can go wrong as result, and, as stated in the syllabus, *does not* provide any support of setting up the system.

3. Running scripts and services in different init levels.

If we only had a different *init* levels and nothing else, that would still be very cool. But the Linux did not stop there. If you may run the ***system*** on different *init* levels... perhaps you also may want to run different ***services*** depending on the *init* level your system is currently on?

And as I often say in the lectures, if you ask "Can I...", in the Linux the answer most likely would be "Yes...".

3.1. The *rc* directories.

Let's take another look at the */etc* directory, and specifically at the entries beginning with ***rc***

ls -ld /etc/rc*

(-d) flag for the **ls** command tells to list directories, not go inside them.

```
cs130@raspberrypi ~ 3 ls -ld /etc/rc*
drwxr-xr-x 2 root root 4096 Dec 25  2019 /etc/rc0.d
drwxr-xr-x 2 root root 4096 Dec 25  2019 /etc/rc1.d
drwxr-xr-x 2 root root 4096 Dec 25  2019 /etc/rc2.d
drwxr-xr-x 2 root root 4096 Dec 25  2019 /etc/rc3.d
drwxr-xr-x 2 root root 4096 Dec 25  2019 /etc/rc4.d
drwxr-xr-x 2 root root 4096 Dec 25  2019 /etc/rc5.d
drwxr-xr-x 2 root root 4096 Dec 25  2019 /etc/rc6.d
-rwxr-xr-x 1 root root  463 Dec 26  2019 /etc/rc.local
drwxr-xr-x 2 root root 4096 Jul  5  2017 /etc/rcS.d
```

Your listing may be different.

We see that there are few ***rc*** directories. If you notice similarity of numbers of the ***rc*** directories to the run level numbers, that is because there is direct correlation between them. In these directories you can place your scripts if you want them to start at certain run level. That is additional granularity – you can control what script started and stopped at what run level. Let's check first few lines of the ***rc*** entry in the run level 5.

```
ls -l /etc/rc.d/rc5.d
```

```
cs130@raspberrypi /etc 18 ls -l rc5.d/
total 4
-rw-r--r-- 1 root root 677 Apr  6  2015 README
lrwxrwxrwx 1 root root  18 Jul  5  2017 S01bootlogs -> ../init.d/bootlogs
lrwxrwxrwx 1 root root  16 Jul  5  2017 S01dhcpcd -> ../init.d/dhcpcd
lrwxrwxrwx 1 root root  14 Jul  5  2017 S01motd -> ../init.d/motd
lrwxrwxrwx 1 root root  17 Jul  5  2017 S01rsyslog -> ../init.d/rsyslog
```

There are quite a few scripts there. Actually, you will see that those are the **links**. And the actual physical files reside into the ***inti.d*** directory under the ***/etc***.

```
cs130@raspberrypi /etc 13 ls -ld /etc/init.d
drwxr-xr-x 2 root root 4096 Dec 25  2019 /etc/init.d
```

Do you remember our discussion about whether we should copy or move the files? Here is a great continuation of our that discussion.

Let's quickly check couple of things:

```
ls -l /etc/rc.d/rc5.d/ | wc -l
```

```
cs130@raspberrypi /etc 24 ls -l rc5.d/ | wc -l
21
```

```
ls -l /etc/rc.d/rc5.d/S* | wc -l
```

```
cs130@raspberrypi /etc 25 ls -l rc5.d/S* | wc -l
19
```

There are 21 lines in the directory that `wc -l` counts, but one is the "***total***", and another is the ***README*** file, which leaves to 19 links to the scripts. From the second screen we see, that the names of all those links start with the capital 'S'. Let's take a note of that.

Now let's do the same for the ***rc1.d***.

```
cs130@raspberrypi /etc 26 ls -l rc1.d/ | wc -l
17
cs130@raspberrypi /etc 27 ls -l rc1.d/S* | wc -l
4
```

Only four of such names. What's the others?

```
ls -l /etc/rc.d/rc1.d/ | awk '{print $9}' | perl -ne 'print "$1\n" if/([A-Z])\d/' \
| sort -u
```

(Note how I use a backslash to break the line: backslash-<enter>. I did not need to do that for the command, but I did it for better readability on the screen)

```
cs130@raspberrypi ~ 5 ls -l /etc/rc1.d/ | awk '{print $9}' | perl -ne 'print "$1\n" if /([A-Z])\d/' \
> | sort -u
K
S
cs130@raspberrypi ~ 6
```

This screen shows, that there are only two types of entries in the directory. One type starts with the capital 'S' (we already saw that), and another one starts from the capital 'K'. Both followed by the digit.

Let's see the full listing of that:

```
cs130@raspberrypi /etc 29 ls -l rc1.d/
total 4
lrwxrwxrwx 1 root root  20 Jul  5  2017 K01alsa-utils -> ../init.d/alsa-utils
lrwxrwxrwx 1 root root  22 Jul  5  2017 K01avahi-daemon -> ../init.d/avahi-daemon
lrwxrwxrwx 1 root root  19 Jul  5  2017 K01bluetooth -> ../init.d/bluetooth
lrwxrwxrwx 1 root root  16 Jul  5  2017 K01dhcpcd -> ../init.d/dhcpcd
lrwxrwxrwx 1 root root  22 Jul  5  2017 K01fake-hwclock -> ../init.d/fake-hwclock
lrwxrwxrwx 1 root root  25 Dec 25  2019 K01isc-dhcp-server -> ../init.d/isc-dhcp-server
lrwxrwxrwx 1 root root  17 Jul  5  2017 K01lightdm -> ../init.d/lightdm
lrwxrwxrwx 1 root root  22 Jul  5  2017 K01triggerhappy -> ../init.d/triggerhappy
lrwxrwxrwx 1 root root  17 Jul  5  2017 K03rsyslog -> ../init.d/rsyslog
lrwxrwxrwx 1 root root  20 Jul  5  2017 K05nfs-common -> ../init.d/nfs-common
lrwxrwxrwx 1 root root  17 Jul  5  2017 K05rpcbind -> ../init.d/rpcbind
-rw-r--r-- 1 root root 369 Apr  6  2015 README
lrwxrwxrwx 1 root root  18 Jul  5  2017 S01bootlogs -> ../init.d/bootlogs
lrwxrwxrwx 1 root root  19 Jul  5  2017 S01killprocs -> ../init.d/killprocs
lrwxrwxrwx 1 root root  14 Jul  5  2017 S01motd -> ../init.d/motd
lrwxrwxrwx 1 root root  16 Jul  5  2017 S02single -> ../init.d/single
cs130@raspberrypi /etc 30
```

First group of scripts ***S***tarts, when system enters that level. The second group of tools will be ***K***illed upon entering that level. That's how the Linux tunes which scripts or tools are run on which level.

What are these numbers that follow the 'S' and 'K' prefixes?

These are the order in which scripts/tools will be started or killed. The low the number is, the sooner in the process its fate will be executed.

Now, again, I want to return to the point that those are links to the */etc/**init.d*** entries, not the actual files. That is super convenient and smart. That allows me to have only one copy of a physical file with links to the different ***init*** levels. If I do not want to have that script in the *init* sequence, I will remove a link.

And as you may expect, you can place other (your) scripts there as well. If you want to add a script to the run level, do not put a copy of the file there. Put a **link** to that file. Do as they did: put a script into ***init.d*** directory, and make a link to the *runlevel* directory. If you do so, you will need to select the number in which order it will start. Do not select the low number, because not all services may start yet. Use some higher numbers within the range of the existing scripts. And make sure you test your script, because, if your script hangs, your system may hang on your script during the switching to the run level (essentially would not start). Bummer.

> You can also use a graphical tool to schedule services (if you are on the init 5 level). Go to **application > system > systems settings > start up and shut down > service manager** and you will see the system services that run on that level.
> Or go to **application > administration > service manager** where you can start and stop the services.

There is some issue with that, at least for some of the distros. I cannot setup services for the different levels. That essentially does not allow me to configure various levels in the graphical mode.... Did I say "Bummer" already?

So, let's see how we can add a new service to run automatically at the **init 5** level. Let's check if we have that services running:

ps -ef | grep mbd

And I don't show the screen, because there is no such service, which is not surprising for me, because I did not install it, to allow myself to run this demonstration.

I am a ***root***. I can go around and copy files. I found some script on one of the user's home location and copied it to the ***/etc/init.d*** directory.

> **You will *NOT* do that, right? You will *NOT* copy some random files to the important system's places just because you can.**

```
root@raspberrypi:~# cp /home/cs130/nmbd /etc/init.d/nmbd
```

Now, I will create a link in the ***rc5.d*** directory. I want that script to run on the level 5.

```
root@raspberrypi:/etc/rc5.d# ln -s ../init.d/nmbd S17nmbd
root@raspberrypi:/etc/rc5.d# ls -l *nmbd
lrwxrwxrwx 1 root root 14 Sep 23 20:18 S17nmbd -> ../init.d/nmbd
```

I used pretty high number chosen among the existing starting numbers. I am a nice person (we know that because the **top** showed that to us), and I will schedule my tools to start after most of the existing ones started. One note here. I created a ***symlink*** before running next command. If I did not do that, the system would still add the script, but will assign it a higher priority, which I did not want. Now system will accept my level of priority.

Alright..... when the sky was high and blue, and the grass was green and soft, that would be enough to have that my service to start when I enter that level. These days we need to do some additional work.

> Your distro and your installation will have it differently. I show it on my Raspberry.

update-rc.d <script_name> defaults

```
root@raspberrypi:/etc/rc5.d# update-rc.d nmbd defaults
insserv: warning: script 'K01nmbd' missing LSB tags and overrides
insserv: warning: script 'nmbd' missing LSB tags and overrides
root@raspberrypi:/etc/rc5.d#
```

I have couple of warnings because I did not write that script per rules; I did not register it with the system... per rules. I just copied it from some place (which I know and trust, but it is still the foreign place). But... it was just warnings, not errors. And that is good enough for me, because, right after that demonstration, the first thing I'll do after the closing the lecture file is to revert everything back.

But... I saw the ***K01nmbd*** file name, which I did not make. What was that about? Let's find out.

```
root@raspberrypi:/etc/rc5.d# find ../ -name K01nmbd
../rc0.d/K01nmbd
../rc1.d/K01nmbd
../rc6.d/K01nmbd
```

When I update the services, system automatically added the instructions to kill that my script in the shutdown/reboot level, and in the maintenance mode level. Nice. Note also, that it scheduled that my service to be terminated very early in the process (See that number 1?). Thus, when I have process to start late, it is scheduled to be terminated early. Makes sense. Good, system took care about some of my housekeeping tasks.

Now, what we have left to do, is to reboot and see if the service runs. The best demonstration here would be to switch the run levels, but that my Raspberry does not want to cooperate with me here, and only can switch the levels after the reboot. Oh, well. People on the RedHat should have better luck.

... And here we are, running my script, and we see, that it started from the place, where I put it.

```
cs130@raspberrypi ~ 1 ps -ef | grep mbd
root         998       1  0 20:22 ?        00:00:00 /etc/init.d/nmbd start
```

Thus, to summarize. You put a ***symlink*** into the ***rc*** directory corresponding to the run level you want script to run, and register that script with the system. Again, people on the RedHat will have it (the service to register it with the system) differently (and likewise on the other distros).

Alright. That was an involved discussion. In my live classes we used to proceed with adding custom scripts to run on the various *init* levels.... But I think we'll stop here today. With diverse distros/systems that we have, it will only make confusion worse. I will only say, that when writing your custom script that you want to register with the system (and, thus, managed by the system processes), it has to follow certain rules. For example, it has to respond to the systems' directives ***start***, ***stop***, ***restart***, and, optionally, ***status***), so that you could control it by these commands:

service <your service> start

Or

systemctl <your service> start

And that would be all that I'll say here about that.

And in the meanwhile I will run this command, to remove the demo service from my system:

update-rc.d <my script> remove

That takes care about that in all the ***rc.d*** directories where references to that had been added.

```
root@raspberrypi:/etc/rc5.d# update-rc.d nmbd remove
insserv: warning: script 'K01nmbd' missing LSB tags and overrides
insserv: warning: script 'nmbd' missing LSB tags and overrides
root@raspberrypi:/etc/rc5.d#
```

```
root@raspberrypi:/etc/rc5.d# ls -l *nmbd*
ls: cannot access *nmbd*: No such file or directory
```

```
root@raspberrypi:/etc/rc5.d# !498
find ../ -name K01nmbd
root@raspberrypi:/etc/rc5.d#
```

The only thing that I need to do manually, is to remove the physical file from the ***/etc/init.d***. That is logical, because I put it there manually myself.

4. Summary and review

/proc file system, memory status, *nice* levels, ***init*** levels, ***rc*** and ***init.d*** directories.

Commands: ***free, diff, pgrep, pidof, nice, systemctl, who, update-rc.d***

Lecture 11. Networking

> *The major difference between a thing that might go wrong and a thing that cannot possibly go wrong is that when a thing that cannot possibly go wrong goes wrong, it usually turns out to be impossible to... repair."*
>
> *Douglas Adams, Mostly Harmless.*

Luckily, we are not in the networking class. We don't need to study the network topology. We don't need to look down at the network schema trying to figure out why two networks do not want to talk to each other despite all the magic commands we send to them in a pseudo-random order... We will simply talk on how to configure a network card on a Linux. That's it. We will leave anything beyond that to that networking class.

One important note to remember, is that UNIX was initially built to live in the networking environment. Because of that, all networking functions and tools are built natively into the kernel, and it makes a great networking device, whether you want to have a general purpose machine, or a dedicated and specialized network unit.

When you install Linux, you have an option to configure network card manually, or let it be configured automatically. Whatever option you select, you can re-configure and manage the network interface later.

1. Brief overview of the networking

Let me first off, very briefly describe the networking environment. Again, this is not a networking course, nor it is a ***sysadmin*** course, so, very briefly and just to bring everyone to the same page:

You have a router/gateway/modem that connects to your service provider through what is now called "cloud", and when I was a student, it was "internet", but with the same drawings of cloud:

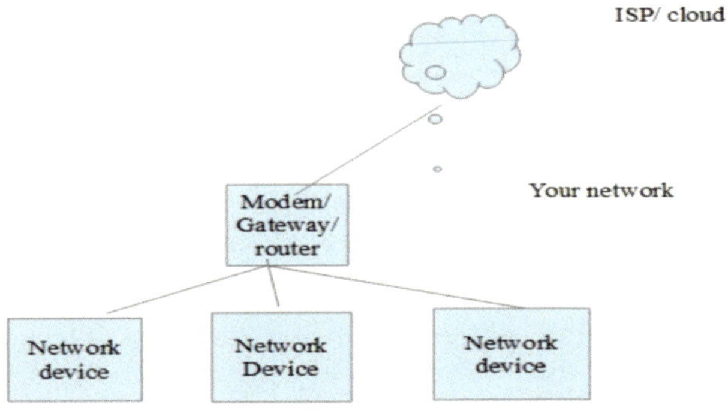

Job of a router is to determine and direct the network traffic, and also provide some firewall. Network devices are all identified by their internet protocol addresses or IP addresses. They have to be unique, otherwise we'll see an IP address collision errors on a network. Note, that we talk ***not*** about "computer" or "phone", or "TV". We talk about network devices. We all know that "computer" or "phone" or "TV" may have more than one network cards or IP addresses. Thus, a network device is something that has a network address, specific, and unique for the given network.

Currently there are two types of IP addresses: version 4 and version 6. Version 4 was introduced with the networking, and it has familiar four 8-bits format. It worked well, but people started raising concerns, that the humankind may run out of addresses if they continue using version 4 schema at the same rate, as it'd been.

Indeed. With 8-bits schema, example of which may look for a home (or small office) network like that:

192.168.0.x

each of its four sections can hold any number between 0 and 255. Thus, theoretically you can have 256 devices connected to your 192.168.0.x network. On practice, it will be less, because you will not use the highest and the lowest numbers, so the range would be:

192.168.0.1, 192.168.0.2, ... 192.168.0.254

You also need an address for the router/gateway.

> – That's bummer! So many addresses taken out of so few! 
>
> – You can also additionally subdivide your network into subnets, which will reduce the number of available addresses even further... But, on the other hand, *while you are inside your network domain*, you can move to the next (higher) bit to the left, and start adding more hosts:

192.168.1.x, 192.168.2.x, ... 192.168.254.x

Each of which will add you another (theoretical) 256 addresses. Thus, (theoretically) your small home or office network can handle 256 * 256 = 65536 network devices, which probably will allow you to accommodate your needs, and still have some few unused addresses spared for future expansion.

As far as theoretical capability of the IPv4 schema, the maximum number of IP addresses it can provide is around 4 billions (4,294,967,296). Of course, the real number is less, because there are unused and reserved addresses, but still, it is an impressive number. Nobody could imagine, that we would need more than that, but after 30-40 years of using the network, people started expressing different opinion. I remember papers, predicting the exact year and month when humankind runs out of address space and vividly picturing the total collapse and chaos on each and every field of economy as result of that. Interestingly, after 20 years, the version 4 is still well in use these days, and it looks like that the danger of all those gloomy scenarios was a little overstated.

1.2. IPV6

At the end of 1990th , the new version of IP protocol started being developed. It was to address problems with the previous version, mainly its "antiquated" address space. With its its 128-bits schema, the IPv6 protocol provides, what sometimes has been said, an unlimited capabilities in that regard.

As we know, when in CS we say "*unlimited*", we mean "*reasonably* unlimited". But still. The number of addresses the 128-bits schema can provide probably would be sufficient to colonize couple of planets in the Solar system, with few addresses still left for their moons (people, taking the Astronomy classes, don't take me on that...). It is indeed an impressive number. But then again... back into 80th, nobody could really think that the IPv4 address space could be exhausted either. So... let's wait for another 30-40 years.

Alright. We know how the IPv4 addresses look like. Let's take a look at the IPv6's one. Note that segments are separated by the colons. The segment may consist of all zeroes, or it may start with zero. In such case leading zeroes are omitted, and if there are all zeroes in two or more segments, they may be replaced with the double colon:

here

```
Link-local IPv6 Address . . . . . : fe80::          50e:c07e%12
```

Remember we did exercise to match the IP addresses? How would we write a ***RegEx*** to extract the IPv6 address?

ifconfig | egrep '([0-9a-f]{,4}:){5,7}'

```
$ ifconfig | egrep '([0-9a-f]{,4}:){5,7}'
        inet6 2600:380:4914:              5:8938  prefixlen 128  scopeid 0x0<global>
        inet6 fe80::              00:55  prefixlen 64  scopeid 0x20<link>
```

Why are there various length? That's how local and global links are shown. ...And in case you ask... I blackened out parts of the addresses not because I was too much concerned that they could be abused, but because I didn't want to give some people an impression that they could be.

But of course, you probably better keep your (global) IPv6 addresses private. We'll return to that later, and now let's proceed to our overview.

Besides an increased address space, what are the other advantages or enhancements of the IPV6?

- It is streamlined – increased efficiency. As an example of that, here is the picture, I borrowed from one of the site, discussing the IPv6 addressing, that was credited to Thierry Erhmann (Flickr) and used here for the educational purposes. It illustrates difference between traffic flow with broadcast (IPv4), and multicast (IPv6) schema. You see, how much less traffic is shown for the IPv6 on the left?

- Nodes can determine their addresses, that would be linked to their physical (***MAC*** address), and thus, more identifying on the network.
- Larger payload, better support for various protocols, more expansion capabilities.
- Better support for the mobile devices
- Each node can now have a unique address – both internal and external. No need for the network address translation (NAT*), network masquerading, which means... increased security and track back capabilities (that's probably was one of the big reason for that version**).

---

* "No need for the NAT". That also means, that you may not be able to build a complex network topology. In that regard I can mention, that none of the (big) organizations I used to work for until the end of second decade of this century, used the IPv6 schema for their internal networking.
** That is strictly my personal opinion, not all people may agree with that statement.

Now, it all looked good, but the companies and organizations did not really eagerly want to switch to the IPv6. Around year 2000 the government made a big push for that switch, but still. Not long before a year 2020 when I checked, the penetration of the IPv6 among the big companies in the US was around 12%. That seems to be a very modest rate of adoption of the new standard during the fifteen or so years, which raises a question: who really needed that, but that discussion is outside of this class.

Because of that modest rate of the adoption, most of the network devices now have to work in a dual stack mode, supporting both IPv4 and IPv6. Sometimes they need to implement an IPv6 by tunneling it through the IPv4, or IPv4 through IPv6, which does not add a nice touch to the picture.

How to find out if you operate on IPv6 or IPv4 protocol? There are number of online tools available for you to check, for example this one from google (https://ipv6test.google.com/) where you can test your network. Here is result of me running the test on my phone:

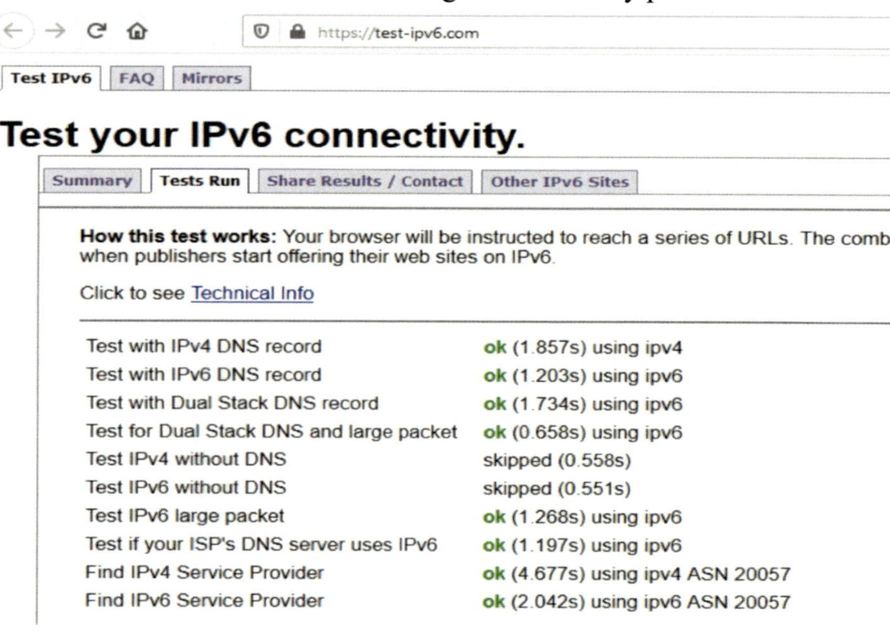

What's interesting, when I did the same test just few months earlier, it showed that my phone only operated on a IPv4 network... But. It's being migrated to. Even while I am writing this lecture, I see sites being migrated to the IPv6, so we can expect more and more global IPv6 addresses on the outside... whereas inside, the companies, at least some of them will still probably hold on the existing infrastructure and configuration, just perhaps out of simple consideration of how much investment had been accumulated into all of that.

Alright. It turned out to be not ***that*** brief introduction. We are in the Linux class, we will not talk about business decisions and rational, we will talk how to configure the IP addresses on Linux. We'll do that for both, IPv4, and IPv6.

– "How to configure the IP addresses"... That means they can be changed?
– Yes.
– And what about identifying device by the IP address then?
– "They can be changed"...

2. Configuring the IP addresses.

2.1. General considerations.

So, the device has to have an IP address. No matter what the protocol is, the IP address must be unique for each network device. Let's start with the IPv4.

When you assign an IP addresses, you have a choice to make it static or dynamic.(and in that case you need to have a DHCP server somewhere, probably it would be on your router). If you configure your network manually, it will be your job to ensure that there is no conflict of IP addresses. In many cases you probably may want to configure your devices with dynamic IP addresses. That way, when new device joins a network, it will be assigned an address from the existing and available pool. Yes, there is such thing as "caching of addresses", to make the job of DHCP server easier, but generally, IP addresses are reused from the available pool. That means, that next time you join the network, your IP address may be different, because your old one is used by someone else. In general, that is flexible and reasonable approach. Why would you need to hold the address if you are not on the network?

What about the static address and why is it needed?

There are cases, when you want to have the IP address to be assigned to the machine "permanently". That is most likely will be the cases for and with all sorts of servers. For the servers it is much more important to have a permanently assigned IP address than for the regular workstation.

And, as always there is more than one way to assign IP addresses. We will not talk about the GUI interface; we will not probably talk much about going and modifying files. We will do examples with couple of commands: The original, ***ifconfig*** (Well, I don't know if it is really an original, but it's been in place all the time I know it), and the newer one: the ***ip***. We will also do IPv4 and IPv6 address assignments. People on RedHat will need to substitute the network interface ***eth0,*** which I will mostly use for the demo with the (likely) ***p2p1***. Note, that ***ethX*** naming convention is probably more ubiquitous.

2.2. Configuring the IP address with ifconfig

When you install the system, you have an option to automatically determine and join the network. If your system is configured with the DHCP option, it will automatically join a network. Suppose it is not the case and you need to manually configure it. We will need to know some information. First, we need to know the network itself. (Let's not consider the subnets now). We also need to know the gateway, and (good to know, but not strictly necessary) the DNS – the Domain Name Server of our network. So we call our network administrator and kindly ask.

Few years back one friend of mine asked me to set his internet TV (to run directly through the ISP). Since I am a good citizen, I wanted to do it "right" way, so, with the TV's manual in front of me I called the ISP and started asking questions as instructed by that manual.... Hmmm. Few years back... The Russian's accent on the phone. Questions about the network...The answering person was not nice to me. Not at all. Not a bit. He was protecting his company's network. He defended it. Right.

So, he did not give me any of the information that TV's manual instructed me to obtain. Thus I said "thank you" and went an easy way then.

Suppose, as it was in my case, you don't have access to the router from where you can get most of the information you need to. But you don't really need it. All you need is to have at least some other device on the existing network. Let it be the Windows machine (which it was). Let's open Window's command prompt and type:

ipconfig

```
C:\Users\Vladimir>ipconfig
```

That will show the status of the network cards, attached to the computer. Find the correct card, and note the IP address of the gateway, associated with that. Here is how the part of output of ***ipconfig*** command looks on my home Windows machine:

```
IPv4 Address. . . . . . . . . . . : 192.168.43.121
Subnet Mask . . . . . . . . . . . : 255.255.255.0
Default Gateway . . . . . . . . . : fe80::               74:f5d
                                    192.168.43.1
```

We want to look at the last line. That is our network.

(You may see, that it is my home (small) network, because it starts with 192..... address.)

What you actually really need is the IP address of the gateway. Here on that screen it is on the last line. But it may not always be shown. Not a big deal, we already know the most important information: The network. And if we know the network, we can find out the gateway. We may do it few different ways. First, the gateways usually use either the lowest host address (1), or the highest one (254). We can just ***ping*** both these numbers and see where response comes from:

```
C:\Users\Vladimir>ping 192.168.43.254

Pinging 192.168.43.254 with 32 bytes of data:
Reply from 192.168.43.121: Destination host unreachable.
```

Not from there.

```
C:\Users\Vladimir>ping 192.168.43.1

Pinging 192.168.43.1 with 32 bytes of data:
Reply from 192.168.43.1: bytes=32 time=18ms TTL=64
```

Yes, from there.
But... Actually. We didn't need all of that guessing. Let's do better:

```
route print
```

And find the right entry (we already know the network from the previous screen):

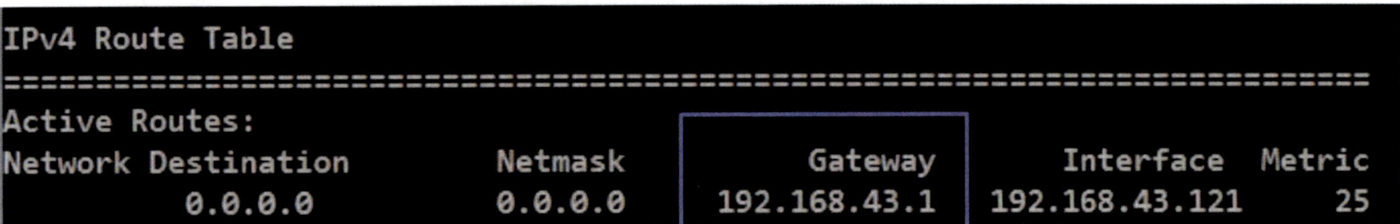

```
IPv4 Route Table
===========================================================================
Active Routes:
Network Destination        Netmask          Gateway       Interface  Metric
          0.0.0.0          0.0.0.0     192.168.43.1  192.168.43.121      25
```

That's what we need.

And... We are almost all done. We also need to know the DNS entry, but if we cannot get it from our network, no big deal. First, we can try to use the Gateway as a DNS. It should very likely work, because gateways often have that information. If not... There are plenty of free Domain Name Servers around, including one (or more) from the largest web search company (I will not give its IP address, it is very easy to look it up). One last thing you need is a network mask, but that is easy to figure out for a simple small network, I'll talk about that in a short while.

With that, you go to the GUI (on that TV setup screen) and fill in the corresponding boxes all that information. So... who won?

But that was a detour to explain where to get all the necessary information to join the network. Of course you will get it from your network admin, right? Now let's configure the Linux network card.

> For this lecture I will do demonstration using two Raspberries, one to be used for the network card changes, and the second one to probe (ping) that network card. How to distinguish between those two, given that I set them with the same host name? We will know which one is which by the ***mac*** addresses of their network cards.
>
> 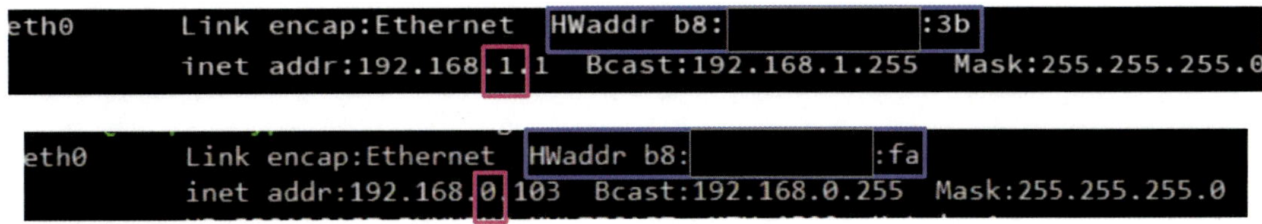
>
> ```
> eth0      Link encap:Ethernet  HWaddr b8:                :3b
>           inet addr:192.168.1.1  Bcast:192.168.1.255  Mask:255.255.255.0
>
> eth0      Link encap:Ethernet  HWaddr b8:                :fa
>           inet addr:192.168.0.103  Bcast:192.168.0.255  Mask:255.255.255.0
> ```
>
> Why ***mac*** address (Physical address of the network device)? You generally cannot make assumptions of the network

> device's identity based on the IP addresses or host names. Actually... the ***mac*** address is not something set in the stone either, but at least it is not ***that*** easy to change....
>
> For convenience, I will call the first Raspberry "*left*", because I connect to it from the terminal, that is on my left side, and the second one, "*right*", because, obviously it sits to the right of the first one on my desk.

Note that these two Raspberries are on different networks defined by the second to the last octet in the IP addresses of the network. Let's not talk about how they talk to each other, that's not in the scope. The bottom line for us now is that they can talk to each other as it is shown here:

```
cs130@raspberrypi ~ 1 ping 192.168.1.1
PING 192.168.1.1 (192.168.1.1) 56(84) bytes of data.
64 bytes from 192.168.1.1: icmp_req=1 ttl=63 time=2.36 ms
64 bytes from 192.168.1.1: icmp_req=2 ttl=63 time=1.36 ms
64 bytes from 192.168.1.1: icmp_req=3 ttl=63 time=1.42 ms
^C
--- 192.168.1.1 ping statistics ---
3 packets transmitted, 3 received, 0% packet loss, time 2003ms
```

Now let's go to the "left" Raspberry and type:

```
ifconfig eth0 192.168.1.20
```

That command sets the interface ***eth0*** to the IP address provided. Note, that there may be more than one interface attached to the computer, in which case they are numbered sequentially starting from zero (computer people start counting from zero). Same goes to the ***wlan*** interface, with the only difference, that its name would be ***wlan***, not the ***eth***.

Going back to the "right" Raspberry:

```
cs130@raspberrypi ~ 5 ping 192.168.1.20
PING 192.168.1.20 (192.168.1.20) 56(84) bytes of data.
64 bytes from 192.168.1.20: icmp_req=1 ttl=63 time=1.93 ms
64 bytes from 192.168.1.20: icmp_req=2 ttl=63 time=1.46 ms
64 bytes from 192.168.1.20: icmp_req=3 ttl=63 time=1.49 ms
^C
```

Good. Again, when I assign the IP address manually, it is my responsibility to ensure that there is no address collisions on the network, which means, there is no such IP address in use by any other devices.

The same **`ifconfig`** command without parameters gives me status of all active interfaces:

```
ifconfig
```

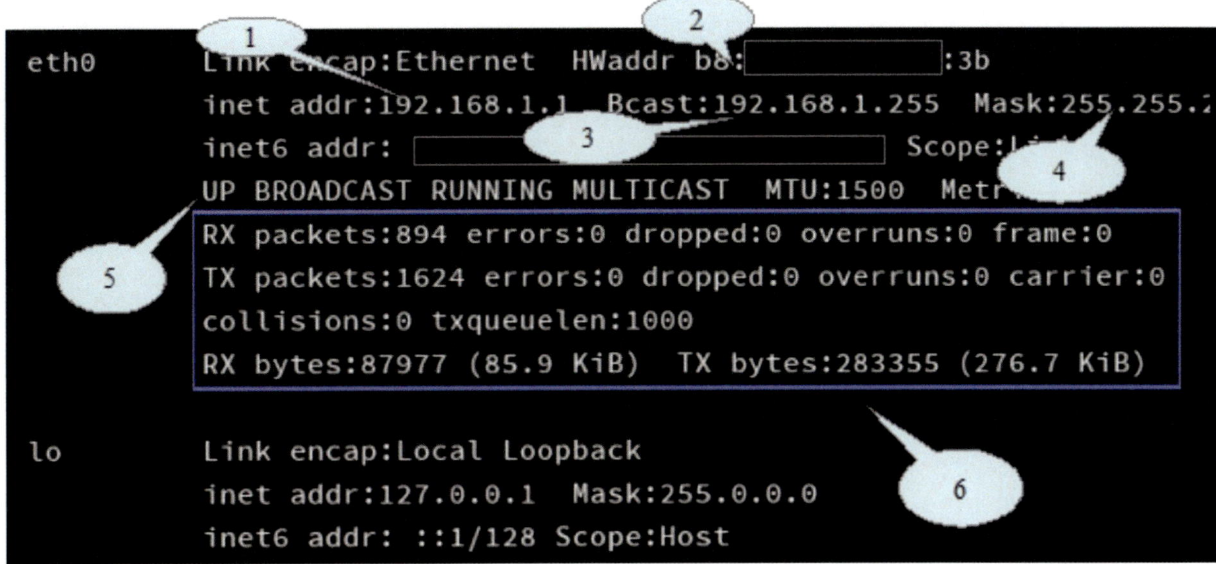

eth0 Link encap:Ethernet HWaddr :3b
inet addr:192.168.1.1 Bcast:192.168.1.255 Mask:255.255.
inet6 addr: Scope:
UP BROADCAST RUNNING MULTICAST MTU:1500
RX packets:894 errors:0 dropped:0 overruns:0 frame:0
TX packets:1624 errors:0 dropped:0 overruns:0 carrier:0
collisions:0 txqueuelen:1000
RX bytes:87977 (85.9 KiB) TX bytes:283355 (276.7 KiB)
lo Link encap:Local Loopback
inet addr:127.0.0.1 Mask:255.0.0.0
inet6 addr: ::1/128 Scope:Host
1
2
3
4
5
6

This screen shows the status of the interface before I changed the address. What we see here, is:

1. IP address.
2. The ***MAC*** address of the interface. That is an unique identifier of the device on the network.
3. Broadcast address (address of the network)
4. Network mask (which defines broadcast). For a simple small network (without subnets), as I have, it is usually 255.255.255.0 (i.e. broadcast goes to all 256 last nodes on the network).
5. This shows that the interface is active (we know that, because by default ***ifconfig*** shows only active interfaces, but still)
6. Some statistics

Note the interface at the bottom with the name "***lo***". That is a local *loopback* interface, and it is needed so that all internal processes could communicate to each other. You generally do not want to make changes there, and you do not want to bring it down. Note its IP address. That's what it usually is.

Thus we re-assigned the IP address within the same network. We can also join different network, in which case we would provide all the necessary parameters:

ifconfig <interface> <ip-address> netmask <255...> broadcast <...255>

And we will need to set a new gateway too.

We will not do that, because it will require a detour from our subject to make devices to see each other.

We can bring the interface down (***don't do it yet!***)

```
ifconfig eth0 down
```

And now our computer is not reachable for anyone through that interface.

Note, that it is different from completely shutting down the network services:

```
service network stop
```

(We can also do ***systemctl***).

But that will stop ***all*** the network services. If we had more than one network card, it will stop all of them, even facing internal network. It will also stop the ***lo*** interface. That may not be something you really want to, and you'll probably use that command to restart service to reload the configuration.

People who access their machines remotely (as I do), and who do not have physical access to them (not as I do):

```
You do not want to run these commands!
```

I will not run them either, but if I did, and tried to ping that address, the result would be the same, what we already saw few screens above: "*Destination host unreachable*".

That is very handy command in the situation where you want to quickly disable some particular interface. For example, you take the laptop with you to that corner coffee house, and the guy next to you looks... not nice. You don't know what he's been doing – browsing the web, or reading your files. And you do not want to guess.

What you do instead is this:

```
ifconfig wlan0 down
```

(assuming that ***wlan0*** is your wireless card interface).

After that you enjoy your coffee with biscuit looking at him with the straight face.

As I mentioned, if the interface is down, it will not be shown with the command:

```
ifconfig
```

To see them all, you'd do:

```
ifconfig -a
```

And you'll see that the interfaces that are not active, do not show the "***UP***" flag on their status.

How to bring the interface back up? As you may guess, it would be:

```
ifconfig eth0 up
```

And the service?

```
service network start
```

You may also need to restart the service in case you did some configuration changes and need them to take effect. In that case it would be:

```
service network restart
```

Remember in one of the previous lectures we talked about parameters that scripts registered with the system should respond to? That is an example of that.

2.3. The *ip link* and *ip address* commands

That was an old and faithful ***ifconfig***. It probably works in many if not all Linux distros, but there are also few other tools.

ip link is to set the device. As with any tool, you can get an online help (sometimes very brief and bare bone, sometimes very detailed and with the examples) by asking... for a help:

```
ip link help
```

There are many various options available to configure the device. Just to compare to what we did with ***ifconfig***, let's bring the device down (again, you may not want to do that; From my examples, looking at the interface's name, you may figure out, that I ran following commands on the CS's lab installation):

```
ip link set p2p1 down
```

and up

```
ip link set p2p1 up
```

and to see status

```
ip link
```

I will not show the screen, because it is analogous to the one from the `ifconfig`'s one and, since I am not on the CS lab's computer, I am too lazy to do all that censoring of the identifying information.

We can also see the status of the specific interface:

```
ip link show p2p1
```

To set the address (you may not want to do that):

```
ip addr add 192.168.56.20/24 dev p2p1
```

to see addresses:

```
ip addr list
```

And so on.

2.4. Assign the IPv6 address

Again, you may want ***not*** to do that. That is for the demonstration and information. I will not provide screens, because it is pretty much analogous to what we've already seen.

To see all information (both, IPv4 and IPv6 addresses):

```
ip addr
```

To see the IPv6 addresses only:

```
ip -6 addr
```

That pretty much filters out the non-IPv6 addresses from the above command.

These two commands are analogous to the:

ifconfig (to see all the addresses)

and

ifconfig | grep inet6 (to filter for the IPv6 only)

To assign IPv6 address, you need to have the ***iproute2*** tools installed. Also, the ***ipv6*** module has to be installed. Then, use the following command to add new IP address:

```
ip -f inet6 addr add 2001:5c0:9168::2/64 dev p2p1
```

How did I know that IP address? I copied the address shown for the ***p2p1*** device and changed couple of last digits. You did not expect me typing all that myself, did you?

Since I am changing the global link, I may need to add the default IP address:

```
ip -f inet6 ro add default via 2001:5c0:9168::1 dev p2p1
```

… but let's steer away from the routing tables.

Here is the screen from my raspberry (Yes, I know, I promised, but for the demo):

```
root@raspberrypi:~# ip -f inet6 addr add  fe80::d7          f:c37f/64 dev eth0.1
root@raspberrypi:~# ip -6 addr | grep eth0.1 -A +2
10: eth0.1@eth0: <BROADCAST,MULTICAST,UP,LOWER_UP> mtu 1500 state UP qlen 1000
    inet6 fe80::d7          f:c37f/64 scope link
       valid_lft forever preferred_lft forever
```

Note how I use the -A flag for the grep to print 2 lines following the match. That is a very handy option.

And finally, since I disclosed the complete v6 IP address (I am always willing to show ***their*** addresses), here is couple of general things of its composition, to explain to you which parts of ***my*** addresses and why I wanted to blacken out on all my screens:

The next screen is from the CS lab's VM; that's why I freely show it:

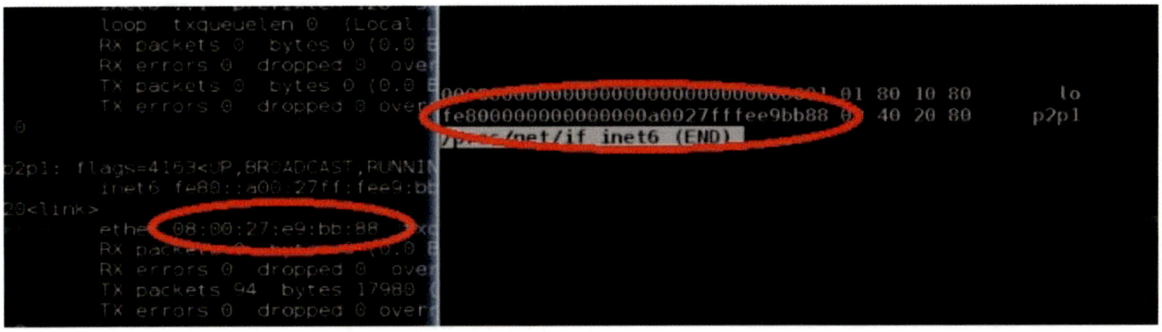

On the left is output of the **ifconfig** showing the physical address of the device (the ***MAC*** address). We already know, that it is a unique identifier of the device on the network. When you buy a new phone, they write down few things from the box. The ***MAC*** address is one of them.

On the right is IPv6 IP address in raw format from the ***/proc/net/if_inet6*** file.

You may see, that part of the v6 IP address includes part of the ***MAC*** address or based on them. And *that* was what I did not want to display for ***my*** addresses.

– What are all these ***fe80*** numbers that strangely seem to start the v6 IP addresses on all those screens, both from your machines and the CS labs' ones?
– These are the prefixes for the local links. They are the same. You may also see some other numbers, for example the 2001. Those are global prefixes (remember, the idea behind the IPv6 was to have a global addressing schema). Here is how these things look from my Windows machine:

```
IPv6 Address. . . . . . . . . . . : 2001:0:34
Link-local IPv6 Address . . . . . : fe80::c34
```

Alright. I think we can wrap up with that now.

– So. You advised not to change the IP addresses, but still you ran examples doing exactly that. Since I know that you, as a Linux user are... I mean you would not do that if you risked losing the connection, would you?
– No, I would not.
– Then... How did you do all that? And also... On the third screen above, I think I saw something strange. The interface name. It was not exactly the ***eth0*** as you told us all along... What was that?

3. Virtual interface.

In the introduction to this lecture I said:

...a network device is something that has a network address, specific, and unique for the given network.

That means, that the IP address has to bind uniquely to the network interface, i.e. it cannot bind to more than one interfaces. But the opposite is not required. There is no restriction, that the given interface has to have one and only one IP address assigned to it.

Sometimes you want to have a card with more than one IP address. There can be various use cases for that, you may want different networks connected to the same card, or you may have different services run for some particular address. So there can be valid cases to have more than one address for a device, and Linux supports that. Various distros may have various tools to do that. It could be as simple as copying and modifying couple of files, or adding an additional address through the GUI window, or running couple of commands on the terminal...

We will do that with couple of commands on the terminal. And since we started our discussion with the ***ifconfig***, let's continue with that.

```
root@raspberrypi:~# ifconfig eth0.1 192.168.1.20
root@raspberrypi:~#
```

That command creates a virtual interface and sets the IP address to that. Now I can see it:

```
root@raspberrypi:~# ifconfig eth0.1
eth0.1    Link encap:Ethernet  HWaddr b8                3b
          inet addr:192.168.1.20  Bcast:192.168.1.255  Mask:255.255.255.0
          inet6 addr: fe80::d                7b/64 Scope:Link
          UP BROADCAST RUNNING MULTICAST  MTU:1500  Metric:1
          RX packets:0 errors:0 dropped:0 overruns:0 frame:0
          TX packets:49 errors:0 dropped:0 overruns:0 carrier:0
          collisions:0 txqueuelen:1000
          RX bytes:0 (0.0 B)  TX bytes:9819 (9.5 KiB)
```

And if you recall my screens pinging that IP address, the responses were coming from that one. Thus, you see one of the usages of the virtual interface. I kept the original configuration to not to lose the connectivity, while I was able to run all those demonstrations. Pretty cool!

As you can expect, I am not limited by just one virtual interface. Let's add another one!

```
root@raspberrypi:~# ifconfig eth0:2 192.168.1.150
root@raspberrypi:~#
```

```
eth0:2    Link encap:Ethernet  HWaddr b8:              3b
          inet addr:192.168.1.150  Bcast:192.168.1.255  Mask:255.255.255.0
          UP BROADCAST RUNNING MULTICAST  MTU:1500  Metric:1
```

And if I did not censored out the ***mac*** addresses, you could see, that they are the same for all those virtual interfaces I so smartly created.

Alright, that was fun. Let's do the same with other tools. As you can expect, the newer tools require you to do more typing, which is good for keeping your fine dexterity in shape. But they also provide more functionality (if you need that). Let's start with simple things:

```
ip link add type veth
```

That will add a new virtual interface, numbered sequentially. You can see it with the

ip link or

ip addr list

commands.

Now let's assign an IP address to it:

```
ip addr add 192.168.1.201/24 dev <….>
```

Hmmm... we need to know a device. But we did not specify a device at time of creation. Not a big deal, we can look it up with the `ip link` command and then just plug it into the dotted part above.

But that was a good lesson. Next time we will specify a device at time of creation:

```
ip link add type veth peer name veth1
```

And if that was successful, we can assign the IP address using that peer name:

```
ip addr add 192.168.1.210/24 dev veth1
```

And we can ping it to see response. We can create a link to the non-existing device:

```
ip link add dev eth3 type veth peer name veth0
```

```
root@raspberrypi:~# ip link add dev eth3 type veth peer name veth0
```

Here I created an interface (virtual) named ***veth0*** (virtual interface) to ***eth3***. Let's assign an IP address to that.

```
ip addr add 192.168.1.150/24 dev veth0
```

And we can ping that as well.
Or we can link an existing device (***eth0***):

```
ip link add link eth0 type name veth3 type vlan id 10
```

And finally, we can use the virtual interface to bridge two networks, so we could ping it like that:

```
cs130@raspberrypi ~ 11 ping -c1 10.7.232.100
PING 10.7.232.100 (10.7.232.100) 56(84) bytes of data.
64 bytes from 10.7.232.100: icmp_req=1 ttl=63 time=1.45 ms

--- 10.7.232.100 ping statistics ---
1 packets transmitted, 1 received, 0% packet loss, time 0ms
rtt min/avg/max/mdev = 1.450/1.450/1.450/0.000 ms
cs130@raspberrypi ~ 12
```

Now, since we are not on the networking class, let me stop here and delete all those devices...

– Wait! You said you created a link to a non-existing device. What would be its ***MAC*** address?
– Good question. But let me defer myself on that one. Why don't you run the `ip link` command and see it for yourself?

```
I remind a rule and condition of this class: Do no harm, and the
instructor is not liable...
```

Now, let's stop here and let me delete all those devices...

```
ip link delete
```

No. Not like that.

```
for i in {0..3}; do ip link delete veth$i; done
```

Yes. That is better.

As always a good source of information is on the man pages of those commands.

4. Network configuration files

If you run the commands we discussed to show the status of the devices... How do you know which IP address assigned dynamically, and which one(s) statically?

And here, probably the easiest way would be to look at the configuration files. Different distros have different places to look at; let's perhaps use the one, probably mostly utilized. People on a RedHat should be able to see that.

Let's go to the ***/etc/sysconfig/network-scripts*** directory and look for the files starting with ***ifcfg***...

In theory, we should see the same suffixes as the network interfaces. But let's open the file ending with ***enp0s3*** (noting, that this is the name of the network card we would see on the network configuration window). If you are in doubt, you can grep that directory for the ***mac*** address of the device you are looking at.

That is the file that keeps all the configuration for that card. Let's note just couple of things.

At the beginning (or close to the beginning) you may see this line:

ONBOOTH=yes

That tells to bring the interface up at the time on start up.

The **BOOTPROTO** directive shows you whether the card is configured dynamically (**=dhcp)** or statically (**=static**, or 'none' as in the RedHad's guide)

If it is static, somewhere near that should be lines similar to that:

IPADDR=192.168.0.12
NETMASK=255.255.255.0

And also there will be an entry telling what is the gateway:

GATEWAY=192.168.0.254

So this is simple. Not a rocket science.

For the Raspberry you may want to look at couple of files: ***/etc/network/interfaces*** and ***/etc/dhcpd.conf***

We started our discussion mentioning that there is one piece of information that is good to know, but not strictly necessary. We talked about the Domain Name Server. Its job is to translate domain name (for example my.domain.com) into the IP address. Computers operate on numbers, not the names. They need to know all these dots and digits. And when human points its browser to the URL "idon.t.know.if.that.domain.exists.com", what internally and without telling us happens, that clever name gets translated to all those scrambled sequence of hexadecimal numbers broken by sections. The job of that translation is on the shoulders of the DNS.

5. The /etc/hosts file

When we configured the network, I said that the DNS entry is not that critical, we may be able to figure that out later. Suppose you listened to me and did not fill in that DNS entry. What would happen?

If we do

```
ping yahoo.com
```

it will reply that the host is unknown.

What can we do?

Let's ask our friend to run that command for us from his/her computer. We can promise something big and good in return. Say, not practicing the violin for half an hour in his/her presence. That would be a good price.

What we want to see is this:

```
C:\Users\Vladimir>ping yahoo.com

Pinging yahoo.com [98.137.11.163] with 32 bytes of data:
Reply from 98.137.11.163: bytes=32 time=89ms TTL=44
Reply from 98.137.11.163: bytes=32 time=104ms TTL=44
```

We want to see the IP address of the responding server. That's what we need to keep ourselves occupied for that half an hour that we so generously promised in return for the favor.

There is file ***/etc/hosts***. That file maps IP addresses to the host names... It maps the host name to the IP address... Yes, that's better. Host name to the IP address. It is useful if you want to create a local map of hosts without need to consulting a gateway, which sometimes may delay the response, especially if the gateways does not know about that host and relays the request up to the DNS chain. Let's open that file with your favorite ***vi*** editor and enter the line:

98.137.11.163 yahoo.com

Save the file, and do ***ping*** again (you may need to restart the network service to re-read the cached DNS table). And we should see the reply. Let's make a change to that file, just to make sure the response we see is indeed because of that file.

Let's change **yahoo.com** to **yahoo.net**. Save the file. Now

```
ping yahoo.net
```

And we should see reply, even though there is probably no real yahoo.net domain at least with the same IP address, as the yahoo.com.

```
cs130@raspberrypi ~ $ ping yahoo.net
PING yahoo.net (98.137.11.163) 56(84) bytes of data.
64 bytes from yahoo.net (98.137.11.163): icmp_seq=1 ttl=47 time=213 ms
64 bytes from yahoo.net (98.137.11.163): icmp_seq=2 ttl=47 time=123 ms
```

Now, it is interesting – if we ping yahoo.com, what happens? We may need to restart the network service to force to re-read the cached DNS table. But basically you will return to the square one, i.e. to the nice message telling you that the host is unknown.

What else the hosts file can be used for? Suppose you want to block some sites from being accessed from your machine, or you want to redirect traffic to some site to another site – for example showing your company's web access policy. The typical way of doing that would be through the router and firewall, but we can do it locally too. Let's open the ***hosts*** file again, and add this line:

```
127.0.0.1    yahoo.net
```

```
127.0.0.1        yahoo.net
```

(Supposedly, you want to redirect all requests to ***yahoo.net*** to the local web server running on your computer, that will show the page you want to). Save, quit, restart network service (if needed):

```
service network restart
```

and

```
ping yahoo.net
```

You should see that the ping comes from your local *loopback* interface, not from the yahoo.

```
cs130@raspberrypi ~ 2 ping yahoo.net
PING yahoo.net (127.0.0.1) 56(84) bytes of data.
64 bytes from localhost (127.0.0.1): icmp_seq=1 ttl=64 time=0.179 ms
64 bytes from localhost (127.0.0.1): icmp_seq=2 ttl=64 time=0.131 ms
64 bytes from localhost (127.0.0.1): icmp_seq=3 ttl=64 time=0.123 ms
```

And that affects all the network protocols on your machine, be it ***http***, ***ftp***, or anything else. Thus, if you open your browser and type in the URL field "***yahoo.net***", the browser will show your local page instead. If you had a web server running on your machine you would see exactly that.

There are quite some other usages of the ***hosts*** file. For example, if you search online, you may see some samples that close your computer to the unwanted visitors (list is quite long), and so on. Note, that I do not endorse them or otherwise advise you to use them. That is just for the information.

6. Routing tables

Very briefly. Routing tables are needed if you want to specify routing from one network to another. For example you want to connect from network A to network B, and you need to add to your router or your gateway information – how to connect, and through which node it should go.

Just to give you the idea, here is part of the routing table from my Windows machine:

```
IPv4 Route Table
===========================================================================
Active Routes:
Network Destination        Netmask          Gateway       Interface  Metric
          0.0.0.0          0.0.0.0    192.168.0.254   192.168.0.100     25
        127.0.0.0        255.0.0.0         On-link         127.0.0.1    306
        127.0.0.1  255.255.255.255         On-link         127.0.0.1    306
  127.255.255.255  255.255.255.255         On-link         127.0.0.1    306
      192.168.0.0    255.255.255.0         On-link     192.168.0.100    281
```

You should recognize some of the lines and fields there. The first line with the Gateway tells you that the destination (first column) is everything. Thus, my gateway allows me to connect to any other network..... hmmm... which would welcome my connection.

The command to see it is (surprise)

route

And for the Windows: **route print.**

7. Few commands to check network.

7.1. ping.

We already saw it here. Very useful if you need to quickly check if there is a route to the host. If you have problem with network, that would be the first command to use. If you cannot ping your gateway, provided the route is allowed – i.e. no firewalls are installed in between, that means that you need to check your basic settings. The network setup is pretty straightforward, and if you cannot ping gateway, that means there are some basic settings need to be reviewed.

7.2. traceroute

traceroute <host> (*tracert* on Windows. We know, there should be some difference between them, right?). That allows you to trace your route to the host, via intermediate nodes. Here is example of tracing route from my machine to yahoo.com. See how many ~~roads~~ nodes the poor packets have to travel through?

```
C:\Users\Vladimir>tracert yahoo.com

Tracing route to yahoo.com [98.137.11.164]
over a maximum of 30 hops:

  1    17 ms    18 ms    12 ms  192.168.0.254
  2    25 ms    18 ms    15 ms  192.168.1.1
  3    32 ms    24 ms    23 ms  192.168.43.1
  4     *        *        *     Request timed out.
  5   103 ms    73 ms    74 ms  107.72.231.164
  6     *        *        *     Request timed out.
  7    71 ms    63 ms    66 ms  12.83.179.49
  8   195 ms    62 ms    69 ms  ggr2.la2ca.ip.att.net [12.122.128.97]
  9   107 ms    52 ms    77 ms  las-bb1-link.telia.net [80.239.193.213]
 10   124 ms    75 ms    90 ms  sjo-b21-link.telia.net [62.115.116.40]
 11   119 ms    94 ms    94 ms  yahoo-ic-328472-sea-b2.c.telia.net [62.115.61.122]
 12   132 ms   104 ms    99 ms  UNKNOWN-216-115-97-X.yahoo.com [216.115.97.107]
 13   111 ms   103 ms   101 ms  et-0-0-0.msr2.gq1.yahoo.com [66.196.67.109]
 14   162 ms   117 ms   112 ms  et-19-1-0.clr1-a-gdc.gq1.yahoo.com [67.195.37.95]
 15   113 ms   100 ms    88 ms  lo0.fab5-2-gdc.gq1.yahoo.com [68.180.235.6]
 16   107 ms   128 ms   126 ms  lo0.fab7-1-gdc.gq2.yahoo.com [98.136.159.241]
 17   133 ms   103 ms   122 ms  usw2-1-lbc.gq2.yahoo.com [98.136.158.193]
 18   112 ms   108 ms   107 ms  media-router-fp73.prod.media.vip.gq1.yahoo.com [98.137.11.164]

Trace complete.
```

And here is the example of running the same (I mean, running the ***traceroute***) command from the Linux. If you want to run it in the IPv6 mode, use a (-6) flag (here I run it in default mode because with -6 flag the picture will be even smaller):

```
cs130@raspberrypi ~ 1 traceroute yahoo.com
traceroute to yahoo.com (74.6.143.26), 30 hops max, 60 byte packets
 1  192.168.43.1 (192.168.43.1)  3.879 ms  4.318 ms  4.449 ms
 2  * * *
 3  107.72.231.188 (107.72.231.188)  77.535 ms 107.72.231.164 (107.72.231.164)  77.280 ms  84.877 ms
 4  * * *
 5  12.83.179.49 (12.83.179.49)  89.829 ms  94.216 ms  95.341 ms
 6  ggr2.la2ca.ip.att.net (12.122.128.97)  89.322 ms  64.167 ms  65.925 ms
 7  las-bb1-link.telia.net (80.239.193.213)  64.012 ms  63.737 ms  65.397 ms
 8  rest-bb1-link.telia.net (62.115.137.36)  128.544 ms ash-bb2-link.telia.net (62.115.137.38)  126.338 ms  126.383 ms
 9  nyk-bb3-link.telia.net (62.115.141.245)  122.299 ms *  104.756 ms
10  buf-b1-link.telia.net (62.115.141.180)  110.559 ms  110.620 ms  109.299 ms
11  yahoo-ic-315726-buf-b1.c.telia.net (213.248.82.10)  109.003 ms  108.120 ms  116.407 ms
12  et-1-0-1.pat1.bfz.yahoo.com (72.30.223.5)  116.472 ms et-19-0-0.pat2.bfz.yahoo.com (216.115.97.105)  122.991 ms et-1-0-1.pat1.bfz.y
ahoo.com (72.30.223.5)  117.313 ms
13  et-18-0-1.msr2.bf2.yahoo.com (72.30.223.27)  111.122 ms  110.658 ms et-1-1-1.msr1.bf1.yahoo.com (74.6.227.135)  143.939 ms
14  et-0-1-0.clr2-a-gdc.bf2.yahoo.com (74.6.122.25)  143.509 ms et-18-0-0.clr2-a-gdc.bf2.yahoo.com (74.6.122.65)  98.185 ms et-19-0-0.c
lr2-a-gdc.bf2.yahoo.com (74.6.122.45)  110.496 ms
15  lo0.fab2-1-gdc.bf2.yahoo.com (74.6.123.243)  110.406 ms lo0.fab6-1-gdc.bf2.yahoo.com (74.6.123.239)  105.480 ms lo0.fab1-1-gdc.bf2.
yahoo.com (74.6.123.244)  116.036 ms
16  usw2-1-lbb.bf2.yahoo.com (74.6.98.139)  116.039 ms  115.977 ms  106.701 ms
17  media-router-fp74.prod.media.vip.bf1.yahoo.com (74.6.143.26)  106.248 ms  100.457 ms  110.362 ms
cs130@raspberrypi ~ 2
```

Not very readable at least for my eyes. But that's what we have the big screens for, right?

Or, depending on the installation you may have that option already set as a default:

```
$ traceroute yahoo.com
 1?: [LOCALHOST]                        0.025ms pmtu 1500
 1:  2600                                3f29          0.406ms
 1:  2600                                3f29          0.199ms
 2:  2600                                3f29          0.195ms pmtu 1430
 2:  2600                                             16.916ms
 3:  2600                                             82.852ms
 4:  no r
 5:  2600                                            104.818ms asymm  4
 6:  2600                                             89.364ms asymm  5
 7:  no r
 8:  2001                                            103.214ms asymm 10
 9:  no r
10:  2001                                            119.161ms
11:  no r
12:  et-7-1-0.pat2.sjc.yahoo.com                     93.037ms asymm 13
13:  ae-9.pat2.dnx.yahoo.com                          99.927ms
14:  ae-9.pat1.che.yahoo.com                         176.575ms asymm 16
15:  v6.ae9.pat2.bfz.yahoo.com                       243.174ms asymm 20
16:  2001:4998:f01b:5::1                             327.906ms asymm 20
17:  2001:4998:58:fc21::1                            342.930ms asymm 22
18:  2001:4998:124:fc03::1                           346.137ms asymm 22
19:  no reply
20:  no reply
21:  no reply
22:  no reply
23:  no reply
24:  no reply
25:  no reply
26:  no reply
27:  no reply
28:  no reply
29:  no reply
30:  no reply
     Too many hops: pmtu 1430
     Resume: pmtu 1430
$
```

7.3. whois

Remember our discussion about the spam on the email. We talked that first thing you never do is to never open that email, because by the fact you have that email, you know it is a fraudulent. And particularly, you know it did not come from the place it claimed to be.

But suppose you want to find out a little more information about the real origin of that email. I'll do that on the example of some email, I received from (supposedly) bank, which I saved into separate folder to be used for the demonstrations like the following.

So, you open the email and you need to look at the message's raw header and find the IP address or the domain name somewhere on the top of that header. Something like these:

these

```
X-Apparently-To: [                    ] Mon, 14 Mar 2016 22:50:01 +0000
Return-Path: <cwebst01@mail.uoguelph.ca>
Received-SPF: pass (domain of mail.uoguelph.ca designates 209.85.192.68 as permitted sender)
X-YMailISG: g4tMVIEWLDtvKSzHdWocaw7KpMPmcl7JSVMOdOtkO6I5pUUA
 d9nnxqpKuvopKScgFhW_8DQwifl7deV66mvIcOdZpRAKV1ILEUYnlRIenx.J
```

By looking at that domain name, you know, that the message did not come from your bank. Well, we knew that even before, but now we know where it really came from. Sometimes, though it would be not a domain name, but the IP address instead.

No problem. We'll return to that in a second, now let's do one more step. We want to know the registrar information for that domain. Why? Because it'll give us some useful information in case we want to press that case forward. These days you can find the tools necessary to do what we'll do next online, but luckily, we are on a Linux. So, we do this:

whois <that domain name>

```
cs130@raspberrypi ~ $ whois uoguelph.ca | more
```

And we should see the complete registrar information for that domain. Here is part of that:

```
Registrant Name: University of Guelph
Registrant Organization:
Registrant Street: 50 Stone Road East
Registrant City: Guelph
Registrant State/Province: ON
Registrant Postal Code: N1G2W1
Registrant Country: CA
Registrant Phone: +1.5198244120
```

No, it is definitely not a bank. There probably were some scripty happy kids, so let them have their fun. And we return to our discussion.

Suppose you did not have the domain name, but only the IP address. Or, suppose, your version of the ***whois*** does not handle the domain name, and, therefore we need to get the IP address first. No problem.

```
cs130@raspberrypi ~ $ ping -c1 uoguelph.ca
PING uoguelph.ca (131.104.93.93) 56(84) bytes of data.
^C
```

It does not matter whether we receive the response or not. We already have what we need – an IP address. We'll use that:

```
cs130@raspberrypi ~ $ whois 131.104.93.93 | more
```

And the reply is:

```
NetRange:       131.104.0.0 - 131.104.255.255
CIDR:           131.104.0.0/16
NetName:        UOGUELPH
NetHandle:      NET-131-104-0-0-1
Parent:         NET131 (NET-131-0-0-0-0)
NetType:        Direct Assignment
OriginAS:
Organization:   University of Guelph (UNIVER-279)
RegDate:        1988-11-04
Updated:        1998-12-22
```

Alright. The really last one for today. You want to see all these nice guys sharing your computer with you?

7.4. netstat

```
netstat | more
```

```
Active Internet connections (w/o servers)
Proto Recv-Q Send-Q Local Address           Foreign Address         State
tcp6       0      0 2600:38           091 2607:f8b0:4023:c06:5228 ESTABLISHED
udp        0      0 100.115.92.2:49260      lax31s12-in-f10.1:https ESTABLISHED
udp        0      0 100.115.92.2:50329      lax17s34-in-f10.1:https ESTABLISHED
udp        0      0 100.115.92.2:38208      lax17s05-in-f202.:https ESTABLISHED
udp6       0      0 2600:38           83 lax17s15-in-x0a.1:https ESTABLISHED
udp6       0      0 2600:38           80 lax30s04-in-x0a.1:https ESTABLISHED
udp6       0      0 2600:38           47 lax31s11-in-x0a.1:https ESTABLISHED
udp6       0      0 2600:38           08 lax17s05-in-x0a.1:https ESTABLISHED
udp6       0      0 2600:38           21 lax17s34-in-x0a.1:https ESTABLISHED
```

(See, I had to do censoring again, however I tried to avoid it at that time of the day.... I even did some examples on Windows ...)

And for comparison, here is what is going on on my internal device:

```
cs130@raspberrypi ~ 2 netstat | head
Active Internet connections (w/o servers)
Proto Recv-Q Send-Q Local Address           Foreign Address         State
tcp        0      0 raspberrypi:ssh         192.168.43.224:41073    ESTABLISHED
Active UNIX domain sockets (w/o servers)
```

And that would be really it for today.

8. Summary and review

```
Everything in this lecture is for educational purposes only. You
should do no harm based on the information you obtain in this or in
any other lectures of this course. Instructor is not liable nor
responsible for any of your actions based off this or any other
lectures of this course.
```

Linux networking, configuring the network cards, virtual interfaces.

Commands: ifconfig, ip, ping, traceroute, netstat

Lecture 12. Linux firewall.

"Computer?" hi hissed.
"Mmmm?" said the computer terminal...
"Is there someone on this ship?"
"Mmmmm" said the computer.

Douglas Adams, Life, The Universe And Everything.

We don't want anyone to be ~~on our ship~~ on our computer without our knowledge... That's why first thing you do before you go online, is to setup and configure a firewall. These days you may expect, that every new contemporary system comes with the firewall pre-installed. That was not so just some years ago. But not for the Linux. As we already know, the Linux was made to live on the network, and all the tools necessary for that were being built into the kernel, which makes them robust, efficient, and reliable. These days if you are on your home of office network, the firewall can be provided by the router. But what if not? I mean, if there is no router and you are wired to the larger network as a part of it (perhaps subnetting)? Or what if you want to create a subnet, or perhaps you want to generously spare a couple of addresses out of your busy 256 nodes to be used by your guests or visitors? Or, even as a good Samaritan you may want to provide a free wifi to your neighbors (or roommates)?

Many years ago, in the middle of night I got lost on a highway. I pulled into the shopping plaza of the nearest town I saw, and sure enough, there was a dentist's office... And sure enough there was a wifi there... And sure enough it was open...

You don't have an open wifi these days, do you? If you do, first thing you should do after reading this lecture is to set a password to it. That is not a full break proof, but at least that tells people that no, you don't want them there... And if you want much higher level of security, you would set your router to allow only devices with the certain ***mac*** addresses that you give to it. We already know the rational for that. And we know how to get those ***mac*** addresses.

Anyways, back to that night. Thank you, doc!

So. Suppose you want to setup a stand alone firewall for your network. And the Linux is an ideal platform to do that.

Let say you have some spare computer that has two network cards. You will need few things.

1. Obviously, you will need to have all packages installed; we will talk about software and package management later; but in most cases, the required packages should be installed by default. If you want to run a DHCP server (which you may or may not need, depending on your configuration), it may probably also be installed by default; just check the package composition during the installation. It should be included in the network packages.
2. Next, you will need two network cards. And if you are like me, you "save" all

spare parts from old computers before taking them to the e-waste station. Thus, in the lower right drawer among other things there are few network cards waiting to be (re)used... Therefore, you will have one card to be connected to the outside network (suppose it would be ***eth0*** device, which what usually it is). That card may be (and probably will be) configured to have a dynamic IP address assigned by your router/gateway, or directly by the ISP. The other card (usually, the ***eth1***) will be connected (through a switch or… a second router) to the internal network. It really does not matter what card faces what network. It could be other way around: ***eth1*** – ***eth0***. You can even have one of these cards wireless, in which case you dub that machine as an wifi extender.

You will need to enable IP masquerading (for the IPv4) and IP forwarding. That allows all the traffic from your internal network to go outside; and for the outside network it will appear as if it comes from one source – which is your linux box; so it will appear as it comes from the ***eth0*** card. As we talked in the previous lecture, with the IPv6 schema, there is no concern (… there is no immediate concern) about exhausting the address space in the nearest perhaps 30-40 years, so the first function is not really needed, but if you operate a small home or office network with the IPv4, it will be a consideration.

Let's start with IP forwarding. It is actually very easy to do.

echo "1" > /proc/sys/net/ipv4/ip_forward

The content of the ***ip_forward*** file is first thing to check if your internal network has no connectivity to the outside world. In many cases it can be as easy fix as to set it back to 1.

And now we are ready to setup our firewall.

1. Setting a firewall with iptables

If you decided to use a really old distro (or if you want to give it a second life), you may discover that the firewall there is implemented by ***ipchains.*** That one is ***really*** old tool. The only reason I mention it here is because if you have it running, it will interfere with the ***iptables***. These two tools cannot work together. But most likely you will not have such antiquated distro.

Newer firewall is implemented with ***iptables.*** If you noted that the plural form is used, it is not a coincidence. Every IP packet coming to your computer can be either an input, output, or passing through.

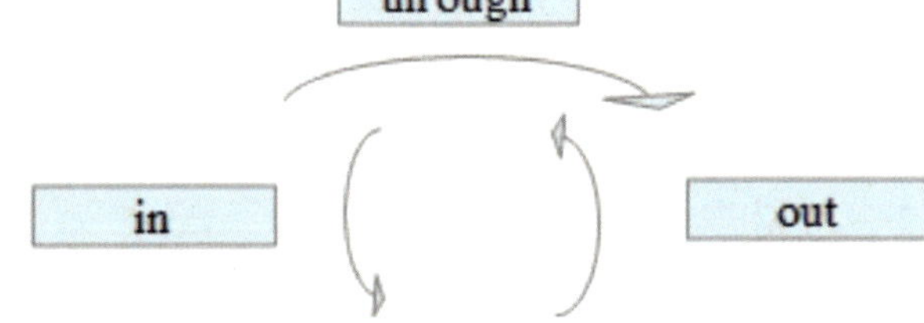

Thus, ***iptables*** have set of rules you establish for each of these three modes, or chains. There are ***INPUT*** chain of rules, ***OUTPUT*** chain of rules, and ***FORWARD*** chain of rules.

When the packet enters a chain, it enters a decision tree, which compares the property of the packet with the set of rules for that chain and decides whether the rule applies to the packet or not. Rules are probed sequentially, and as soon as the match is found, the corresponding rule will be applied; if no match is found, the default rule will kick in. People taking programming classes should be familiar with that concept (if-else or switch). Visually it can be represented like that:

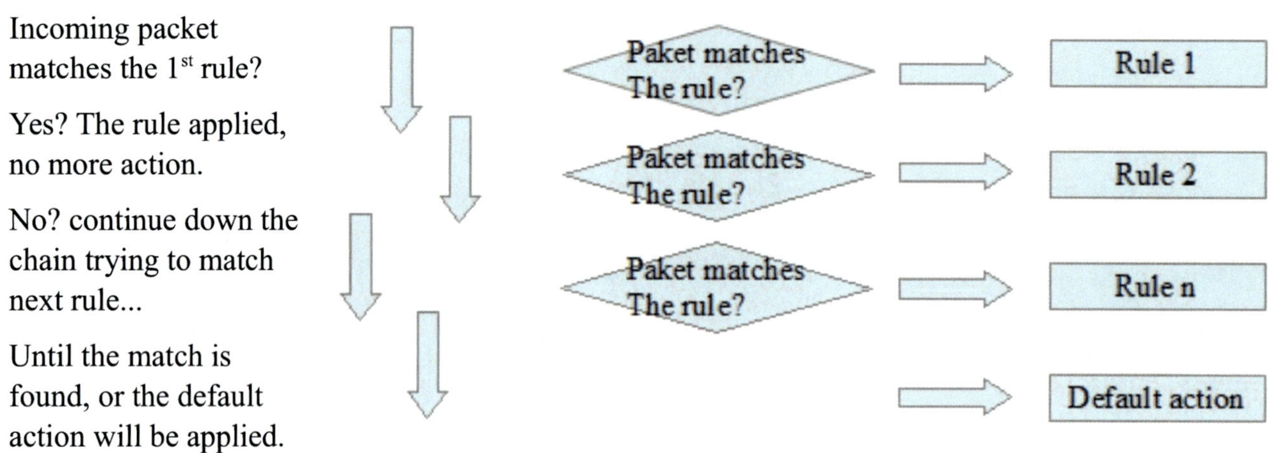

Because of that, there are two strategies of setting the firewall:

Permission-based model and restriction-based model. In the first one you list the conditions permitting packets to go through, and drop everything else. In the second model you list all those conditions that will restrict packets and allow everything else. Clearly, the first model is more secure; you don't need to be worried about some things that you forgot to restrict. The second model is very relaxed; it also requires you to specifically list every condition that you want to restrict, not forgetting even a single one. So again, the first model is preferable.

There are many options exist for the ***iptables.*** That makes the ***iptables*** very flexible and powerful, but on the other hand you need to memorize number of things. That is not a big deal however, since you will only probably need to setup the firewall once or once in a while, and you always can easily find a lot of good references, examples, and tutorials available online.

So, let's setup a simplest firewall. First, let's restrict all input traffic from a certain IP address (for simplicity, let's operate on the IPv4 model):

iptables -A INPUT -s 192.168.0.200 - j DROP

That tells to drop all the traffic coming from the source 192.168.0.200 without explaining the reason (-j

DROP). The source will not see anything; it will appear as the connection is lost. That is very good option. If you used the **BLOCK** switch, source would see message like "forbidden", and that message would indicate that there is a system there, which by itself may provide some useful information for people who want to see that information (and therefore we don't want them to see that information).

Now, I mentioned, that there are three chains in the ***iptables***: *INPUT*, *OUTPUT*, and *FORWARD*. You need to indicate which chain the rule should be applied to. In that case – it is an *INPUT* chain. With the (-A) flag you also say that you want to ***append*** the rule at the end of the chain. You can also insert the rule in any position in the table. For example

iptables -I INPUT 1 -s 192.168.0.200 - j DROP

would insert the rule into the first position of the *INPUT* chain, ***causing that rule to be evaluated first***.

What if you want to block ***your*** computer from connecting to that IP address? Change the *INPUT* to *OUTPUT* and change -s (source) flag to -d (destination)

iptables -A OUTPUT -d 192.168.0.200 -j DROP

Or, you may want to insert that rule into the first position of that chain as well (-I … 1). These two rules will block all traffic to and from the 192.168.0.200 address to your computer.

That is good. The problem is, as we discussed last week, the IP addresses can change and thus, the next time request from that computer comes in, it will look like it comes from different source. They also can be dynamically allocated and in such case, there is no guarantee, that another computer will not acquire that IP address and because of that will be restricted from accessing that network node. So, relying on an IP address is not very good strategy. Let me repeat, since it is important. When you rely on the IP address,

1. There is no guarantee you will block that same node on its next attempt (allowed due to failure of positive identification)
2. There is no guarantee you will not erroneously block different node because you mis-identify it to the one you actually wanted to block (denied due to false positive identification)

Last time I mentioned, that every network device has an unique ID, associated with that; which is the ***MAC*** address. Theoretically, that is not only unique, it is also identifying. If someone tells me that they identified some illegal activities coming out from my IP address, I would laugh at their face and tell them to take the CS130 class to begin with. If, however, they tell me that they linked that activity to my ***MAC*** address, I would take that much more seriously. Although not ***that*** seriously to lose the nighttime sleep perhaps. Because guess what – the ***MAC*** address can also be changed or (re)assigned.

So, it can be changed; but it still is much more reliable source than the IP addresses. Therefore, let's restrict traffic based on the ***mac*** address, not based on the IP address. Of course, you need to know the ***MAC*** address to do that. Which we suppose would be the case, because it is on your internal network, and it is you who are setting that network. So.

iptables -A INPUT -m mac --mac-source 08-00-27-E9-BB-88 -j DROP

You will need to have a ***mac address*** package installed. And in case you ask, that is the CS lab computer's ***MAC*** address, the same, that I used in the previous lecture too.

Anyways...

That drops all traffic from that computer. No. Not right. Let me try that again. *That drops all traffic from **that** network device.* That is the correct and accurate statement.

We can also restrict traffic based on the protocol, on the interface, we can close certain ports, and we can redirect traffic to another port, another computer, or another server.

iptables -A INPUT -p tcp -i eth0 --dport 22 -j ACCEPT

Here I opened incoming connection through the ***eth0*** network interface for the ***ssh*** using the ***tcp*** protocol. When I do this, in most cases I probably may also want to open the second protocol as well:

iptables -A INPUT -p udp -i eth0 --dport 22 -j ACCEPT

For a well-known ports, I also may say to use ***ssh*** instead of port 22 (i.e. verbose mode).

And if you cannot recall what is one of those well-known ports that you want to use verbosely, no big deal. Do ***less /etc/services*** and find that port there:

```
ftp             21/tcp
fsp             21/udp          fspd
ssh             22/tcp                          # SSH Remote Login
ssh             22/udp
telnet          23/tcp
smtp            25/tcp          mail
time            37/tcp          timserver
```

Or:

```
cs130@raspberrypi ~ $ egrep '^http' /etc/services
http            80/tcp          www             # WorldWideWeb HTTP
http            80/udp                          # HyperText Transfer Protocol
https           443/tcp                         # http protocol over TLS/SSL
https           443/udp
http-alt        8080/tcp        webcache        # WWW caching service
http-alt        8080/udp
```

Alright. So, we have these rules in our *INPUT* chain added to the queue. They are:

```
iptables -I INPUT 1 -s 192.168.0.200 - j DROP
iptables -A INPUT -m mac --mac-source 08-00-27-E9-BB-88 -j DROP
iptables -A INPUT -p tcp -i eth0 --dport 22 -j ACCEPT
```

Let's see what happens if user from the computer with **08-00-27-E9-BB-88** mac address tries to access my computer using the ***ssh***. The connection's request will hit the first rule that is based on the IP address. Suppose, that user changed that IP address and because of that was able to avoid detection. The packet goes down to the next rule that looks at the source's mac address. That matches. The rule triggers its action. The action is "**DROP**". Sorry, that's the end of the game, no further rules will be processed.

What if I wanted to allow an ***ssh*** connection, but still restrict anything else from that source?

I would need to move the rule allowing ***ssh*** connection up, perhaps even to the first place in the chain, and certainly above any other rules dealing with that source:

iptables -I INPUT 1 -p tcp -i eth0 --dport 22 -j ACCEPT

That way, when user from that computer tries connecting using the ***ssh***, the packet will hit the first rule that says "**ACCEPT**"; the ***iptables*** will accept connection and bail out of the decision tree, thus, no other rules for that source will be applied. If, however, user from that computer will want to access anything else besides ***ssh***, for example web, or mail server, the condition will fell through the first rule because it is not the ***ssh***, and will hit the next rule that says "*drop anything else from that source*".

ssh

not ssh

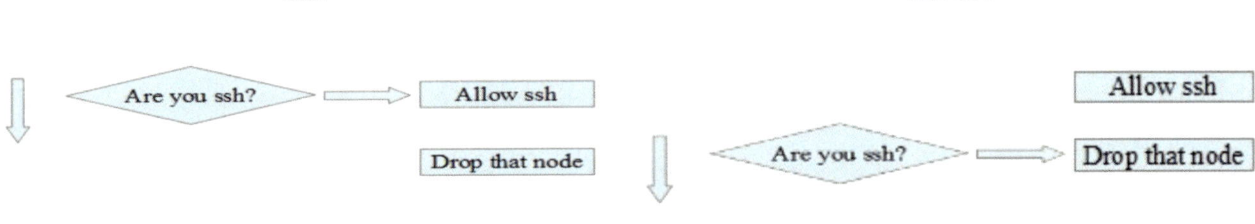

Thus, the order of the rules is important. It gives you much flexibility in setting out rules of access.

We mentioned the web traffic? If I want to open a web connection, I need to open port 80 for ***http.*** I can also open ***https*** port (443), 8080 (secondary), or any other custom port that could be needed should the web server be configured that way:

iptables -A INPUT -p tcp -i eth0 --dport 80 -j ACCEPT

And similarly, for the ***udp***.

Again, for the well-known ports, you may use names instead of number. Thus, for the ***http*** connection, you can use ***"www"*** instead of number 80.

What if I wanted to allow services that use several ports (for example ***NFS***?) or if I wanted to allow many different services? It would be too tedious to use a separate line for each of them. I can do this:

iptables -A INPUT -p tcp -i eth0 -m multiport --dports 80, 443, 22, 137, 138,139, 445, 113, 25 -j ACCEPT

Here I open the connections to ***http***, ***https***, ***ssh***, ***samba***, ***nfs***, and ***mail***.

What if I want to allow all connections coming from one particular interface? We started our discussion by saying that we want to configure a firewall for our network, not a firewall for an individual computer. In that case we probably trust all internal connections that come into the ***eth1*** interface.

iptables - A INPUT -i eth1 -j ACCEPT

What's really good about firewall, you can redirect traffic to different port or even computer:

iptables -A PREROUTING -t nat -i eth0 -p tcp --dport 8080 -j DNAT --to 192.168.100.200:80

In which case you will also need to forward packet to a new destination:

iptables -A FORWARD -p tcp -d 192.168.100.200 --dport 80 -j ACCEPT

That redirects web traffic from port 8080 (often used secondary port for the web sites) to another computer's (**192.168.100.200**) standard web port (:80). That way you can separate web hosting for a single domain to host two different web sites or applications without configuring virtual server on the apache. That way you can also run dedicated servers for each site.

Did I say “that's cool!” already?

Next thing, you may want to allow only traffic, that originated from your computer. To do this, you use the ***established*** flag:

iptables -A INPUT -m state --state ESTABLISHED,RELATED -j ACCEPT

Basically that says, that unless you initiated a connection, you do not want to accept anything else. If you run a web or any other server, you may want to put that rule after the web (or other corresponding) port rule, otherwise users will not be able to connect to that server. Again, what it says is this: “and in addition to all of the above, allow everything, that has been initiated and established from this computer”. That line would probably be the second to the last. And the last one for the *INPUT* chain would be that:

iptables -A INPUT -j DROP

Nice and simple. I listed everything I wanted to accept, and everything else is not a mine realm. That is how the default rule will be. Just like that.

Be careful with that command. Make sure you have it last, and make sure you have an ***ssh*** port or other means of connection open ***before*** that. Otherwise, you will immediately lock yourself (and others) out of system, and the only way you can get back to it – is accessing it physically from the terminal.

- Most everything I tell you in these my lectures are based on my direct hands on experience.
- That includes...
- Yes, that includes the above statement too.

As for the *OUTPUT* chain, you set up it similarly to the *INPUT*, with one important addition.

You want a line to be on that chain.

You probably want to have that line to be a first one on that chain.

You do not want to forget about that line.

Here is that line:

iptables -A OUTPUT -o lo -j ACCEPT.

That line allows any traffic originated from your local loopback interface.

You do not want to forget about that line.

1.1. Finishing up with the iptables firewall.

Now we have only couple of things to do still.

We want to forward the internal incoming traffic to the outside network. And (applicable to the IPv4), we want to masquerade our traffic such that for the outside network it will appear as coming out from one node. We already set the forwarding flag in the the ***ipv4_forward*** file, but we also need to specify a rule for that in the firewall:

iptables -t nat -A POSTROUTING -o eth0 -j MASQUERADE

iptables -A FORWARD -i eth0 -o eth1 -m state --state RELATED,ESTABLISHED -j ACCEPT

iptables -A FORWARD -i eth1 -o eth0 -j ACCEPT

And that sets the firewall. Again, you list all the rules specifically how you want them to be implemented, and in the order you want them to kick in, and you drop everything else by default.

To enable the changes in the firewall, you need to restart network. Any appropriate command will do, for example:

service network restart

You can see all your rules with the command:

iptables -L

You can flash the chain (or the table) with

iptables -F INPUT

and you can delete individual rule with

iptables -D INPUT 1

Now you are done with that, you can save these rules to the file:

iptables-save > iptabales_rules

After which you can restore your firewall as simple as that (and here is finally a good example of ***stdin*** redirect):

iptables-restore < iptables_rules.

And in case I have not said that, it is a really good idea to make a backup copy before you start modifying your firewall rules. To make a backup copy of the important configuration file(s) is always a very good idea.

Finally, you may want to put everything into the script and register the script to run with levels 3 and 5.

2. RedHat firewall with the firewalld

Some years back RedHat added an additional layer on top of ***iptables*** by creating a ***firewalld*** interface to the kernel's ***netfiters***.

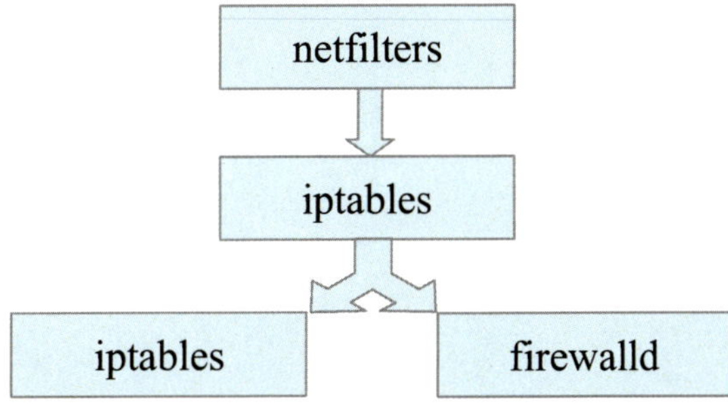

Because both ***firewalld*** and ***iptables*** run on the same level, they both end up managing the ***iptables,*** that in turn manage kernels' ***netfilters***. Thus, you can have only one of them active. It can be either ***firewalld***, or ***iptables*** service; you cannot run both of them at the same time.

iptables is a system's tool. Let's see if it is registered:

systemctl status iptables

That will probably show us nothing.

What about the ***firewalld***?

systemctl status firewalld

and we should see that it is running.

Let's do:

firewall-config

And it should start the graphical tool. This is the same tool which can be started from the

Applications > Settings > Firewall.

It provides a lot of options, you can specify zones, you can set rules for each zone, you can allow/deny ports; for the external zone you may see the masquerading options selected; you can see port forwarding tab and so on.

What are the advantages of ***firewalld*** as compared to the ***iptables*** service as stated by the RedHat? First, is that firewall can be managed dynamically, i.e you don't need to restart network service after changing rules. I personally would say it could be somewhat controversial, because it may take away from you an option of do a check before applying changes, but it is my opinion, and not all people may agree with that. Again, with the ***firewalld*** the changes in the rules applied immediately, and on the other hand that may be an important advantage, as I will show just in a minute.

Another advantage, as they say is that you can have zones and you can see there is a lot of zones here – work, home, trusted, public etc. You can select any zone, and set different rules for each the zone. I may sound aged, but I personally think, that while it may ***sound*** as a good idea, it is ***actually*** a big disadvantage. Security is only good if it does not rely on you not forgetting to do something. If you take your laptop from home or office, from the supposedly trusted environment and join the public network which is not, you should rely on your memory not forgetting to switch to a new zone. Thus, you may open yourself to a risk. That is ironically, because that system clearly designed with the mobile users in mind. So for that reason alone, I think that this may not be a good idea.

But there is something else. If you look at those zones, you may start wondering: What is the difference between "home" and "trusted"? Or "work" and "trusted"... The system should be very clear and unambiguous. Because when you need to act fast, you want to act right.

But that's, again, just my opinion.

Finally, they say the ***firewalld*** has the advantage of having graphical interface, which I will not comment on. But that is my opinion, and your opinion may be different.

So, the ***firewalld*** has a graphical UI, but it also can be configured with command lines. You can do with ***firewalld*** pretty much everything that you can do with the ***iptables***, which should not be a surprise, as they are just the layers for the same system. For example to list all the services with the ***firewalld***:

firewall-cmd --get-services

It should show the list of all services that are allowed from the computer. Which is actually good thing, because it provides much more clear output than you may get with the ***iptables***

Another nice feature, you can stop all traffic at once by enabling a panic mode:

firewall-cmd --panic-on

For example:

ping <some host >

That should work.

Now:

firewall-cmd --panic on

ping <some host>

Now it should not.

To restore back:

firewall-cmd --panic-off

ping <some host >

and it should work again.

That would be analogous to the following commands for the ***iptables***:

iptables -I INPUT 1 -j DROP

iptables -I OUTPUT 1 -j DROP

Two commands vs one, and not forgetting to restart the service. Here the ***firewalld*** wins... But... it shuts the entire traffic. What if you want to keep other network card working? Or local device?

Remember the ***ipcofing***? You can bring a specific interface down. So, that could be a good alternative here.

3. Now let's see few examples of working with the firewalld

There are a lot of guides and tutorials available. There are a lot and lots of various and different commands and options. The tutorial on the ***firewalld*** is pretty tick. I will show just few examples.

To see the ports on the internal zone:

[root@localhost ~]# firewall-cmd --zone=internal --list-ports

To add a port to the internal zone.

[root@localhost ~]# firewall-cmd --zone=internal --add-port=8080/tcp

[root@localhost ~]# firewall-cmd --zone=internal --list-ports

And you should see:

```
8080/tcp
```

Let's remove that port:

[root@localhost ~]# firewall-cmd --zone=public --remove-port=8080/tcp

[root@localhost ~]# firewall-cmd --zone=public --list-ports

Should be nothing there.

Adding interface to the zone.

[root@localhost ~]# firewall-cmd --zone=public --change-interface=p2p1

To see the default zone:

[root@localhost ~]# firewall-cmd --get-default-zone

```
public
```

To see what's on the public zone:

[root@localhost ~]# firewall-cmd --zone=public --list-all

```
public
 interfaces: p2p1
 sources:
 services: mdns dhcpv6-client ssh
 ports:
 masquerade: no
 forward-ports:
 icmp-blocks:
 rich rules:
```

What's the active zone?

[root@localhost ~]# firewall-cmd --get-active-zones

```
public
 interfaces: p2p1
```

To see the zones:

[root@localhost ~]# firewall-cmd --get-zones

```
work drop internal external trusted home dmz public block
```

Assign work zone to the interface eth0

```
[root@localhost ~]# firewall-cmd --zone=work --change-interface=eth0
```

[root@localhost ~]# firewall-cmd --get-active-zones

```
work
 interfaces: eth0
public
 interfaces: p2p1
```

Now the interesting question. We discussed that it can be a security risk if you forget to change the zone when you switch over the different network. But isn't there some tool to help us with that?

Don't forget, we are on the Linux.

4. How to determine network

Let's see if we can create a tool to determine the network changes.

The idea is that we want to monitor the changes in the gateway. Because it is a gateway that defines the network. If the gateways changes, that means we switched over to a new network. As soon as we found that out, we check the new gateway against our existing table of safe networks, and if it is not there, we assume that it is not a safe network. How we determine the changes? By the changes in the IP address? Not. We know that answer. We will look by the changes in the ***MAC*** address of the gateway.

Let's do it step by step:

route

```
cs130@raspberrypi ~ $ route
Kernel IP routing table
Destination     Gateway         Genmask         Flags Metric Ref    Use Iface
default         192.168.43.1    0.0.0.0         UG    303    0        0 wlan0
10.7.232.0      *               255.255.255.0   U     0      0        0 veth0
link-local      *               255.255.0.0     U     202    0        0 eth0
```

This commands shows you the routing table. We already saw it. We a[re] interested in the Gateways line. We know the gateway by the flags: 'G' (gateway) and 'U' (Up).

route | grep 'UG'

```
cs130@raspberrypi ~ 2 route | grep 'UG'
default         192.168.43.1    0.0.0.0         UG    303    0        0 wlan0
```

The second field there will be an IP address, let's grab it:

route | grep 'UG' | awk '{print $2}'

```
cs130@raspberrypi ~ 3 route | grep 'UG' | awk '{print $2}'
192.168.43.1
```

But we don't need an IP address, we need the ***MAC*** address... So, we are not done yet. We've met the ***arp*** tool ("address resolution protocol"); it can translate an IP address to the ***MAC*** address. Let's feed it with the IP address of the gateway, and it should give us back its ***MAC*** address:

route | grep 'UG' | awk '{print $2}' | xargs arp

```
cs130@raspberrypi ~ 4 route | grep 'UG' | awk '{print $2}'| xargs arp
Address                  HWtype  HWaddress           Flags Mask            Iface
192.168.43.1             ether   24:             :d3   C                     wlan0
```

That's good. Now let's grab just the ***MAC*** address and feed it into the file of known networks.

route | grep 'UG' | awk '{print $2}' | xargs arp | grep ether | awk '{print $3}'

```
cs130@raspberrypi ~ 5 route | grep 'UG' | awk '{print $2}'| xargs arp | grep ether | awk '{print $3}'
24:            d3
```

route | grep 'UG' | awk '{print $2}' | xargs arp | grep ether | awk '{print $3}' >> known_network

```
cs130@raspberrypi ~ 5 route | grep 'UG' | awk '{print $2}'| xargs arp | grep ether | awk '{print $3}'
24:            d3
```

We want to keep that file safe. We want to make sure that nobody accesses that file, and nobody changes that file. We know how to set the permissions. But here we probably may want something else. We want to make sure that we know if that file has been accessed and changed.

How can we assure ourselves on that?

By looking at the modification/access/change time stamp?

No.

By looking and comparing the size of the file with that of the original one?

No.

We want to compute a checksum (a hash) of that file, and then we want to keep the file with the checksum outside of that file system. Some other place. Yes, that's what we want.

As you can expect, the Linux comes with everything you need to do your work:

```
cs130@raspberrypi ~ ? md5sum known_network
7925c578e32c0fd944e9bbf89f28343c  known_network
```

The property of the hash (checksum) is such, that even if one single bit of the file changes, the entire checksum changes. Here is the example:

```
cs130@raspberrypi ~ ? md5sum known_network
7925c578e32c0fd944e9bbf89f28343c  known_network
cs130@raspberrypi ~ 8 echo "1" >> known_network
cs130@raspberrypi ~ 9 md5sum known_network
985ad08704f4b4bb669b534a308c25d5  known_network
cs130@raspberrypi ~ 10
```

I added just one character to the file, and you can see, that the hash has changed. That's how we can know that the file was changed. Well... That was not a very good example, because I also changed a size of the file. The good example would be me changing some character *inside* the file, but... Then I would disclose the ***MAC*** addresses there, so I went an easy way. You will take my word on it, won't you?

Now, when we built the list of all known networks we trust, if we join a new network, and grepping the gateway against that list does not produce any matches, we should automatically assume we are not on the trusted network. In which case we do:

firewall-cmd --zone=public –change-interface=wlan0

And that, Ladies and Gentlemen, is the power of the Linux.

And that would be it for today.

5. Summary and review

Linux firewall

Commands: ***iptables, firewalld***

Lecture 13. Connecting to the remote server; Network File System; Samba

"That ship?.. What happened to it?.."
"It hated me because I talked to it."
"You talked to it?.. What do you mean you talked to it?"
"Simple... I went and plugged myself into its external computer feed. I talked to the computer at great length and explained my view of the Universe to it"
"And what happened?" pressed Ford.

Douglas Adams, The Hitchhiker Guide To The Galaxy.

We are not interested that much, what happened with that ship next. We want to know how to connect to our machine through the "external computer feed", or, stated differently, remotely. Throughout the semester I've repeatedly been saying that if you work with the Linux, in most majority of cases you will be working with the remote machine. That means, you need to be able to remotely connect to it, and do it securely. Today we will talk about that.

1. Connections over the network. Telnet. The old does not always mean trusty.

I would start with the very old tool, which is probably little used or even little known today, yet the reason why I still want to discuss it hopefully should be clear after I do that virtual demonstration.

But before we proceed to that, please read the following:

Disclaimer.

> **The following demonstration is intended for educational purposes only. By participating in that demonstration you agree not to abuse that knowledge and not to use it to make or try to make any harm. Furthermore, instructor is not liable for any your actions if you try to use that demonstration for any purposes.**

I will not provide any screens for the following demo; just the commands and explanations.

Every mail service has a mail exchange records that define the mail server over the internet. We can query these ***mx*** records with the following command:

nslookup -query=mx <name of email server>

It should give you **mx** entries for that server.

Now let's do:

>telnet <address from the above query> 25

we should see reply:

220

We type:

>ehlo

Should see some reply:

....

We type:

>mail from: <my email address for that server>

Se should see:

250 ok

We type

>rcpt to: <you will *not* send the email like that, right?>

We should see:

250 ok

We type:

>data

Reply:

go ahead

We type:

>(Our message, i.e. : hello there)

(empty line followed by a single dot on a separate line)

.

We see

250 ok message accepted

We type:

>quit

So what happened? We opened a connection with the mail server of **<email server>**, we initiated the email exchange for the user name, which is real, and which exists on a system. We know that such user exists, and if we did not, it is not a hard thing trying to figure out whether that user exists or not...

What's important here, is that we initiated an email exchange for that user, **AND the email server did not ask us for the password authentication, or in fact any authentication besides valid user name!!!**

I repeat: the email exchange did not ask us to authenticate user before accepting an email from us.

Recall our example with the Linux email – we were able to send emails with ***-r*** flag and specifying the return address, which is different from the real user's email address. But this one is even better. So, the point I want to make, is the one I already made: if you receive some strange email, even from someone you know, it may not necessarily be the real email from that real user.

Because of that reason, more and more servers are closing the anonymous relay (that's what we did above), but it is still possible to do that.

With such dramatic introduction to the ***telnet***, what is it?

It is a tool to connect to a host over the network. Note, that with that you can specify any port (for our demonstration we used port 25, which is an ***smtp*** port), therefore it gives you technical ability to talk to any server. You can use it to connect to your account on a server, but you probably do not want to do that, because the entire session ***is not encrypted, including transmission of the password***. It is just a plain text. But again, it gives you ability to connect to the server specifying the port. One example I just showed. Here is another example (we will use port 80, which is a web port):

telnet yahoo.com 80

may be a blank screen, keep typing

get / http 1.0

And we should see the http page from yahoo retrieved and displayed on your terminal. It does not matter what the page says; what matters, that we established connection to the yahoo.com on port 80 (which is http port) and were able to fetch something from there.

If that is such a bad tool, shouldn't we block it with the firewall? The question is – how? If we close port 80, nobody will be able to get the web pages with legitimate requests, If we close port 25, nobody will be able to get the emails with legitimate requests... and so on. You see, where I am leading to? Just because you have some ports in a firewall presumably open for a legitimate services, it does not guarantee you from being exploited by something that you may not expect.

```
Again, do not try to reproduce the demo that I described above for
whatever reason you may think is a good one. You may be liable.
```

With such an introduction, what is the tools to connect to the remote server?

Probably the *de-facto* standard is the ***ssh*** (the secure shell). We already saw it. Let's talk about that now.

2. ssh

Back in the very old days people were connecting to the remote machines using ***telnet*** – the way we just talked above. The problem with that tool, is that it sends everything in a plain text, without any encryption. Including the passwords. That was very quickly recognized as probably not a good idea. As soon as network made its way out of the labs' doors, people realized, that not only the user name and password should be sent securely, but so the entire session should. ***Ssh*** quickly became an alternative, and probably is a *de-facto* standard how you connect to the server remotely. ***Ssh*** is almost always installed on your Linux; it comes with the default installation for probably most (if not any) of the (major) distros. For the window, it is obviously not a case, so if you want to be able to connect from your windows machine to the Linux, you need to install ***ssh*** client for windows. There are quite a few clients available; some with GUI, some are just command line; some have more features, some less; some are easy in installation and configuration, some other require you to do quite some work and so on, but you should find the one that suits your taste. There are some that allow you to run the X-windows (which is graphical terminal) over an ***ssh***, probably the most famous ones (without any endorsement) would be ***Xming*** or ***Cygwin*** (I think one is installed in the lab's computers). You can easily find the list of ***ssh*** clients for windows by googling it.

So, how does the ***ssh*** work? First, it encrypts your traffic. Not only the password, but the entire traffic is encrypted. It works by public/private keys encryption. You encrypt your packets with one key, and for that key it can only be decrypted with the matching key. There are few encryption algorithms available; probably the most used one is the ***RSA*** public/private keys encryption. Without exaggeration, that tool made possible all our modern life experience – online shopping, online banking... everything. But before we start discussing it, I want to make a short comment.

The purpose of the encryption is not to make your communication to be not possible to decrypt. Any encryption can be broken, given sufficient resources (time, money, computing power etc). The best example probably would be when British broke the encryption for the German's navy during the WWII. They were able to direct the unlimited state resources and thus, were able to analyze the encryption.

So, the purpose of encryption is not to be not possible to decrypt; don't think it is.

What's then? 

The purpose of the encryption is to make the cost of crypto-analysis to far exceed the value of the information obtained. So, when you do the online shopping and the bad guy listens to your conversation trying to analyze it and to get the session key, by the time he is able to break your encryption, your online session supposedly should long terminate. That's BTW why it is always a good idea to always logout, and close the browser, to make sure the session is indeed ended (who knows what the programmers on the other side think they did?)

Alright. With that, let's briefly discuss the private/public keys.

You generate a pair of keys using a certain algorithm in such a way, that they match each other. And only ***they*** match each other. The theory of numbers teaches us, that no other key(s) can match that pair. That is also basis of the online identity. If something was decrypted by your public key, you cannot successfully deny that it was not your private key that was used to encrypt that message (principle of non-repudiation). That means... Yes, as I always say, keeping your account secure is your responsibility and may be your liability too.

Let's generate an ***rsa*** keys (and of course, the Linux comes with all the tools to do that and if that package is not installed on your distribution, you can easily install it with the command like that: ***`pkg install openssh`***; your package installation tools may be different).

ssh-keygen

```
$ ssh-keygen
Generating public/private rsa key pair.
Enter file in which to save the key (/data/data/com.termux/files/home/.ssh/id_rsa):
Enter passphrase (empty for no passphrase):
Enter same passphrase again:
Your identification has been saved in /data/data/com.termux/files/home/.ssh/id_rsa
Your public key has been saved in /data/data/com.termux/files/home/.ssh/id_rsa.pub
The key fingerprint is:
SHA256:MoGkzmQhaTdpOIkEDj6d8lwllrgUj125VWq1qJhQTFk u0_a52@localhost
The key's randomart image is:
+---[RSA 3072]----+
|Bo+.B=+E. .o     |
|**.@B=+. .+ .    |
|.=0=++. o+ .     |
| ==.o ooo        |
|  oo oo.S        |
|      o          |
|                 |
|                 |
|                 |
+----[SHA256]-----+
$ 
```

You will be asked for a passphrase. Make sure it is a good passphrase. It will ask you couple other questions to the effect where to store the keys, to which you can just accept the default values, and as result there will be couple of files created (we know meaning of a "couple" in this class):

```
$ ls -l .ssh/
total 28
-rw------- 1 u0_a52 u0_a52    0 Oct  6 16:59 authorized_keys
-rw------- 1 u0_a52 u0_a52 2655 Oct  6 17:00 id_rsa
-rw------- 1 u0_a52 u0_a52  570 Oct  6 17:00 id_rsa.pub
-rw------- 1 u0_a52 u0_a52   93 Sep 25 13:52 known_hosts
$
```

Let's look at the **~/.ssh/id_rsa.pub**

```
ssh-rsa AAAAB3NzaC1yc2EAAAADAQABAAABgQCyZv9M
H7VdFsTMTYfg6CdJCG5ynHqGk0tM0wPbk7T5sCxkMNgr
F0cmTboyVBjC1KbeIXFhzXmd1MQ82bGeW18FJqnS1nAT
nBz9pZY816TVqaem56pzhSp6wbymH7D/0YexbbUj1Ks+
35oxdC+U529Tljy46j4UrEIeUYpirL3dILaApowv5DZW
_a52@localhost
.ssh/id_rsa.pub (END)
```

That file will have your public key which is a pair to the private key. Inside that file you will see the long string of the numbers and characters. If you change just one of that character, it will not match the private key any longer. And good luck to figure out the correct key by the brute force.

Again, that is your public key, which you can send to anyone whom you want to establish a connection to. Now let's look at this file: **~/.ssh/id_rsa**

```
-----BEGIN OPENSSH PRIVATE KEY
b3BlbnNzaC1rZXktdjEAAAAACmFlcz
KhW1r9xMknjbfBAAAAEAAAAAEAAAGX
He6cYLd9XRaf62W6PbmDV2HDmy8J9a
MTYfg6CdJCG5ynHqGk0tM0wPbk7T5s
Yaffoi1Yxpi73j0XrCaFk48rEhL25v
JqnS1nATbtt4N0+DBqKjg8AnefcCaY
```

That is your private key. If you thought the public key was a long string of the numbers and characters, take a look at the private key. That's what the "long" means. You keep that key secure. No one should be able to read it or to get handle to it. (Look at the permissions of that file from the screen above).

…………………………

```
I70t4f70TAYsBWPceHu/gGNv/QlecH
FrAYhqA7u+STUFH5QxxX3Mwmutq+HN
P2H2R1W//Gp/Jd2/ZhgZhfLMYM0mSV
CEK4k7nfQbDqVz2L2Rj4zrG0DbcIaw
MmyTem7qcheYTBkXKvFdTf7GqSVWh1
FZ8ZfHBbxXxKkEsJQYtuisS/YDI=
-----END OPENSSH PRIVATE KEY--
.ssh/id_rsa (END)
```

Now, when we have keys, let's set up an ***ssh*** connection to another machine (actually we did not need to generate keys just for the purpose of ***ssh*** connection, but because we will use them for something else, that was a good start).

> To do that demonstration, I usually start two virtual clients (for that purpose, I have one installed on the USB stick), but it is equally possible (although not as demonstrative) to just ***ssh*** to yourself from the other terminal of the same virtual machine. If you do it with two virtual machines on the same host, make sure you set the network adapters for both to "bridged" to the host.

On one window we type:

ssh <host>

host could be an IP address, or the host name.

```
$ ssh -l cs130 raspberrypi
The authenticity of host 'raspberrypi (192.168.43.124)' can't be established.
ECDSA key fingerprint is SHA256:K3uKf0woyX2jG8wMRa0tQBGo7kxafa3wwyH0YrvkeLY.
Are you sure you want to continue connecting (yes/no/[fingerprint])?
```

When you connect to the host for the first time, it sends you its public key. Usually you would see the message:

> Authentication of host .... followed by a string of a scrambled characters... cannot be verified. Are you sure you want to connect....

If you say "yes" , it will add that key to the list of known hosts (which is under the same **~/.ssh/** directory).

```
-rw------- 1 u0_a52 u0_a52   93 Sep 25 13:52 known_hosts
$
```

Note, that you say "*yes*" to this question only if you know that the message is legitimate. If you already connected to that host and receive that message upon any of the following connection, watch out! There can be something not nice going on. At that point it is better to pause and figure out why is that message shown.

```
Warning: Permanently added 'raspberrypi,192.168.43.124' (ECDSA) to the list of known hosts.
```

And what's inside that file? Just fingerprints of the known hosts, which, as you can guess is a … string of a scrambled characters.....

```
raspberrypi,192.168.43.124 ecdsa-sha2-nistp256 AAAAE2VjZHNhLXNoYTItbmlzdHAyNTYA
```

Boring...

If your user name on the remote machine is the same, as on the local one, you can skip the user part in the above command and just type: **ssh <host>** , otherwise you specify it with the (*-l, small el*) parameter… Alright, let's finally connect to that:

```
$ ssh -l cs130 raspberrypi
cs130@raspberrypi's password:

The programs included with the Debian GNU/Linux system are free software;
the exact distribution terms for each program are described in the
individual files in /usr/share/doc/*/copyright.

Debian GNU/Linux comes with ABSOLUTELY NO WARRANTY, to the extent
permitted by applicable law.
Last login: Sat Oct  3 19:20:47 2020 from 192.168.43.224
cs130@raspberrypi ~ 1
```

You may see the message informing you about date and time of your last login. You can check that it is indeed the same machine you wanted to log in:

```
cs130@raspberrypi ~ 1 uname -a
Linux raspberrypi 4.9.35-v7+ #1014 SMP Fri Jun 30 14:47:43 BST 2017 armv7l GNU/Linux
```

Or, if you prefer:

```
cs130@raspberrypi ~ 3 ifconfig | grep HWaddr
eth0      Link encap:Ethernet  HWaddr b8:          :3b
```

Thus, after a successful login, you can work on that remote machine, which could be sitting across the hall or across the globe, just as you worked on the local terminal. And the entire session is encrypted.

You can copy files between hosts. From the remote to the local:

scp user@host:/path/myfile .

or from the local to the remote:

scp myfile usert@host:

That will copy the file to your home directory on the host <***host***> Do not forget the colon at the end, otherwise you would copy the file to the one named ***usert@host*** on your ***local*** machine.

And of course, if your user name on the remote host is the same as the local, you can skip the user name part:

scp myfile host:

you can also provide the full path on the remote host.

scp myfile user@host:/home/user/path/

But you need to know that path. For that reason sometimes it is easier first to copy to your home directory, and then log in there, and move it to the desired location.

Let's copy couple of files, just to see how it works:

```
scp cs130@raspberrypi:/home/cs130/somexmllog .
```

```
$ scp cs130@raspberrypi:/home/cs130/somexmllog .
cs130@raspberrypi's password:
somexmllog                                    100%  303    27.3KB/s   00:00
$ ls -l somexmllog
-rw------- 1 u0_a52 u0_a52 303 Oct  6 18:22 somexmllog
$
```

With that command, running from a ***local*** machine I copy the file from the ***remote*** machine named ***raspberrypi*** to my local current directory:

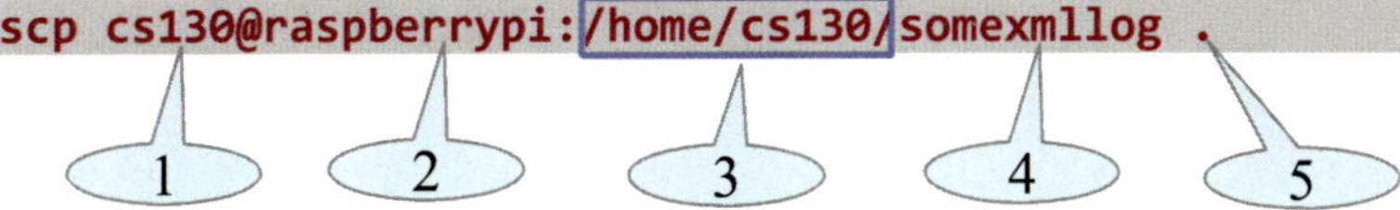

1. My user name on the remote machine
2. Name of the remote machine. You can also use an IP address. I use the name because... the IP address can change.
3. You need to know the exact path. Good thing, you should know your home directory, and you were smart enough to put that file there before you started that.
4. The file name I want to copy to the local machine.
5. And finally, the dot always refers to my current place. From here I can place it anywhere on the local machine I want to and have permissions to.

And I do `ls` to see, that it is here.

You can also run command on a remote host without login in; but you still should provide password:

ssh <host> <command>

Do you know the IP address and want to find out the hostname? You don't need to log in to do that:

```
ssh cs130@192.168.43.124 hostname
```

```
$ ssh cs130@192.168.43.124 hostname
cs130@192.168.43.124's password:
raspberrypi
$
```

Do you want to see the list the IP addresses there?

```
ssh cs130@192.168.43.124 ip addr | grep 'inet '
```

```
$ ssh cs130@raspberrypi ip addr | grep 'inet '
cs130@raspberrypi's password:
    inet 127.0.0.1/8 scope host lo
    inet 192.168.1.1/24 brd 192.168.1.255 scope global eth0
    inet 169.254.19.223/16 brd 169.254.255.255 scope global eth0
    inet 192.168.43.124/24 brd 192.168.43.255 scope global wlan0
    inet 192.168.1.10/24 brd 192.168.1.255 scope global eth0.1
$
```

One of the great feature of ***ssh*** is that you can forward a remote X-windows to the local terminal, **if** remote server runs the X-windows, and local terminal supports it. To see if remote server runs the X-windows, you use command:

who -r

```
$ ssh cs130@raspberrypi who -r
cs130@raspberrypi's password:
         run-level 5  2020-10-06 17:17
$
```

If it shows the run level 5, you can login to it with option -X to forward the X windows:

ssh -l <user> <host> -X

```
$ ssh -l pi raspberrypi -X
pi@raspberrypi's password:

The programs included with the Debian GNU/Linux system are free software;
the exact distribution terms for each program are described in the
individual files in /usr/share/doc/*/copyright.

Debian GNU/Linux comes with ABSOLUTELY NO WARRANTY, to the extent
permitted by applicable law.
Last login: Tue Oct  6 17:17:10 2020
pi@raspberrypi:~ $
```

And then you can run a GUI tools there, which I will not be able to do because it is my ***client*** that does not run at the ***init*** 5 level.

When you are done, don't forget to logout

```
pi@raspberrypi:~ $ logout
Connection to raspberrypi closed.
$
```

Now let's return to the public / private keys.

You can send the ***public(!!!)*** key to the remote host (or copy it there) to add into the ***.ssh/authorized_keys*** file. After that, you can login to the remote host using the ***passphrase*** instead of the password. Thus, even though your public key is known, to login to the host, you still need to enter the ***passphrase***. That's why it is important to have a strong passphrase, not an empty string.

scp ~/.ssh/id_rsa.pub <otherhost>:

```
$ scp .ssh/id_rsa.pub cs130@raspberrypi:/home/cs130/
cs130@raspberrypi's password:
id_rsa.pub
$
```

ssh <otherhost>

cat id_rsa.pub >> ~/.ssh/authorized_key

rm id_rsa.pub

logout

```
cs130@raspberrypi ~ 3 cat id_rsa.pub >> ~/.ssh/authorized_keys
cs130@raspberrypi ~ 4 rm id_rsa.pub
```

and then, when you want to login to that host again, you will use a passphrase.

```
$ ssh -l cs130 raspberrypi
Enter passphrase for key '/data/data/com.termux/files/home/.ssh/id_rsa':
```

I am not sure, and cannot comment on whether that method is more preferable to the password's authentication. The argument can be made that it gives you an option to configure various tools that use ***ssh*** protocol (for example accessing your remote files repository) by not providing your password to the remote machine. Again, I cannot really comment on that. Once you are in, you are in. You are authenticated to the system, and from that point it does not matter, what means of authentication has been used. But.... there is more than one way of doing things.

You can also add your public key to the ***ssh agent***. After that you will ***not*** need to provide a passphrase when login to that host. But... I am not sure if that is a good idea. So I just mention, that there is such option, without discussing it further.

One more thing before we will go to the next topic.

You can forward ports over the ssh.

Why would you need to forward ports? To make a secure connection that otherwise is not secure. For example while traveling (and not trusting the local providers), you can forward regular traffic which is not secure, over the ***ssh*** tunneling and the whole thing will become encrypted.

Other use – to overcome network restrictions over the ports (without much elaboration here).

How to use that?

ssh -L 12345:somehost:6789 somehost

What it does, it tells ssh to listen on the local host port 12345 and forward it to the remote port 6789 of the **somehost** machine. You may need to provide a user name to the **somehost**:

user@somehost

```
Note, that this information is for educational purposes only. I do not
endorse or advise you doing that when it is not expected or
appropriate. As always, the instructor is not liable for your actions.
```

Note, that these days the virtual private networks (VPN) are becoming more and more widely used.

Now, ***ssh*** daemon is of course controlled by the config files. There are quite a number of options there, but some are:

KeepAlive

You set the time interval to keep session from timeout. That is useful if you have short timeout.

User account

To specify the username for a remote machine, so you would not need to use ***-l*** option.

And, probably, the most important option is to disallow root's access to the system via the ***ssh***. That is very good security feature, which is probably universally recommended to use. And I fully agree with that and recommend you to use it.

2. FTP

File ***T***ransfer ***P***rotocol. It is a nice small utility to transfer files between computers. You may see that some web hosts allow to download files using the ftp, not http. To use ftp you would do:

ftp <host>

if you are already on the ftp session, you can open another connection:

>open <host>

The file transfer itself is very simple. You may need to use binary (*b*) option to preserve correct end of line, but the basic session would look like following:

if you want to get file from the host:

get <file>

or if you need to change directory first:

cd <directory>

get <file>

you can also use **mget** to get multiple files:

Or you can put files in that directory:

put (or mput) file(s)

and to close the session:

bye.

That's it very simple. And pretty fast. With ***ssh*** clients that I mentioned before you can run ***sftp*** (secure ftp session) and also do file transfer by drag and drop.

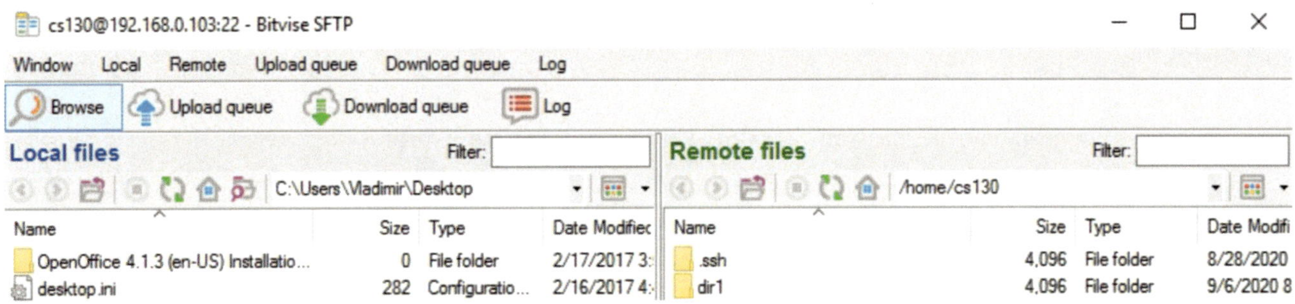

3. NFS

The next topic that I want to talk about is sharing not just files, but the entire directories (sub-) tree across the network; and not just using, but using them as it was mounted to be a local one. People who are familiar with the mapping and sharing folder over the network, should immediately see very close similarity here. And again and again, I would like to point out, that all this was done back in the times when the grass was green, and the sky was high...

Suppose you have computer that hosts some file system that you frequently use. Of course you can copy files to your local machine, but first, that would use space, second, if files are large, you will need to wait until it copies over; and third, and most important one, there may be situation that you will need to figure out, how you would synchronize the files if you do that. If you have many files to work with, it would be more and more an issue.

Wouldn't it be nice, if, while I keep those files remotely, I could use and access them just as they were local?

That exactly solution that the Network File System or ***NFS*** provides. It allows you to work with remote directory tree mounted to be part of the local one. And by "remote" we understand the distance across the hall, or across the globe.

You will need to have few things.

First, obviously, the required packages should be installed. And most likely, they are installed even with the default Linux installation.

We need to have required services run. That may or may not be the case, in which case you need to start them.

And we need to do some configuration. And as everything with the Linux it is … easy.

If you do that on a virtual machine, you need to correctly setup the network adapter (i.e. to have it bridged).

Now let's try to setup the ***NFS.*** (I will do that based off the CS lab's VM installation of Fedora, and this time no screens will be provided... well... by this time of the semester you probably start trusting me):

Obviously, you need to be a root on both machines.

1. If you are on VM, make sure IP addresses are good (use bridged network adapter on a VM setting if needed), and are on the same network (we are not in the networking class to talk about how to talk across the network, so let's do it simple):

For example:

First machine:

ifconfig p2p1 10.7.232.3 (or whatever IP address it will be, but it has to be unique on the network)

Second machine:

ifconfig p2p1 10.7.232.5 (or whatever IP address it will be, but it has to be unique on the network)

You may want to disable the ***SELInux***: (command is: **setenforce 0)**

For the duration of the configuration (as with any other network configuration changes) you may temporary modify or turn off completely the system's firewall (which means you want to be alone on your machine).

You may also want to disable the Windows firewall.

On the “donor” machine let's make the directory which we will export:

mkdir /export

Let's make changes to the configuration file:

vi /etc/exports

And add the line telling that we want to export the entire directory **/export** to the machine **10.7.323.5** allowing the read and write permissions.

/export 10.7.323.5(rw)

You can specify a lot of other parameters and options, among those are the parameters telling what to do with the files, owned by the ***root***, but let's keep it simple.

Save the file, quit.

On both machines:

Check ***rpcbind*** service. If it stopped working start and then try starting ***nfs*** service.

service rpcbind start

service nfs start

You may do ***restart***, if these services already run.

Alternatively, same thing using the ***systemctl***:

systemctl restart rpcbind

systemctl restart nfs

Now we need to add some rules to the firewall (if it is managed by the ***firewalld***):

for i in "service=rpc-bind" "service=mountd" "port=2049/tcp" "port=2049/udp" ;

>firewall-cmd --permanent –add-$i; done

(Note, that you need to use a double minus sign for a verbose parameters)

(Note, that you would probably do that with the separate commands, I just wanted to use that example to show you that you can use loop with the strings as well)

Thus, in reality it will probably be more like that:

firewall-cmd --permanent –add-service=rpc-bind

…..

and all other options from the above list.

After that reload the firewall.

firewall-cmd --reload

just to verify to see that all these ports and services were added:

firewall-cmd --list-all

If your firewall is managed by the ***iptables***, you still need to allow all the above services and ports. But generally, when you do network configuration, you may want to disable firewall entirely to exclude possibility of interfering it with your setup in progress. If that is your home machine, that should not be the problem, but if not?.. What if that is a multi-user machine? You may want to politely not to allow any user besides yourself there. How? By switching to the run level 1? But then you will not have a network on that level. Well. There is more than one way, but you may probably do something like that:

> Here is what I am going to do:
>
> 1. I will make a symlink of the ***nologin shell*** to some distinct name
> 2. For each user except the ***root***, I will modify the ***shell*** to the above name
> 3. That will disable all users except the ***root*** to login
> 4. After I am done with the configuration, I will revert users to their ***login shell***.
> 5. The reason I do "some distinct name" instead of directly using the ***nologin***, is because if there is anyone already with ***nologin***, on the step (4) above, I would set that to the real ***login shell***.

6. And yes, since I am touching the original ***bash*** file, I will make a copy of it just in case.

```
root@raspberrypi:~# cp -p /bin/bash /bin/bash_to_change
root@raspberrypi:~# for i in `grep bash /etc/passwd | awk -F ':' '$1 != "root" {print $1}'`;
> do usermod -s /bin/bash_to_change $i; done
```

And then (**Always have a backup copy of important files!!!**):

```
root@raspberrypi:~# cp -p /bin/bash /bin/bash.ori
root@raspberrypi:~# rm /bin/bash_to_change
root@raspberrypi:~# which nologin
/usr/sbin/nologin
root@raspberrypi:~# ln -s /usr/sbin/nologin /bin/bash_to_change
root@raspberrypi:~#
```

You should understand everything I did there, with probably one question to ask: Why did I remove that ***bash_to_change*** file?

I am so scared to make a mistake here. Because if I do.... I better not to. Thus, I want to take advantage of the feature of the **ln** command that will not allow me to make a link to the existing file (thus, overwriting it). I do not want to have any chance of overwriting the original ***bash***. No, I don't want to... Thus, if I do **ln** and it tells me that the file exists, I'd better check it twice – what I am linking to at?

Alright. After that when user tries to login, there will be a nice friendly message displayed:

```
$ ssh -l cs130 raspberrypi
Enter passphrase for key '/data/data/com.termux/files/home/.ssh/id_rsa':

The programs included with the Debian GNU/Linux system are free software;
the exact distribution terms for each program are described in the
individual files in /usr/share/doc/*/copyright.

Debian GNU/Linux comes with ABSOLUTELY NO WARRANTY, to the extent
permitted by applicable law.
No mail.
Last login: Sat Oct 10 16:39:18 2020 from 192.168.43.224
This account is currently not available.
Connection to raspberrypi closed.
$
```

Of course, you will notify users that the system will undergo the maintenance, in advance right?

And when you are done...

```
root@raspberrypi:~# for i in `grep bash_to_change /etc/passwd | awk -F ':' '$1 != "root" {print $1}'`;
> do usermod -s /bin/bash $i ; done
root@raspberrypi:~# rm /bin/bash_to_change
root@raspberrypi:~# grep bash /etc/passwd
root:x:0:0:root:/root:/bin/bash
pi:x:1000:1000:,,,:/home/pi:/bin/bash
cs130:x:1001:1001::/home/cs130:/bin/bash
newuser:x:1002:1002:,,,:/home/newuser:/bin/bash
root@raspberrypi:~#
```

And now you also should see the reason why I used that placeholder ***bash_to_change***, it is because I need it to know which accounts to switch back to ***bash***. And also, you should see why I did not use the ***nologin***. Because if I did that, I would risk to switch to the ***bash*** the real ***nologin*** accounts on the last step.

And then when user tries to login:

```
$ ssh -l cs130 raspberrypi
Enter passphrase for key '/data/data/com.termux/files/home/.ssh/id_rsa':

The programs included with the Debian GNU/Linux system are free software;
the exact distribution terms for each program are described in the
individual files in /usr/share/doc/*/copyright.

Debian GNU/Linux comes with ABSOLUTELY NO WARRANTY, to the extent
permitted by applicable law.
No mail.
Last login: Sat Oct 10 17:06:34 2020 from 192.168.43.224
cs130@raspberrypi ~ 1
```

Everything is good.

But we deviated significantly from our discussion of the ***NFS*** setup. Let's return to it.

We talked to the changes in the firewall, before we took a detour. We did that for one machine, but we need to do exactly the same things on the other one. The good thing, we know how to copy files to a remote computer. So, copy all the above firewall commands and:

cat > firewall-cmds

...paste it here. And we know, that when we do it like that, we preserve the exact formatting.

Now take that file to another machine:

scp firewall-cmds <second-machine>:/<abs_path_here>

Then ***ssh*** there yourself and.... And just do:

source firewall-cmds

And that should be almost all the configuration needed.

On the first machine:

showmount -e

You may need to do

showmount -e 127.0.0.1

That should show the file system (directory tree) that you are exporting to the remote machine. In our case it should be the **/export** directory:

```
root@raspberrypi:~# !464
systemctl restart rpcbind
root@raspberrypi:~# !465
systemctl restart nfs-kernel-server
root@raspberrypi:~# !466
showmount -e
Export list for raspberrypi:
/export 192.168.0.0/255.255.255.0
root@raspberrypi:~#
```

The IP address shown here is different from what I used in the demonstration, because the screen is from my home's Raspberry.

On the second machine:

showmount -e 10.7.232.3 (The IP address of the first machine)

That should show the same directory tree available for export from the first machine.

Now we need to mount the remote directory to the local file system. We need a place for that.

mkdir /net

mount 10.7.232.3:/export /net

That's it. To see how it works, we can create, change, modify etc files, directories etc there and the changes will be visible on ***both*** machines.

One note. There is file **/etc/fstab** that specifies how the file system is mounted at the time of boot. In the guides and tutorials you may see advice to add that mount instruction to that file, so it would be mounted automatically at the boot. Contrary to the general trend, I would not advise to do that because if there is problem with the connection to that machine, your system may hang and wait for that line to be resolved. It may take some time before the timeout. So it is better to *manually* mount the network shares after the system was booted. "*Manually*" obviously means by placing that command into the corresponding ***rcd*** directories. But that is my personal opinion and not all people may agree with that.

Yet one more note. You can also mount a windows share to the Linux. You will need to specify the partition type and user name.

4. Samba

What we just did, we exported the network share over to another Linux machine. Can we export that to a Windows?

Linux provides special service – ***Samba***, that allows Linux directories to be accessible from the windows. You need to have ***samba*** client running, so let's check:

ps -ef | grep smb

ps -ef | grep nmb

If not, we can start them with

service samba start

Or

service smbd start

service nmbd start

You can configure samba directories with the samba config file, or with the graphical tool, which also should allow you to do that.

Samba config file located in

/etc/samba/smb.conf

Go to the end of the file. It should give you some basics settings. You specify the directory, you specify permission and users who will be accessing the directory; you also specify whether the home directories should be accessible, you can specify printing options; whether directories are browse-able or not, etc.

You can create samba password with the command

smbpasswd -a user

To add a new user to the samba.

When you done with the configurations, you need to restart the samba daemons, and after that you can connect to that share from the window explorer on Windows machine:

<IP address of Linux>

Note the double backslash.

You will need to provide your samba's user name and password.

5. Summary and review

Connection over the network. Telnet, ssh, ftp. Network File System. Exporting network share to other systems (Samba). ***/etc/exports*** , ***/etc/fstab*** .

Commands: ***telnet, ssh, ftp, mount***

Lecture 14. Miscellaneous topics; RAID

1. Package management

It used to be that software management in Linux was a terrifying job. To install a package you would need to do a lot of tedious and manual work. You needed to find the package that is suitable for your distro and your platform. You needed to download that package, decompress it, after which the exciting things would begin.

To install a package you needed to run three or four simple commands:

make

make test

make install.

On the first step the package would be built and compiled. For that, your compiler needed to be compatible. Then, your system needed to have all libraries required. Then... you had to have all dependencies met. If anything was not resolved, you needed to do it manually..... aghrrrrr.

Thus, you go to the step one, search for those missing packages, download them, build them, install them.... hoping that they would not generate similar kinds of errors themselves. If they would... if they would...

If they would you may just decide that you did not need that first package after all.

So, back into the old days  of dark ages the package installation was quite a daunting task.

Not any more.

In all modern (modern meaning anything since the end of the last millennium) distros, this task is managed by the package management tools, which takes all that job and does it for you. They search and resolve dependencies, they download and install the packages, if needed they upgrade the necessary packages... All is done automatically by the tool. You only need to provide your final approval for the actual package installation. They also handle the job of upgrade/downgrade and removal of the packages. Yes, you can downgrade a previously upgraded package. That sometimes can be helpful or needed.

The package management can be done with the GUI, or, of course with the command line. Again, the command line may differ between distributions. For the ***RedHat*** it is ***rpm***.

rpm allows to query packages

rpm -q nfs-utils

to see if the nfs utility package is installed.

Back in the dark age, to query a package, you needed to know its exact name and version. Not anymore. All you need to provide to the package manager, is the package name, and the tool will report back to you what version and version number is installed. Convenient.

You can also query for more than one package:

rpm -q samba samba-common samba-client

Here I query for three packages, responsible for the samba client tools.

Suppose we did not have a ***samba*** package. Not a big deal. We don't need to take a Sunday off to install that. It takes away some excitement too. You are no longer able to impress your friends by saying that you spent your weekend installing and configuring the ***samba*** on your Linux. Back then, you would hear a "Whoa! So cool!".

These days that would be more like:

"Ahhh, so boring....".

So, what you'd do to install a samba package:

yum install samba

For other systems it may be ***apt-get***, based on the aptitude:

apt-get install samba-client

or some other tools, depending on your distro.

So, you type command, hit "*enter*", sit back, and watch how all the dependencies are resolved, the packages are checked, and the list of packages to be modified is presented to you for your approval. Then you hit "***yes***", and after a couple of minutes your system has a new package installed and configured...

Here is the example of package installation on my Raspberry:

```
$ pkg install dnsutils
Testing the available mirrors:
[*] https://dl.bintray.com/termux/termux-packages-24: ok
[*] https://grimler.se/termux-packages-24: ok
[*] https://main.termux-mirror.ml: ok
[*] https://termux.mentality.rip/termux-packages-24: ok
Picking mirror: https://termux.mentality.rip/termux-packages-24
Ign:1 https://dl.bintray.com/grimler/game-packages-24 games InRelease
Ign:2 https://dl.bintray.com/grimler/science-packages-24 science InRelease
Get:3 https://dl.bintray.com/grimler/game-packages-24 games Release [5344 B]
Ign:4 https://termux.mentality.rip/termux-packages-24 stable InRelease
Get:5 https://dl.bintray.com/grimler/science-packages-24 science Release [6191 B]
Get:6 https://termux.mentality.rip/termux-packages-24 stable Release [8255 B]
Get:7 https://dl.bintray.com/grimler/game-packages-24 games Release.gpg [475 B]
Get:8 https://dl.bintray.com/grimler/science-packages-24 science Release.gpg [475 B]
Get:9 https://termux.mentality.rip/termux-packages-24 stable Release.gpg [821 B]
Get:10 https://termux.mentality.rip/termux-packages-24 stable/main i686 Packages [120 kB]
Fetched 141 kB in 4s (30.2 kB/s)
Reading package lists... Done
Building dependency tree
Reading state information... Done
12 packages can be upgraded. Run 'apt list --upgradable' to see them.
Reading package lists... Done
Building dependency tree
Reading state information... Done
The following additional packages will be installed:
  libuv resolv-conf
The following NEW packages will be installed:
  dnsutils libuv resolv-conf
0 upgraded, 3 newly installed, 0 to remove and 12 not upgraded.
Need to get 1282 kB of archives.
After this operation, 5513 kB of additional disk space will be used.
Do you want to continue? [Y/n] y
```

You see, that tool reads the mirrors, builds the list of dependencies, determines what additional packages need to be installed or upgraded, and shows to you the final information for you to accept it or not. If you accept, then it proceeds with the installation:

```
Selecting previously unselected package libuv.
Preparing to unpack .../archives/libuv_1.39.0_i686.deb ...
Unpacking libuv (1.39.0) ...
Selecting previously unselected package dnsutils.
Preparing to unpack .../dnsutils_9.16.7_i686.deb ...
Unpacking dnsutils (9.16.7) ...
Setting up resolv-conf (1.3) ...
Setting up libuv (1.39.0) ...
Setting up dnsutils (9.16.7) ...
$
```

So, once you initiated the package installation, everything is done pretty much without your involvement.

Boring... 

2. Archiving

These are tools that used to compress files and entire directories and directories tree, and also for archiving purposes. There are quite a few of them, with probably the most well-known is ***tar***. The name is an acronym for the ***T***ape ***A***rchive, because that was the media where early people put their archives on... These days, when even the optical drives are long forgotten past, the only thing that left out of that name is... that name.

That is pretty powerful utility. You can compress files, directories, check the content of the archive, add to the archive etc. The general command is

tar cvf <name_of_archive.tar> <path to dir>

c stands for create, ***v*** for verbose, ***f*** for files. It is the only commands that does not require the minus or dash sigh for the options.

In the simplest form to create an archive, you would do:

tar cvf archive.tar dir1/

Be careful not to put the archive in the directory you are archiving – otherwise you will be recursively adding archive to itself.

After you created the archive, you will have file with .tar extension. You can check the content of the archive with ***-t***

tar tvf archive.tar

To extract files from the archive, you use ***x*** option:

tar xvf archive.tar

When you create you archive, you may use additional compression. There are number of tools you can use – ***zip***, ***gzip***, ***bz***, etc. They all differ in efficiency of compressing padded zeroes. Because all files are created differently, it is not possible to predict, how well these utilities will compress them. You just need to run them and check the sizes of the compressed files for it may very well be, that after you did an additional compressing to the ***tar***, the size of your archive may become roughly the same, or may even increase! In which case you may want to use different tool or you may try switching their order, first compressing with (say) ***gzip***, and then with the ***tar***.

You can uncompress gzip files with one command:

tar -xzvf archive.tar.gz

Or you can first do **gzip -d, then tar.**

Why do you need to archive? First, obviously, for archiving files and directories. To make a backup copy. For example, you want to archive your entire web directory. Second, if you want to move directory or copy it, the simplest way would be

tar cf archive.tar dir/

cp archive to other place, and then

tar xf archive.tar.

After that the entire directory structure should be placed into a new location.

If you do not need to compress, but just need to copy directory to the same or different machine, you can also do this with the ***rsync*** command or with ***cp -pr*** (if on the same server). ***cp -pr*** means ***p*** - preserve file information, ***r*** - does a recursively copy.

A good thing about ***rsync*** is that it can copy only the difference between the source and destination.

rsync source dest.

Suppose you want to copy directory tree over the network to keep a backup copy. That means you will need to periodically sync them between the original directory and its copy. If you use a ***rsync***, the first time it copies the entire directory, and then just the difference. That may save you some time when do a copy.

Another good feature of ***rsync*** is that it makes the checkpoints. That means that if something happens during the copying, it will resume from the last checkpoint, so you do not need to start all over. And that is actually a good thing to have. Suppose you upload some video file to the cloud. It could be several gigs. You uploaded 90% of it, and then the connection dropped.

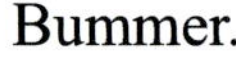
Bummer. 

But if on the other side, to do the copy the tool like the ***rsync*** was used, things may become much brighter. You perhaps still lose few megs, but you nevertheless look to upload only remaining 10%, essentially just resuming the procedure.

That's not that bad. 

When making a backup copies (or archive copies), it is very useful to preserve the original timestamp. The ***tar*** does so by default, for the ***cp*** and ***rsync*** you need to specifically request it. For ***cp*** that would be ***-p*** option, for the ***rsync*** that would be ***-a***..

What else? ***Rsync*** is probably the tool that you would use when copying a directory(ies), while the ***cp*** - when you only need to copy just one or few files.

Finally, using these tools along with hard links allows you to create incremental backups that takes much less space – by only copying the files that changed, leaving unchanged files as hard links.

2.1. Incremental backup with hard links.

Suppose I have a directory **dir1** with couple of files: **file1**, and **file2**.

```
cs130@raspberrypi ~/dir1 10 tree dir1
dir1
├── myfile1
└── myfile2
```

Let's create a backup directory:

mkdir bk1

Let's copy to the ***bk1*** the source directory ***dir1***. We will use the ***cp*** command with the (*-a*) flag for archiving.

cp -a dir1/ bk1/dir1

```
cs130@raspberrypi ~/dir1 12 tree bk1/
bk1/
└── dir1
    ├── myfile1
    └── myfile2
```

Now we want to create an incremental backup (for example weekly or monthly). First, we make a second backup directory that has files hard linked to the original backup (the first backup should be real files; everything after that – hard links. The reason – when we change the original file, we also change all other files hard linked to it, thus we will lose the original file if we do not break the links from it.

Let's copy **bk1** to the **bk2** with the option to create hard links, which is (***-l***).

cp -al bk1 bk2

```
cs130@raspberrypi ~/dir1 13 cp -al bk1 bk2
cs130@raspberrypi ~/dir1 14 tree bk[12]
bk1
└── dir1
    ├── myfile1
    └── myfile2
bk2
└── dir1
    ├── myfile1
    └── myfile2
```

If we check the ***inode*** numbers, we should see that the files in these two directories are hard linked to each other.

```
cs130@raspberrypi ~/dir1 15 ls -li bk[12]/dir*
bk1/dir1:
total 0
43070 -rw-r--r-- 2 cs130 cs130 0 Oct 12 19:47 myfile1
43071 -rw-r--r-- 2 cs130 cs130 0 Oct 12 19:47 myfile2

bk2/dir1:
total 0
43070 -rw-r--r-- 2 cs130 cs130 0 Oct 12 19:47 myfile1
43071 -rw-r--r-- 2 cs130 cs130 0 Oct 12 19:47 myfile2
```

Now let's change the **myfile1** from the first directory by adding some text there

```
cs130@raspberrypi ~/dir1 21 cat >> dir1/myfile1
sdjcskldjc
```

and re-sync the directories with the option to delete the hard links if the files are different.

rsync -a --delete dir1 bk1

```
cs130@raspberrypi ~/dir1 24 rsync -a --delete dir1 bk1
cs130@raspberrypi ~/dir1 25 ls -li bk[12]/dir*
bk1/dir1:
total 4
17607 -rw-r--r-- 1 cs130 cs130 11 Oct 12 20:10 myfile1
43071 -rw-r--r-- 2 cs130 cs130  0 Oct 12 19:47 myfile2

bk2/dir1:
total 0
43070 -rw-r--r-- 1 cs130 cs130 0 Oct 12 19:47 myfile1
43071 -rw-r--r-- 2 cs130 cs130 0 Oct 12 19:47 myfile2
cs130@raspberrypi ~/dir1 26
```

If we do ***ls -li*** on those directories now, we should see, that file that we changed no longer linked to its sibling, and these files are replaced with the real files, whereas the other (unchanged) files are still hard linked. Again, that is useful in saving space if you have large directories and do a regular backups.

3. Disk partitioning.

When you install Linux, you will probably partition your disk. It used to be, that you needed to do it manually, in which case you should be very careful creating your partitions. Not these days. If you skip that step, the system will do a partition for your. If you still want to do it yourself, it is often considered a good idea to make separate partitions for the system, for the data (especially if you know you will have a lot of data), perhaps a separate partition for the mounted network devices, and for the user space. In addition, you will need to create a special partition for the swap. Advantages of partitioning is that if one partition fails, you may have better chances to recover data from it, or at least it may not affect other partitions.

You can see list of your partitions with the command:

fdisk -l

```
Device         Boot   Start      End  Sectors  Size Id Type
/dev/mmcblk0p1         8192  3140625  3132434  1.5G  e W95 FAT16 (LBA)
/dev/mmcblk0p2      3140626 15564799 12424174  5.9G  5 Extended
/dev/mmcblk0p5      3145728  3211261    65534   32M 83 Linux
/dev/mmcblk0p6      3211264  3346431   135168   66M  c W95 FAT32 (LBA)
/dev/mmcblk0p7      3350528 15564799 12214272  5.8G 83 Linux
```

You need to be a root to run this command. Note, that it is different from the ***df*** command, which gives information about the mounted points:

```
root@raspberrypi:~# df
Filesystem     1K-blocks    Used Available Use% Mounted on
/dev/root        5880120 4420448   1137932  80% /
devtmpfs          468148       0    468148   0% /dev
tmpfs             472756       0    472756   0% /dev/shm
tmpfs             472756   30116    442640   7% /run
tmpfs               5120       4      5116   1% /run/lock
tmpfs             472756       0    472756   0% /sys/fs/cgroup
/dev/mmcblk0p6     66528   21418     45110  33% /boot
tmpfs              94552       0     94552   0% /run/user/1000
/dev/mmcblk0p5     30701     398     28010   2% /media/pi/SETTINGS
tmpfs              94552       0     94552   0% /run/user/1001
root@raspberrypi:~#
```

With the ***fdisk*** we should see the disks and their partitions. Usually on a standard installations with "old fashioned" EIDE-like disks, you may expect disks listed to be labeled like that: **/dev/sda.** If we there is more than one disk, we would see all of them listed, for example:

sda, sdb, etc.

If you want to see just one disk you may use:

fdisk -l /dev/sda

For each disk, you will see its partitions, usually numbered sequentially, their sizes, starting and ending sectors, whether it is bootable or not, whether it is primary or extended, their types, and type ids.

```
Device           Boot   Start      End  Sectors  Size Id Type
/dev/mmcblk0p1           8192  3140625  3132434  1.5G  e W95 FAT16 (LBA)
/dev/mmcblk0p2        3140626 15564799 12424174  5.9G  5 Extended
/dev/mmcblk0p5        3145728  3211261    65534   32M 83 Linux
/dev/mmcblk0p6        3211264  3346431   135168   66M  c W95 FAT32 (LBA)
/dev/mmcblk0p7        3350528 15564799 12214272  5.8G 83 Linux
```

We can format (or re-format) any disk that is installed or attached to the system. To do that, the disk should not be in use. Since I use Raspberry with only one "disk", let's see what would be the steps to (re)format a disk here, but we will not save the changes. The disk partitioning table is not changed until you write the changes you made. That is good.

> Disclaimer. I do not advise you to run the examples below on your home computer, including a virtual machine. *Instructor is not Liable* for anything that can go wrong as result, including, but not

```
limited to loss of data.
```

To start formatting the disk you do:

fdisk /dev/<disk>

Note, that you do not provide a (*-l)* flag to list the partitions.

You probably do not want to format the disk you are using; although, you may need to manage unused partitions, or you may want to reformat some partition, and to restore it from the backup. Because it may happen that some partition becomes bad. If the partition becomes bad, it is not usable. And that is one of the main reason why you want to have more than different partitions on your system – if one becomes corrupted, you may still be able to use rest of your disk and may even be able to recover the data from the bad partition.

So, because I have just one disk, let's do some simple formatting session on it, but again, we will not write the changes.

fdisk /dev/mmvblk0

```
root@raspberrypi:~# fdisk /dev/mmcblk0

Welcome to fdisk (util-linux 2.25.2).
Changes will remain in memory only, until you decide to write them.
Be careful before using the write command.


Command (m for help):
```

There is nice welcome message There is also nice message telling me to be careful. Yes, thank you, I know that. I will try. Let's start with the ***m*** for help, because the prompt is waiting

m

It shows available commands, some of them I show on the screen below:

```
  d   delete a partition
  l   list known partition types
  n   add a new partition
  p   print the partition table
  t   change a partition type
  v   verify the partition table
```

Let's print partition table

p

```
Command (m for help): p
Disk /dev/mmcblk0: 7.4 GiB, 7969177600 bytes, 15564800 sectors
Units: sectors of 1 * 512 = 512 bytes
Sector size (logical/physical): 512 bytes / 512 bytes
I/O size (minimum/optimal): 512 bytes / 512 bytes
Disklabel type: dos
Disk identifier: 0x0007aa0e

Device          Boot   Start      End  Sectors  Size Id Type
/dev/mmcblk0p1          8192  3140625  3132434  1.5G  e W95 FAT16 (LBA)
/dev/mmcblk0p2       3140626 15564799 12424174  5.9G  5 Extended
/dev/mmcblk0p5       3145728  3211261    65534   32M 83 Linux
/dev/mmcblk0p6       3211264  3346431   135168   66M  c W95 FAT32 (LBA)
/dev/mmcblk0p7       3350528 15564799 12214272  5.8G 83 Linux
```

And that should give us the list that we saw when we did ***fdisk*** on that device.

Let's add a new partition:

n

It tells us that we have 2 available partitions to create; we can create up to 4 primary partitions.

```
Command (m for help): n
Partition type
   p   primary (1 primary, 1 extended, 2 free)
   l   logical (numbered from 5)
Select (default p): 
```

p

For primary partition.

We need to say what's the partition number. The two partitions are already in used, so we can start with the number 3. It is what should be shown by default. Let's accept it:

3

```
Select (default p): p
Partition number (3,4, default 3): 3
First sector (2048-15564799, default 2048):
```

Now it tells me to start selecting size of the partition by selecting the first sector. Your drive may be different, and if you don't have a raw space, you will be told so, ***but you do not follow me on your system, do you?*** Do you?

I don't want to mess with the partition table absolutely. No one wants to. Because of that, I just accept the default parameters by hitting an <*enter*> key:

```
First sector (2048-15564799, default 2048):
Last sector, +sectors or +size{K,M,G,T,P} (2048-8191, default 8191):
```

Next, I need to select the size of the partition. Here I have an option to do so by specifying the last sector, or the size of the partition. Thus, I can just say:

+5G

To create a partition of 5 Gigs. But again, you should not make a mistake here. If you select position on the disk that overlaps or goes to the different partition, you will corrupt that partition. You do not want to do that. Luckily, the system gives you very good help by giving you the suggested values. We'll take the value the system suggests us as by hitting an <***enter***> key.

```
Created a new partition 3 of type 'Linux' and of size 3 MiB.

Command (m for help):
```

And now we can see a new partition created:

```
Device         Boot   Start      End  Sectors  Size Id Type
/dev/mmcblk0p1         8192  3140625  3132434  1.5G  e W95 FAT16 (LBA)
/dev/mmcblk0p2      3140626 15564799 12424174  5.9G  5 Extended
/dev/mmcblk0p3         2048     8191     6144    3M 83 Linux
/dev/mmcblk0p5      3145728  3211261    65534   32M 83 Linux
/dev/mmcblk0p6      3211264  3346431   135168   66M  c W95 FAT32 (LBA)
/dev/mmcblk0p7      3350528 15564799 12214272  5.8G 83 Linux
```

And partition is type Linux (which is set by default). Let's display help again to see the commands:

m

```
d   delete a partition
l   list known partition types
n   add a new partition
p   print the partition table
t   change a partition type
v   verify the partition table
```

And this time let's change a partition's system ID (the file system):

t

We need to select a partition to modify and new file system. We want to select 3rd partition (the one we currently work with).

```
Command (m for help): t
Partition number (1-3,5-7, default 7): 3
Hex code (type L to list all codes):
```

We can see the list of all available codes, but let me skip this here, because it is a long list. In that list you can find all types you ever wanted to have, including DOS, Solaris, NTFS, FAT, even FAT16.... So, let me skip this list. Let me just type one type that I want:

```
Hex code (type L to list all codes): fd

Changed type of partition 'Linux' to 'Linux raid autodetect'.

Command (m for help):
```

This is Linux RAID. We will talk about RAID in the last section of this lecture (and, therefore, this class).

We are done. Let's print partitions:

```
Device         Boot   Start      End  Sectors  Size Id Type
/dev/mmcblk0p1         8192  3140625  3132434  1.5G  e W95 FAT16 (LBA)
/dev/mmcblk0p2      3140626 15564799 12424174  5.9G  5 Extended
/dev/mmcblk0p3         2048     8191     6144    3M fd Linux raid autodetect
/dev/mmcblk0p5      3145728  3211261    65534   32M 83 Linux
/dev/mmcblk0p6      3211264  3346431   135168   66M  c W95 FAT32 (LBA)
/dev/mmcblk0p7      3350528 15564799 12214272  5.8G 83 Linux
```

And let's list the available codes for the file systems:

Again, changes to the partition table is not written to the disk until we do so. Again, we will not do so. But one thing left here. Let's delete the partition. If you disk has not free space, or if all available partitions taken, before you can create a new partition, you will need to delete one first. Why would you delete a partition and then create a new one in its place? You may have various reasons.

1. Split partition into more than one
2. Or, join two or more partitions into one.
3. You may want to delete partitions, to quickly erase all the data on it.
4. You may try to re-arrange the partitions to fix the corrupted or incorrect partition's table
5. You may want to re-do the partitions schema with different sizes and/or types...

So, there could be various reasons. Let's just delete that new partition that we worked so hard to create just a minute ago:

```
Command (m for help): d
Partition number (1-3,5-7, default 7): 3

Partition 3 has been deleted.
```

Let's print the partition's table to see that there is no such partition there:

```
Device         Boot   Start      End  Sectors  Size Id Type
/dev/mmcblk0p1         8192  3140625  3132434  1.5G  e W95 FAT16 (LBA)
/dev/mmcblk0p2      3140626 15564799 12424174  5.9G  5 Extended
/dev/mmcblk0p5      3145728  3211261    65534   32M 83 Linux
/dev/mmcblk0p6      3211264  3346431   135168   66M  c W95 FAT32 (LBA)
/dev/mmcblk0p7      3350528 15564799 12214272  5.8G 83 Linux
```

And, as I promised, I quit the ***fdisk*** without writing any changes I made thus far:

```
Command (m for help): q

root@raspberrypi:~# fdisk /dev/mmcblk0 -l

Disk /dev/mmcblk0: 7.4 GiB, 7969177600 bytes, 15564800 sectors
Units: sectors of 1 * 512 = 512 bytes
Sector size (logical/physical): 512 bytes / 512 bytes
I/O size (minimum/optimal): 512 bytes / 512 bytes
Disklabel type: dos
Disk identifier: 0x0007aa0e

Device          Boot   Start      End  Sectors  Size Id Type
/dev/mmcblk0p1          8192  3140625  3132434  1.5G  e W95 FAT16 (LBA)
/dev/mmcblk0p2       3140626 15564799 12424174  5.9G  5 Extended
/dev/mmcblk0p5       3145728  3211261    65534   32M 83 Linux
/dev/mmcblk0p6       3211264  3346431   135168   66M  c W95 FAT32 (LBA)
/dev/mmcblk0p7       3350528 15564799 12214272  5.8G 83 Linux
```

That's how you would do the partitions. After you partitioned your disk, you can install the system, and you can use partitions for separate mount points.

4. Copy partitions

> Disclaimer. I do not advise you to run the examples below on your home computer, including a virtual machine. *Instructor is not Liable* for anything that can go wrong as result, including, but not limited to loss of data.

You just read the statement above, right? You really do not want to run any of the below commands.

On some early days at the beginning of times, I said that there are couple of commands that scary me to death every time I need to run them. We already know one of that command. The time has come to talk about the other one.

Let me describe a situation. You boot the system, and... it does not boot. You start looking at the problem, and see the message that the partition's table is corrupt. You look at your partition's table and see that one partition starts on the boundary when the previous partition ends. That should not be so. When you create a partition, the next partition should start after the end of the previous one. Otherwise it will not be valid. But somehow the partition table becomes corrupted, and your system is not bootable. What you do? Not only you have a system that you built and configured – with all those beautiful wallpapers, and nice desktop and gadgets, and so on, but it also keeps a lot of your data. And the value of the data – personal value, is absolutely far greater than the cost of the entire box and all the disks and everything. So what you do? If not that data, you would probably say “It's OK, I'd reinstall, and re-configure it. I will spend my time. It's the price we pay for the technology and convenience.”

But with the potential of the personal data loss you cannot afford to say that.

Thus you take a new disk, you partition it with the same way your old disk was partitioned – you take the old disk, and you write down the partition schema. Then you plug both disks to another Linux computer, and you copy partitions from the old disk to the new one. After that, you install the new disk into your dead computer, boot it up and bingo – magic – you have your system, including all your settings, colors, wallpapers, gadgets and everything, and most of all – you have all your data!

Couple things here. You may need to take special care about copying a booting sectors – which is outside of any partition; and you should be extremely careful to specify which partition is source and which is destination. As simple as it sounds, when you have two disks which only differ in they number, and nothing else – you want to be really, really cognate about source and destination. You may want to mount one of the partition to the available mount point and check the data there. That would be the good test; and after that – you double and triple check the order of the copy command. So. What is the command?

dd if=/dev/sdb1 of=/dev/sdc1

That should do ***byte by byte*** copy first partition of disk **sdb** to disk **sdc**.

I want to point out, that unlike the regular copy, that we used to do so far, that is ***byte by byte*** copy of the entire partition.

There are number of options that control how much blocks to copy and so on, but the base command is that.

You can do some other things with ***dd***, for example, to create an ISO disc image of your partition or the entire disk:

dd if=/dev/sda of=disk.img

Create an image file of the **/dev/sda** hard drive. That is very useful command – to keep image of your entire disk, which you can restore if something goes wrong with your original disk. To restore that image:

dd if=disk.img of=/dev/sda

Also, that is very useful, if you want to have number of computers with the standard installation of the system. You make one installation, you configure that, make an disk image, and then for every new computer you just install the system from that image.

Have not I said already "that is cool"?

Linux RAID

Data safety is always a big concern. It is little help to have a big disk and powerful computer, if the disk fails. And if the disk fails and you cannot restore your data – you don't care how powerful computer was, you just don't really care. Moreover, you could more easy tolerate data loss from a small disk than the large one. Just because with the larger disk you will have more data to lose.

You can also tolerate loss of restorable data, however unpleasant it could be, rather than non-restorable data. Family archive. If you lost it, and if it is not restorable, you don't care if it was insured, uninsured, and so on. It is just lost. That's it.

How you protect yourself from that?

First, of course – is data backup. If you want to sleep well during the night, you would make at least two backups and store it in different places. If you don't have your backup of your important data, make one tonight.

Make backup in different formats, as an archive, and as a disk image. Make your backups on a regular disks and store them in a fire-safe box.

OK. The topic here is to how to make your data survive the loss of a disk.

The obvious approach would be to make redundant copies. Perhaps you would have two disks and keep the backup copies of the data on these two disks.

You have a backup copy. Good. Now if one disk fails, we have data on another disk; and we can use that disk as a source to create another copy on the new replacement disk.

That's good. There is just a small problem here. What if the disk did not fail, but instead some file became corrupted? How would we know, which copy of the file is good, and which one is bad? In other words, which copy to use for the restore procedure? In such scenario, we have 50% chances of choosing the corrupted copy to overwrite the good one. Well, of course that also means that we still have a 50% chance to recover the data, which, by itself is not bad, considering that without that, the probability of full loss of the data would be twice as high.

But that is not good enough. Twice as high – is not high enough. Let's look for other options.

Let's add another disk. And instead of using that disk for data, let's store checksums of files on that disk.

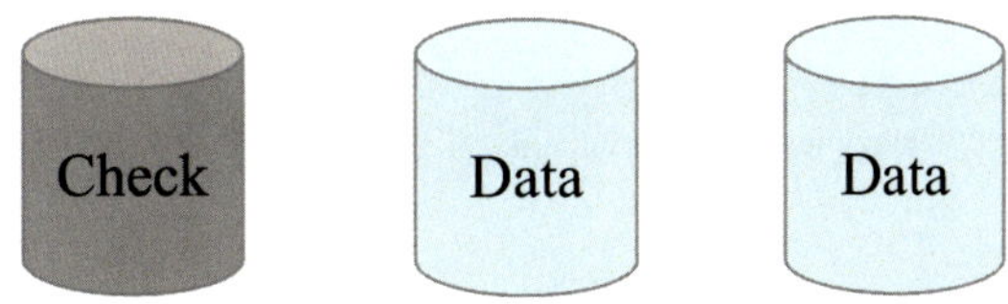

Now, when one of the disk fails, we can always restore that disk from another two. If the disk with checksum fails, we can re-calculate checksums from the existing data, if the disk with the data fails, we can restore the data from another disk with the data and the disk with checksum.

And now, let's make another small step, and strip the disks. And for each disk and for each strip we will store different things there:

Now we have what is called RAID level 5. RAID stands for the ***R**edundant **A**rray of **I**nexpensive **D**isks.* Why inexpensive is clear. Disks are cheap. Why redundant is also clear – the data are redundant, and not only redundant, they also backed by the checksum.

Why level 5? There are several implementations of RAID. Level 0 is just two disks that are intended not for a data redundancy, but for the speed of read/write operations: the data is split between two disks to increase the speed.

Level 1 is a first level to achieve data redundancy through the disk mirroring. That is our first diagram, and as we discussed, it is designed to withstand one disk total failure.

Level 4 is our second diagram – that adds a third disk, but does not strip the disks. Level 4 is slow, and it is not supported by Linux.

Level 5 is our last and greatest drawing. Through the disk stripping we achieve speed of level 0, and data redundancy of level 4. It tolerates total or partial failure of one disk; and it also restores corrupted file, or checksum. Reliability of data storage with level 5 far exceeds 99.9 %. You really need to have two disks to fail to lose your data. Because probability of such event happening simultaneously is very remote (unless something really bad happens with the entire computer system), you should feel relatively good. You need to operate two disks with failed disk being undetected for a prolonged period of time to that to happen. The idea of that level is that when you detect the disk failure, you have enough time for a disk replacement. Now there is important moment here. The system relies on the fact, that no two disk may fail at the same time. How to minimize such event?

One of the best advise is probably to buy disks from different manufacturers and different batches. Next, you can add a spare disk to your RAID. In normal circumstances it is unused, but if one disk fails, system will automatically take the spare and add it into the array. With such setup, you can tolerate two disk failure without data loss. And that should really give you peace of mind for quite prolonged period of time.

And of course, you can build your RAID 5 into other combinations – for example you can add your RAID 5 system into RAID 1, to form higher levels – 6, 10 etc. But that is probably really overkill, not usually needed.

So. What you need to setup a RAID? And we'll talk about level 5. Obviously, you need three disks of the same size. When you do RAID 5 with 3 disk, system will see them as one disk of the size of the smallest out of three ones. So you need to have 3 disks. Don't try to buy the largest size disks – they are less reliable than the ones with one or two notches down.

Next, you will need a Linux. Someone once asked me – what could be the reason his RAID 5 failing and error-ing all the time? I asked what was the system he used, and he said – "<.....>". And I said – that is the reason. Use Linux. In general, if you want to make a file server, use Linux.

You will have an option to make a hardware RAID, or software RAID. Hardware RAID would be faster, but it will set you back several hundreds of dollars perhaps; and the production grade will easily set you back several thousands dollars.

While Linux software RAID .... is free, but still very reliable.

You will need a motherboard that supports several disks.

You need a package installed, which is probably installed with your system by default, if not – you need to install **mdadm** package.

Have three disks. Make sure they are not mounted. Format them with one partition and set the type to **fd** - Linux raid.

I will not go over each and every steps how to make a Linux's RAID. There are a lot of tutorials and guides available. For example, this one:

http://www.linuxhomenetworking.com/wiki/index.php/Quick_HOWTO_:_Ch26_:_Linux_Software_RAID#.VTwMjfBiCM4

Just very briefly following their steps:

To create the raid:

mdadm --create /dev/md0 --level=5 --raid-devices=3 /dev/hde1 /dev/hdf2 /dev/hdg1

Here we create a RAID level 5 with three disks (e, f, g) and name the resulting device **md0** (that's what usually the RAID systems named on the Linux)

Check the raid:

cat /proc/mdstat

You should see something like the following:

```
Personalities : [raid5]
read_ahead 1024 sectors
md0 : active raid5 hdg1[2] hde1[1] hdf2[0]
      4120448 blocks level 5, 32k chunk, algorithm 3 [3/3] [UUU]

unused devices: <none>
```

You should see that there are three disks, and they all are up (note the three UUU flags). You will periodically check these flags when you operate your RAID device to see if all disks are up. If any of them is down, it is time to replace it.

Format the raid:

mkfs.ext4 /dev/md0

Create the config file

mdadm --detail --scan > /etc/mdadm.conf

Create a mount point

mkdir /mnt/raid

This time you probably may want to mount the RAID device automatically at a boot time.

Add a mount point to the **fstab** file:

/dev/md0 /mnt/raid ext4 defaults 1 2

mount your raid:

mount /dev/md0 /mnt/raid

And I think the above guide misses couple of steps: You need to initialize the RAID, and start the it, which would be:

mkraid /dev/md0

raidstart /dev/md0

The **mdadm** administrative package for the RAID is very powerful. You have all the options you need. You can remove device, add a new device etc. You can start and stop the RAID, check the status and so on.

Finally, For each RAID level the setup procedure is slightly different, so make sure you follow the procedure that is for your level.

And that concludes all the topics that I wanted to cover for this course.

Afterword

When I was done with the text, and looked over the code examples, I noticed that because of different systems they'd been written on, some have indentations with the spaces, and some – with the tabs... Well. I did not have good compelling reasons to go over all of them and change them... After all, the good linux user is a lazy linux user.

All icons, clip arts, and images with free license are from: https://pixabay.com

Table of Contents

Made in the USA
Las Vegas, NV
31 January 2024